Religion Journals and Serials

Recent Titles in
Annotated Bibliographies of Serials: A Subject Approach
Series Editor: Norman Frankel

Library and Information Science Journals and Serials: An Analytical Guide
Mary Ann Bowman, compiler

Philosophy Journals and Serials: An Analytical Guide
Douglas H. Ruben, compiler

Dentistry Journals and Serials: An Analytical Guide
Aletha A. Kowitz, compiler

Agricultural and Animal Science Journals and Serials: An Analytical Guide
Richard D. Jensen, Connie Lamb, and Nathan M. Smith, compilers

Economics Journals and Serials: An Analytical Guide
Beatrice Sichel and Werner Sichel, compilers

Financial Journals and Serials: An Analytical Guide to Accounting, Banking, Finance, Insurance, and Investment Periodicals
William Fisher, compiler

Marine Science Journals and Serials: An Analytical Guide
Judith B. Barnett, compiler

History Journals and Serials: An Analytical Guide
Janet Fyfe, compiler

Serials on Aging: An Analytical Guide
Shirley B. Hesslein, compiler

Anthropology Journals and Serials: An Analytical Guide
John T. Williams, compiler

Cancer Journals and Serials: An Analytical Guide
Pauline M. Vaillancourt, compiler

Education Journals and Serials: An Analytical Guide
Mary Ellen Collins, compiler

Religion Journals and Serials

An Analytical Guide

Compiled by
Eugene C. Fieg, Jr.

Annotated Bibliographies of Serials:
A Subject Approach, Number 13

Greenwood Press
New York • Westport, Connecticut • London

Library of Congress Cataloging-in-Publication Data

Fieg, Eugene C.
Religion journals and serials : an analytical guide / compiled by Eugene C. Fieg, Jr.
p. cm.—(Annotated bibliographies of serials : a subject approach, ISSN 0748-5190 ; no. 13)
Bibliography: p.
Includes indexes.
ISBN 0-313-24513-4
1. Religion—Periodicals—Bibliography. I. Title. II. Series: Annotated bibliographies of serials ; no. 13.
Z7753.F53 1988
[BL1.A1]
016.200'5—dc19 87-32276

British Library Cataloguing in Publication Data is available.

Library of Congress Catalog Card Number: 87-32276
ISBN: 0-313-24513-4
ISSN: 0748-5190

First published in 1988

Greenwood Press, Inc.
88 Post Road West, Westport, Connecticut 06881

Printed in the United States of America

The paper used in this book complies with the Permanent Paper Standard issued by the National Information Standards Organization (Z39.48-1984).

10 9 8 7 6 5 4 3 2 1

Dedicated to My Parents
Carl and Jerry Fieg

Contents

Series Foreword ix

Preface xiii

How to Use This Book xv

Abbreviations xix

Indexes and Abstracts 3

History of Religions 11

Primal Religions 20

Spiritualism 22

Religion and Society 26

Eastern Religions 31

Near Eastern Religions 36

Judaism 40

Christianity 45

Bible Studies 45

History of Christianity 66

Denominations 74

Theology 99

Practical Theology. 132

Christianity and Society. 151

Christianity and Science. 158

Christianity and Literature 160

Ecumenism 162

Islam. 166

Modern Faiths. 168

Geography Index 171

Title Index 179

Publisher Index 186

Subject Index 199

Audience Index 211

Series Foreword

The effects of the "information explosion" have been pronounced in the area serial of publishing. Encouraged by the availability of word processing and computer printing, masses of material have been flowing from the presses. Many of the new journals and serials have proved to be ephemeral, ceasing publication as a result of financial difficulties, mergers, or loss of interest by the editorial staff. However, a large number of useful new publications remain, augmenting older titles, which have undergone important editorial changes. On-line bibliographic databases and electronic publishing have also affected the direction of serial publishing. Despite modern technology, as the amount and type of material in most disciplines have proliferated, subscription prices for serials have been maintaining a steady upward trend while library budgets generally have been declining.

The intent of the series ANNOTATED BIBLIOGRAPHIES OF SERIALS: A SUBJECT APPROACH series is to make the task of serial selection and use more systematic through identifying, collecting, annotating, and indexing currently published English-language serials in the major fields of knowledge: social, natural, and applied sciences; humanities; medicine; and business. The scope of the series is worldwide. Serials cited are from the many countries where English is a primary or important language, notably the United States, Canada, the United Kingdom, Ireland, Australia, New Zealand, South Africa, Nigeria, India, Pakistan, and Israel. It is worth noting that journals of international importance from areas of the world where the national language is not widely understood outside the country are often published wholly or in part in English.

Series Foreword

Each series volume provides comprehensive coverage of English-language serials in one subject area with extensively annotated entries for each serial. Titles are included if their primary focus is on the discipline of the particular volume. Many fields overlap, and it is sometimes difficult to decide where the dividing line should be. Occasionally, the same serial will appear in more than one volume, with the annotation pointing to its applicability to the subject area in question. The comprehensiveness of coverage and informative annotations, both exceeding that of other guides of serial literature, will aid librarians in deciding whether a particular title is appropriate for their collections and will aid scholars in determining whether the title will be useful for their research.

For the purposes of this series, the term "serial" is applied to periodicals having a frequency of issue of at least one per year. This includes journals, publications of professional associations, magazines, selected newsletters, almanacs, and conference proceedings. Newsletters are included only if they publish significant articles or have unique features. The newsletter literature is voluminous, and in many disciplines would provide enough material for a separate volume. The same can be said for government documents. Only the most important government publications are included in these series volumes.

The serial entries are culled from extensive searches of manual and computerized information sources. Basic indexing and abstracting services, thorough searches of the most important resource collections, contacts with library associations and other professional associations in the pertinent disciplines, all have been utilized by the volume editors. Wherever possible volume editors have personally examined representative issues of each serial and have acquired information directly from publishers.

Frontmatter contains introductory material, including a "How to Use this Book" section, an abbreviations table, and directories of microform and reprint companies and/or .fo xii databases as appropriate. Abbreviations or acronyms for indexes, abstracts, and databases may be included in the abbreviations table or, if an extensive list, may be given in one or more separate tables. Depending on the subject matter, some volumes are divided into chapters according to classified subdisciplines, while others are arranged in one unclassified sequence. Entries are alphabetical by title. Most volumes will include a geographical index, an index of publishers, and a subject or classified title index. Depending on the organization of the volume, an alphabetical title index may be added.

It is hoped that the information provided by ANNOTATED BIBLIOGRAPHIES OF SERIALS will facilitate access to and help strengthen bibliographic control of the rapidly growing body of serial titles.

Norman Frankel
Series Editor

Preface

A compiler of a bibliography in a field of study always wants to make the finished product as complete as possible. That definitely was my intention with this book, but my lofty intentions were cooled by the fact that there are over 1,900 English-language journals in the field of religion. From those, 300 to 400 had to be chosen for the book. In order to bring the number of journals to a manageable amount, stringent selection criteria were required. The first types of serials to be excluded were newsletters, annuals, proceedings, directories, and bulletins. This, however, did not reduce the number of periodicals to the desired point. Therefore, journals that were of little interest or only of interest to those in special professions--for instance, serials directed toward Christian lawyers--were excluded. While it is true that Christianity is concerned about the world and how the faithful should behave in it, those journals concerned with how Christians behave in their professions center more on the profession than on the religion. Such selection, therefore, seemed justifiable.

Letters were sent out to the publishers requesting them to complete a questionnaire and to send sample copies of their journals. Not all of the questionnaires were returned and not all of the respondents sent sample copies. In order to supply any missing information, several reference sources were used: Ulrich's International Periodical Directory, Standard Periodical Directory, Union List of Serials, New Serial Titles, Directory of Serials, and Faxon's Librarians' Guide to Serials. In addition, collections of serials in the seminaries in Chicago were checked. In spite of these efforts, some information remained elusive, and, accordingly, the descriptions of certain publications are rather brief. Where data and description are minimal, usually the titles of such journals will suggest the broad subject area that is covered by the journal.

The order of the chapters was dictated by both historical considerations and by moving from the more general to the more specific. Therefore, journals in the field of the history of religions are treated before any on a specific religion and journals focusing on Islam follow those on Christianity. The category of modern faiths should be self-evident from perusing the journals covered in that chapter. It should be noted here that while atheism is included in this chapter, it is hardly a modern faith. However, it did receive much support during the period of the Enlightenment and from the spread of popular scientific methods and discoveries in the nineteenth century, and therefore is listed here alongside journals dealing with other modern faiths such as humanism and Mormonism.

This book is aimed primarily at helping the librarian to select journals for the library and at the scholar who wishes to read or subscribe to journals that fit his or her particular interests. To this end four indexes have been produced: by geography, title, subject, and intended audience. An index of publishers is included as well.

While it is too much to expect that this book will be free from errors, I hope that they few and insignificant and that this book will be helpful to those who use it.

Thanks are gratefully given to the editors of this series for their patience with me in producing this book. Finally, thanks are due to my wife, who encouraged me throughout this project.

How to Use This Book

The titles in this book are arranged under broad subject headings. More detailed subject access is provided by the subject index. Access by place of publication, publisher, title, and intended audience is also provided through the appropriate indexes.

Generally, each entry has two main parts. The first contains bibliographic information about the title; the second is a descriptive and evaluative annotation. If, however, the entry is based only on the response from the publisher, the annotation may be very brief or omitted altogether. The first part containing the bibliographic data contains the following information:

1. An entry number.

2. TITLE: The title as provided by the publisher, or as printed on the title page, or as found in reference sources.

3. DATE FOUNDED: As provided by the publisher, or as listed in reference sources.

4. TITLE CHANGES: Previous titles are listed with dates when the information was provided or as could be derived from reference sources.

5. MERGERS: Titles of previous journals combined to produce the current periodical or one of its predecessors listed under TITLE CHANGES as supplied by the publisher or derived from reference sources.

6. FREQUENCY: How often the title is published.

7. PRICE: Subscription price as provided by the publisher or as found in reference works, and in the currency listed.

8. PUBLISHER: Name and address as provided or found in reference works.

9. EDITOR: Name(s) as provided or found in reference works.

10. ILLUSTRATIONS: Descriptor used if the title contains illustrations or if the publisher stated so without sending a copy of the serial.

11. INDEX: Descriptor used only if title has an index.

12. ADVERTISEMENTS: Descriptor used only if title has advertisements.

13. CIRCULATION: As provided by the publisher or as found in reference sources.

14. MANUSCRIPT SELECTION: How materials are selected for publication.

15. MICROFORMS: Descriptor used only if available. Abbreviations are supplied to indicate the vendor. Consult the abbreviations.

16. REPRINTS: Descriptor used only if available. Hard copy availability from the publisher is indicated. Abbreviation of vendor is supplied. Consult the abbreviations.

17. BOOK REVIEWS: Descriptor used only if the title contains reviews. The nature, length, and number of the reviews is provided in the annotation.

18. SPECIAL ISSUES: Descriptor used if special issues are published.

19. INDEXED/ABSTRACTED: Descriptor is used only if the title is indexed or abstracted. Abbreviations for indexes and abstracts are given. For the full name, consult the abbreviations. Note that some of the indexes and abstracts, such as Social Sciences Index and Historical Abstracts are available from database vendors.

20. DATABASE: Descriptor used only if title is available on-line. Abbreviation of on-line database is supplied. Consult the abbreviations.

21. TARGET AUDIENCE: Indicates the intended audience or audiences of the journal.

22. SAMPLE COPIES: Descriptor used if sample copies are available. If they are not free, that is also noted.

Abbreviations

ABBREVIATIONS OF INDEXES AND ABSTRACTS

db refers to database

AATechAbs = Art and Archaeology Technical Abstracts

ABC = ABC Clio

AbrRG = Abridged Reader's Guide to Periodical Literature

ABS = ABS Guide to Classical Studies

AEI = Australian Education Index

AES = Abstracts of English Studies

AfrAb = African Abstracts

AFS = Abstracrts of Folklore Studies

AHCI = Arts and Humanities Citation Index

AHI = American Humanities Index

AHSearch (db) = Arts and Humanities Search

AI = Art Index

ALA = American Literature Abstracts

Abbreviations

America (db) = America: History and Life

America = America: History and Life

AMHA = Adolescent Mental Health Abstracts

AP = L'annee philologique

APAIS = Australian PAIS

API = Alternative Press Index

ATLA (db) = ATLA Religion Database (BRS)

Avery = Avery Index to Architectural Periodicals

BABH = Bulletin analytique bibliographie hellenique

BELL = Bibliography of English Language and Literature

BHI = British Humanities Index

BI = Biography Index

Biblica = Biblica

BM = Bibliografia Missionaria

Bowker = R. R. Bowker (International Serials Database)

BP = Bibliographia Patristica

BRD = Book Review Digest

BRI = Book Review Index

BRM = Book Reviews of the Month

BullSig = Bulletin signaletique: histoire des sci. des rel.

CA = Chemical Abstracts

Can = Canadiana

CC = Current Contents

CDA = Community Development Abstracts

CERDIC = CERDIC

ChLit = Christianity and Literature

CHR = Canadian Historical Review

CIJE = Current Index to Journals in Education

CLA = Canon Law Abstracts

CLI = Current Law Index

CPG = Catholic Periodical Guides

CPI = Christian Periodical Index

CPLI = Catholic Periodical and Literature Index

Dustbooks = Dustbooks

EI = Education Index

EightCent = Eighteenth Century: A Current Bibliography

ElencBibBib = Elenchus Bibligraphicus Biblicus

Elenchus = Ephemer. Theolog. Lovan.: Elenchus Bibliograph.

ExMed = Excerpta Medica

FLI = Film Literature Index

Francis (db) = Francis: histoire des sciences des religions

GCP = Guide to Christian Periodicals

GSScRel = Guide to Social Sci. and Rel. in Per. Literature

HA = Historical Abstracts

HA (db) = Historical Abstracts

HI = Humanities Index

HI (db) = Humanities Index

HLI = Hospital Literature Index

IAJS = Index of Articles on Jewish Studies (Kirjath Sepher)

Abbreviations

IAPV = Index of American Periodical Verse

IBBRev = International Bibliography of Book Reviews

IBPL = International Bibliography of Periodical Literature

IBRevHum = Index to Book Reviews in the Humanities

IBZL = Internationale Bibliographie der Zeitschriften Liter.

IJP = Index to Jewish Periodicals

IM = Index Medicus

Infodex = Infodex

IntMedBib = International Medieval Bibliography

ISAP = Index to South African Periodicals

IZ = Internationale Zeitschriften

IZBG = Internat. Zeitschriften. fuer Bibelwiss. u. Grenz.

JES = Journal of Ecumenical Studies

JPCI = Journal Processing Citation Index

LCR = Literary Criticism Register

LISA = Library and Information Science Abstracts

LLBA = Language and Language Behavior Abstracts

LRI = Legal Resource Index

Magazines = Magazines for Libraries

MHRA = MHRA Bibliography

MI = Magazine Index

Miss. = Missionalia

MLA = Modern Language Association

MLA Abstracts = MLA Abstracts

MLAInt = MLA International Bibliography

MPI = Mosher Periodical Index

MRD = Media Review Digest

MusInd = Music Index

NEBPI = NEBPI Press

NTA = New Testament Abstracts

OTA = Old Testament Abstracts

OT/ANE = OT/ANE Permucite Index

PA = Psychological Abstracts

PAIS = Public Affairs Information Service

PCCA = Pastoral Care and Counseling Abstracts

PI = Philosopher's Index

PI (db) = Philosopher's Index

PII = Public Issues Index

PMR = Popular Magazine Review

PRG = Psychological Reader's Guide

PSA = Political Science Abstracts

RAA = Repertoire d'Art et d'Archeologie

RBIC = Repertoire bibliographique des institutions chretien.

RBP = Repertoire bibliographique de la philosophie

RevHE = Revue d'histoire ecclesiastique

RG = Readers' Guide to Periodical Literature

RG (db) = Readers' Guide to Periodical Literature

RGScRel = Repertoire generale de sciences religieuses

RI (db) Religion Index (Dialog)

RILA = Internatinal Repertory of the Literature of Art

RIO = Religion Index: One

Abbreviations

RPI = Religious Periodical Index

RPTA = Religious and Philosophical Theological Abstracts

RTA = Religious and Theological Abstracts

SA = Sociological Abstracts

SA (db) = Sociological Abstracts

SBPI = Southern Baptist Periodical Index

SCA = Social Citation Review

SIBPL = Strasbourg Intern. Bibliog. of Periodical Literature

SISPerLit = Subject Index to Select Periodical Literature

SocScisearch (db) = SocScisearch

SP = Scholars Press

SPD = Standard Periodical Directory

SRA = Science of Religion Abstracts and Index of Recent Art.

SSCI = Social Sciences Citation Index

SSI = Social Sciences Index

SSI (db) = Social Sciences Index

TA = Theology Abstracts

ThDig = Theology Digest

TK = Theologie im Kontex

TLZ = Theologische Literaturzeitung

TRI = Theological and Religious Bibliograpies

TvF= Tijdschrift voor Filosofie (Bibliograph. Repertorium)

UKCH = United Kingdom Christian Handbook

UMI = University Microfilms International

UMPI = United Methodist Periodical Index

Willings = Willings Press Guide

Zdienst = Zeitschrifteninhaltsdienst

ZdienstTh = Zeitschrifteninhaltsdienst Theologie/Indices Theologici

Zwets = Zwets and Zeitlinger

AUDIENCE ABBREVIATIONS

AC = Scholars

GP= General Public

HS= High School Students

SP= Specialists

UndSt= Undergraduate Students

MICROFORM AND REPINT ABBREVIATIONS

AMS = AMS Press, Inc., 56 East 13th St., New York, NY 10003.

ATLA = ATLA Preservation Board, 1118 E. 54th Place, Chicago, IL 60615.

Bell and Howell = Bell and Howell, Microphoto Division, Old Mansfield Rd., Wooster, OH 44691.

Canner = J. S. Canner, 49-65 Landsdowne St., Boston, Massachusetts 02215.

Abbreviations

CIS = Congressional Information Service, 4520 East-West Highway, Washington, D. C. 20014.

Dawson = William Dawson and Sons, Ltd., Back Issues Department, Cannon Houe, Folkestone, Kent, England.

Hein = William S. Hein and Co., 1285 Main St., Buffalo, New York 14209.

Johnson = Johnson Associates, POB 1017, Greenwich, Connecticut 06830.

Walter J. Johnson = Walter J. Johnson, 355 Chestnut St., Norwood, New Jersey 07648.

Kraus = Kraus Reprints, Kraus Microform, Route 100, Millwood, NY 10546.

KTO = KTO Microform Division, Rte. 100, Millwood, NY

MIM = Microforms International Marketing Co., Maxwell House, Fairview Park, Elmsford, NY 10523.

UMI = University Microforms International University Microfilms International, 300 North Zeeb Rd., Ann Arbor, Michigan.

Microform = Microform Academic Publishers, Bradford Rd., East Ardsley, Wakefield, West Yorkshire WF3 2JN, England; North America distributor: Clearwater Publishing Co., Inc., 1995 Broadway, New York, NY.

Micromedia = Micromedia, Ltd., P. O. Box 502, Station S, Toronto, Ontario M5J 2L7, Canada

NCR Corporation = NCR, 1700 S. Patterson Blvd. Dayton, Ohio 45479

Newsbank = Newsbank, Inc., 58 Pine Street, New Canaan, CT 06840

Swets = Swets and Zeitlinger, Heereweg 547B, Lisse, The Netherlands.

Xerox = Xerox, 300 North Zeeb Rd., Ann Arbor, MI 48106.

OTHER ABBREVIATIONS

a = annual

bm = bimonthly

bw = biweekly

d = daily

irr = irregular

m = monthly

q = quarterly

sa = semiannual

sm = semimonthly

w = weekly

Religion Journals and Serials

Indexes and Abstracts

1. America: History and Life. DATE FOUNDED: 1964. FREQUENCY: 3/yr. PRICE: Based on service. PUBLISHER: ABC-Clio, 2040 Alameda Padre Serra, P. O. Box 4397, Santa Barbara, CA 93140-4397 or Clio Press, Ltd., 55 St. Thomas St., Oxford OX1 1JG, England EDITOR: Pamela R. Byrne. DATABASE: America. TARGET AUDIENCE: AC, SP.

This exhaustive abstracting publication is published in four parts: article abstracts and citations, an index to book reviews, bibliography, and annual index. Only the first comes out three times a year; the index to the reviews is published twice semiannually while the others appear annually. The journals covered are international, ranging from Austria to Zimbabwe. Each volume of abstracts covers North America (in general), Canada, and the United States. Most of the abstracting articles are devoted to the latter. There seems to be little or no emphasis on Mexico except as that country is involved with its northern neighbors. While volume one was published in 1964, there is a volume 0 which covers the years 1954-1963.

2. The American Humanities Index. DATE FOUNDED: 1975. FREQUENCY: q. PRICE: $165.00/yr. PUBLISHER: The Whitston Publishing Co., Troy, New York. EDITOR: Eamon O'Brien. CIRCULATION: 200. TARGET AUDIENCE: AC, SP.

This index attempts to fill a void: to index journals not indexed elsewhere or indexed only in publications not universally available. Review articles are also indexed. The index is arranged in one alphabetic index; each entry is subdivided to help the user find the subject he is interested in. It is cumulated at the end of the year. It was produced from photographic typescript pages and the printing was very clear for such a publication. Currently the index is printed in a more standard way.

3. Arts and Humanities Citation Index. DATE FOUNDED: 1976. FREQUENCY: 3/yr.; the third issue is a cumulation of the other two. PRICE: $2,200/yr. PUBLISHER: Institute for Scientific Information, Inc., 3501 Market St., Philadelphia, Pennsylvania. ADVERTISEMENTS: In-house. DATABASE: AHSearch. TARGET AUDIENCE: AC, GP, SP.

This index is one of the most extensive in the field of humanities. It indexes material from approximately 7,000 journals; some are covered selectively while others are covered in full. This material is then indexed four different ways: by subject, cited item, the item itself, and by geography. All fields in the humanities are covered. The selectively covered journals come from the Science Citation Index and the Social Sciences Citation Index. Any material which is found in this index represents journals that were received by ISI during the period covered; there is very little lag time.

4. Bibliographia Patristica. DATE FOUNDED: 1959. FREQUENCY: a. PUBLISHER: Walter de Gruyter, Berlin and New York. EDITOR: Wilhelm Schneemelcher. INDEX: yes, author index. TARGET AUDIENCE: AC.

As the title suggests, this is a bibliography devoted to those works on non-scriptural material or on the patristic literature; however, articles on the New Testament and its Apocrypha are also indexed. It includes works on patrology in general, the New Testament and its Apocrypha, the patristic fathers, liturgics, councils and confessions, doctrines, Gnosticism, exegesis of the Old and New Testaments in the Fathers, and finally books received. The main drawback of this index is the gap between its publication and that of the material that is indexed.

5. Bulletin signaletique: histoire et science des religions. DATE FOUNDED: 1947. TITLE CHANGES: Bulletin signaletique: sciences religieuse. FREQUENCY: 4 fascicles per year. PRICE: France: 350 francs/yr.; foreign: 368 francs/yr. PUBLISHER: Centre de documentation sciences humaines, 54 blvd. Raspail, B. P. 140, 75260 Paris Cedex 06, France. EDITOR: Raymond le Boubennec, Daniel Louys, Louis Brix. INDEX. ADVERTISEMENTS: In-house. DATABASE: Francis. TARGET AUDIENCE: AC, SP.

This index will probably cover anything that is missed in another indexing or abstracting periodical. Compared to other indexes such as Elenchus Bibliographicus or Elenchus

Bibliographicus Biblicus, this one offers current coverage; it seems to cover the literature appearing mostly in the year prior to its own publication. Its coverage is extensive. It covers history of religion, ancient religions, Judaism, Christianity (its history, exegesis of Scripture), Islam, African religions, religions in the Americas and the Pacific, and those in Asia. Each issue has several indexes; those indexes are cumulated at the end of the year.

6. Canon Law Abstracts. DATE FOUNDED: 1958. FREQUENCY: sa. PRICE: 5.00 pounds/yr. PUBLISHER: Canon Law Society, Archbishop's House, Westminster, London SW1P 1QJ, England. EDITOR: Rev. I. Payne. CIRCULATION: 1,000. MANUSCRIPT SELECTION: Editor. TARGET AUDIENCE: AC, SP.

This journal abstracts articles on Roman Catholic law from about ninety four journals from around the world. The abstract is divided into several parts; first, general discussions of canon law are annotated followed by those on the history of canon law; then come abstracts of articles dealing with the various subjects in the Roman Catholic canon law. There is no table of contents indicating where each section begins. None of the abstracts is signed.

7. Elenchus Bibliographicus. DATE FOUNDED: 1925. FREQUENCY: a. PUBLISHER: Universite Catholique de Louvain, Bibliotheque de l'Universite, Louvain, Belgium. EDITOR: R. Boudens. INDEX: Author and partial subject index. TARGET AUDIENCE: AC, SP.

As fascicles 2-3 of the Ephemerides Theologicae Louvaniensis, this bibliography is one of the most complete; it covers religion in general, the history of religions, the Old Testament, the New Testament, as well as theological topics dating from the first century to the current one; it does not, however, cover popular works. Each section is compiled by a special editor or editors. One area where it is strong compared to other indexes is in the field of dogmatics.

8. Elenchus Bibliographicus Biblicus. DATE FOUNDED: 1920 FREQUENCY: a. PUBLISHER: Pontifical Institute, Biblical Press, Rome, Italy. EDITOR: Robert North. INDEX. TARGET AUDIENCE: AC.

This is one of the most extensive indexes to yearly works in the field of biblical studies in the world. It covers not only periodical literature but also monographs, books, and reviews of those books. This is a standard index needed for serious academic study of the Bible. The yearly volume ends with an index of authors, languages treated, and biblical books studied.

9. Historical Abstracts. DATE FOUNDED: 1955. FREQUENCY: q. PRICE: Based on service; write for price quotation. PUBLISHER: ABC-Clio, Inc., 2040 Alameda Padre Serra, P. O. Box 4397, Santa Barbara, California 93140-4397 or Clio Press, Ltd., 55 St. Thomas St., Oxford OX1 1JG, England. EDITOR: Pamela R. Byrne. INDEX: Cumulated every five years. CIRCULATION: 1,400. DATABASE: HA. TARGET AUDIENCE: AC, SP.

This is another of the abstracting services from the American Bibliographic Center. It is published in two parts: modern history abstracts, 1450-1914; and twentieth century abstracts, 1914-present. This is the counterpart to America: History and Life; that covered North America, excluding Mexico; this one covers the rest of the world. Book reviews are included. It should be noted that starting with volumes 26-35, volumes 26-30 (1980-1984) contained articles prior to 1979, and volumes 31-35 (1980-1984) contained abstracted articles after 1979.

10. Humanities Index. DATE FOUNDED: 1974. TITLE CHANGES: International Index to Periodicals (1907-1955); International Index (1955-1965); Social Sciences and Humanities Index, (1965-1974). FREQUENCY: q. PRICE: $90.00/yr., minimum; price depends on the subscriber's periodical holdings. PUBLISHER: H. W. Wilson Co., 950 University Ave., Bronx, New York 10452. EDITOR: Joanna Greenspon. CIRCULATION: 4,200. MANUSCRIPT SELECTION: Journals covered selected by the subscribers. DATABASE: HI. TARGET AUDIENCE: AC, GP, SP.

This Wilson index is divided into two sections: an author/subject index, and a book review index. It covers about 300 journals. Those periodicals chosen for coverage are selected based upon the subscribers' vote. The index asks the subscribers to place primary emphasis on the reference value of the journals.

11. International Bibliography of the History of Religions = Bibliographie internationale de l'histoire des religions. DATE FOUNDED: 1954. FREQUENCY: a. PUBLISHER: E. J. Brill, Leiden, The Netherlands. EDITOR: Dr. C. J. Bleeker, Salih H. Alich. INDEX: Authors. TARGET AUDIENCE: AC, SP.

This index of published literature is limited to the objective study of religion, be it of the main religions of the world or of those that have no scriptures. Apologetic materials are omitted; the emphasis is on the history of religion. The index is arranged alphabetically by main entry with special subject fields; monographs as well as periodicals are indexed. One drawback is its late date of publication; it is published about six years after the indexed material has been published. It is sponsored by both the International Association for the History of Religions and Unesco.

12. New Testament Abstracts. DATE FOUNDED: 1956. FREQUENCY: 3/yr. PRICE: $20.00/yr. PUBLISHER: Weston School of Theology, 3 Phillips Place, Cambridge, Massachusetts 02138. EDITOR: Daniel J. Harrington, General Editor; Elizabeth Burr, Managing Editor. INDEX. ADVERTISEMENTS. CIRCULATION: 2,100. MANUSCRIPT SELECTION: Selection for abstracting on the basis of their relevance to the New Testament and related fields. REPRINTS: Back issues available from the publisher. SPECIAL ISSUES: Occasionally. TARGET AUDIENCE: AC, SP, UndSt. SAMPLE COPIES.

New Testament Abstracts contains abstracts of articles from about 300 journals from all countries. The abstracts are arranged by broad subject areas: New Testament, General; Gospels-Acts; Epistles-Revelation; Biblical Theology; and New Testament World. Following the abstracts of the journals are abstracts of new books arranged according to the same subject categories. Along with Old Testament Abstracts, Religious and Theological Abstracts, and Religion: One, this is a standard theological index for studies in religion. It is very attractively printed; it does not have as small a print face as does the Elenchus Bibliographicus Biblicus, for instance. Like the latter, it not only has an index of authors, there is also one for biblical passages discussed, books reviewed, book notices, and a list of the abstractors. All the abstractors are either academics or clerics and the abstracts are signed.

13. Old Testament Abstracts. DATE FOUNDED: 1978. FREQUENCY: 3/yr. PRICE: $11.00/yr. to individuals and libraries. PUBLISHER: Catholic Biblical Association, Catholic University, Washington, D. C. 20064. EDITOR: Bruce Vawter, DePaul University, Chicago, IL 60614. INDEX: ADVERTISEMENTS. CIRCULATION: 1,800. REPRINTS: None; back issues available from the office of the Catholic Biblical Association. DATABASE: ATLA, RI. TARGET AUDIENCE: AC, GP, SP. SAMPLE COPIES: To both individuals and libraries.

This publication of about 110 to 130 pages abstracts articles and books. The first part is dedicated to periodical abstracts which are arranged from a discussion of general articles to those on the intertestamental literature. Next books are abstracted. At the end of the publication are the sigla of the journals abstracted as well as a list of the abstractors.

14. Readers' Guide to Periodical Literature. DATE FOUNDED: 1900. FREQUENCY: sm, m. PRICE: $100.00/yr. PUBLISHER: H. W. Wilson Co., 950 University Ave., Bronx, New York 10452. EDITOR: Jean Marra. DATABASE: RG. TARGET AUDIENCE: GP.

This index covers about 160 journals aimed at the general public. It is divided into two parts; the first part is an author/subject index followed by a listing of book reviews. All of the journals covered are in English. It should be noted that the entries in the index are subdivided.

15. Religion Index One: Periodicals. DATE FOUNDED: 1949. TITLE CHANGES: Index to Religious Periodical Literature, 1949-1976. FREQUENCY: a. PRICE: $314.00/yr. PUBLISHER: American Theological Library Association, Religion Index One: Periodicals, 5600 S. Wooodlawn Ave., Chicago, Illinois 60637. EDITOR: Paul D. Peterson. CIRCULATION: 1,200. MICROFORMS: Comfiche. DATABASE: ATLA, RI. TARGET AUDIENCE: AC, GP, SP.

After starting out as a small, slim volume in 1949, this index has grown to the point that it is necessary now to split the publication into two parts: periodicals and multivolume works. It indexes 369 journals from all over the world and in all fields relevant to religion; while many of the journals are in a foreign language, most are in English. The index is split into three sections: subject index, author index with abstracts, and a book review index; the second part is only selective. This index will start to be published in two volumes starting with volume 16. It lists the journals and their addresses, but at least for the U. S. journals, no zip codes are supplied.

16. Religious and Theological Abstracts. DATE FOUNDED: 1958. FREQUENCY: q. PRICE: $44.00/yr., institutions; $22.00/yr., individuals. PUBLISHER: Religious and Theological Abstracts, Inc., P. O. Box 215, Myerstown, Pennsylvania. EDITOR: J. Creighton Christman, D. D. INDEX. CIRCULATION: 1,000. MANUSCRIPT SELECTION: Editor. Articles selected from over 200 journals. MICROFORMS: Publisher. TARGET AUDIENCE: AC. SAMPLE COPIES: To libraries.

Religious and Theological Abstracts contains precis of journal articles from about 200 journals; these abstracts are arranged topically: Bible, theology, history, and practical theology. There are about 4,000 abstracts per year. The indexes to each volume is located in the fourth issue; they are organized by author, subject, citations from

Scripture. Additionally, there are lists of the abstractors, the list of journals abstracted and their addresses. While the title implies that articles about religion are abstracted, most of the abstracts are centered either on Judaism or Christianity; the abstracts on ecumenism and world religions are in the minority.

17. Religious Studies Review. DATE FOUNDED: 1975. FREQUENCY: q. PRICE: $18.00/yr., for members of the Council of Societies for the Study of Religion; $24.00/yr., for others. PUBLISHER: Council of Societies for the Study of Religion, Mercer University, Macon, Georgia 31207. EDITOR: Dr. Harold Remus. INDEX. ADVERTISEMENTS. CIRCULATION: 2,625. MANUSCRIPT SELECTION: Editors. REPRINTS: Back issues from the Council of Societies for the Study of Religion. BOOK REVIEWS. INDEXED/ABSTRACTED: IZBG, NTA, RIO, SRA. DATABASE: ATLA, RI. TARGET AUDIENCE: AC. SAMPLE COPIES.

This journal is one of the very few that is devoted to reviewing current books in the field of religion. Besides the six major review essays that may be either on specific books or on contemporary academic problems as exemplified in recent books, the Religious Studies Review has many short reviews of books arranged by subject. Every issue has 300 reviews, all signed; in addition to those, the signed essays are 4,000 to 6,00 words; the critical notes are written in 200 words. Each issue also has a bibliography devoted to a particular subject, and a list of dissertations, both completed and in progress. The section, "Personalia," lists experts in various fields. For a scholarly review of current literature in the academic study of religion, this journal is a must. The only caveat would be that it may take a year or more after publication for a book to be reviewed; that could mean that the book may be out of print when a library, relying on this journal, decides to buy one of the books reviewed.

18. Social Sciences Citation Index. DATE FOUNDED: 1969. FREQUENCY: 3/yr.; cumulated at the end of the year. PRICE: $2,300.00/yr. PUBLISHER: Institute for Scientific Information, 3501 Market St., Philadelphia, Pennsylvania 19104. ADVERTISEMENTS: In-house. DATABASE: SocScisearch. TARGET AUDIENCE: AC, GP, SP.

This publication indexes 4,500 journals, 1,400 of which are fully covered. Like its relative, the Arts and Humanities Index, it indexes the journals four different ways: by subject, by citation, by author, and by geography. It covers the full range of the fields in the social sciences as well as some that might be considered to be in the field of humanities, such as history and philosophy. The 3,100 selectively covered journals are derived from the Science Citation Index. The coverage is very wide; the print is very small.

19. Social Sciences Index. DATE FOUNDED: 1974. TITLE CHANGES: International Index to Periodicals, 1907-1955; International Index, 1955-1965; Social Sciences and Humanities Index, 1965-1974. FREQUENCY: q. (bound at the end of the year). PRICE: $75.00/yr. or less depending on the periodical holdings of the library. PUBLISHER: H. W. Wilson Co., 950 University Ave., Bronx, New York 10452. EDITOR: Joseph Bloomfield. CIRCULATION: 4,400. MANUSCRIPT SELECTION: Journals covered are chosen by the subscribers. DATABASE: SSI. TARGET AUDIENCE: AC, GP, SP.

This index is similar in format to the Humanities Index except that it indexes about the same number of journals in the social sciences. The index is divided into two sections: an author/title alphabetic listing and a listing of the books reviewed in the journals indexed. All of the journals indexed are in English.

20. Southern Baptist Periodical Index. DATE FOUNDED: 1966-1985. FREQUENCY: a. PRICE: $32.95/yr., for previous volumes. PUBLISHER: The Historical Commission of the Southern Baptist Convention, 901 Commerce Street, Suite 400, Nashville, Tennessee 37203-3620. MICROFORMS: Back issues are available. AUDIENCE: SP.

This denominational index, while defunct, is included because it covered the literature produced by the agencies of the Southern Baptist Convention, one of the largest denominations in the United States. Some important journals, like the Review and Expositor, still list it as an indexer of its articles. The index was computer produced and made camera ready for printing; unfortunately, the resulting copy is not too clear and is hard to read. It is arranged in one alphabetic list with both authors and subjects combined. There is no separate breakdown by subject as is found in the abstracting services.

History of Religions

21. American Quarterly. DATE FOUNDED: 1949. FREQUENCY: 5/yr. PRICE: Individuals: varies with membership dues to the American Studies Association; libraries: $30.00, domestic; $35.00, foreign. PUBLISHER: Trustees of the University of Pennsylvania, Philadelphia, Pennsylvania 19104. EDITOR: Janice Radway, Richard R. Beeman. ILLUSTRATIONS: Occasionally. INDEX: Partially. ADVERTISEMENTS. CIRCULATION: 4,400. MANUSCRIPT SELECTION: Editors and outside readers. MICROFORMS: UMI, MIM. BOOK REVIEWS. SPECIAL ISSUES. INDEXED/ABSTRACTED: AHCI, CC, HI, MLA, RIO, LCR. DATABASE: AHSearch, ATLA, HI, RI. TARGET AUDIENCE: AC, SP. SAMPLE COPIES: To libraries.

American Quarterly is not only a journal of history, but a journal of cultural life. Its articles, numbering about five and written by American academics, aim to give direction to the studies of American culture, both past and present. Writers are encouraged not only to write about what they know best but to relate it to the entire American culture. In general, such articles will explore behaviour and social ethics, whether it be on "civilization" and the war with Spain or on the deeper meanings for American culture as found in Uncle Tom's Cabin. The articles on religion also are culturally based as the article on the ghostlore among the Afro-American slaves shows. The articles are documented. The three to five signed reviews, consisting of two to five pages apiece, are both long and penetrating.

22. Greek, Roman, and Byzantine Studies. DATE FOUNDED: July 1958. TITLE CHANGES: Greek and Byzantine Studies,

vol. 1, issues 1-2. FREQUENCY: q. PRICE: $18.00/yr. (10% discount through agencies). PUBLISHER: Duke University, 329 Perkins Library, Durham, North Carolina 27706. EDITOR: D. Keith Stanley. ILLUSTRATIONS. INDEX. ADVERTISEMENTS: In house. CIRCULATION: 900. MANUSCRIPT SELECTION: Editor in consultation with editors with special subject expertise. MICROFORMS: Kraus. INDEXED/ABSTRACTED: AHCI, AP, CC, HI, RILA, RIO. DATABASE: AHSearch, ATLA, HI, RI. TARGET AUDIENCE: AC, SP. SAMPLE COPIES: Occasionally.

This journal of about 100 pages per issue, is devoted to studying all aspects of the Greek world from its prehistory through the Byzantine period. Articles concerned primarily with Latin are excluded; the reference to "Roman" in the title is geographical only. It is very similar to the _Journal of Greek Studies_ or the _Bulletin of the American Society of Papyrologists_. It does not have a book review section. Its annual indices not only include a listing of the journal articles by author and a subject index, but also an index of Greek words cited in that year's issues. The subject index is very complete.

23. _History of Religions_. DATE FOUNDED: 1961. FREQUENCY: q. PRICE: $23.40/yr., individuals; $38.25/yr, libraries. PUBLISHER: University of Chicago Press, Journals Division, P. O. Box 37005, Chicago, Illinois 60637. EDITOR: Joseph M. Kitagawa, Frank E. Reynolds, Wendy D. O'Flaherty. ILLUSTRATIONS. INDEX. ADVERTISEMENTS. CIRCULATION: 2,000. MANUSCRIPT SELECTION: Editors and referees. MICROFORMS: MIM, UMI. REPRINTS: UMI, ISI; also from the University of Chicago Press. BOOK REVIEWS. SPECIAL ISSUES. INDEXED/ABSTRACTED: AHCI, America, CC, GSScRel, HI, IZBG, NTA, OTA, RIO, RTA. DATABASE: AHSearch, America, ATLA, HI, RI. TARGET AUDIENCE: AC, SP, UndSt.

This quarterly is dedicated to the study of historical religious phenomena, either within particular traditions or across cultural boundaries; it seeks to integrate the results of the several disciplines of the science of religion. The writers are academics from all over the world; the articles, averaging four per issue, are signed. If articles are submitted in any of the major foreign languages, they are translated into English. In addition to the four to six signed, 1,000 word book reviews, there are "Book Notes," which are shorter reviews that are one fourth as long. The articles do not exhibit any; confessional stance; instead the writers attempt to be objective and scientific. In coverage and outlook, this journal is very comparable to _Religion_.

24. _Journal of Dharma: An International Quarterly of World Religions_. DATE FOUNDED: 1975. FREQUENCY: q.

PRICE: $15.00/yr., surface mail; $20.00/yr., air mail. PUBLISHER: Dharma Research Association, Dharmaram College, Bangalore-560 029, India. EDITOR: Thomas Kadankavil. INDEX. CIRCULATION: 1,000. MANUSCRIPT SELECTION: Editorial board. REPRINTS. INDEXED/ABSTRACTED: AHCI, CC, PI, RIO. DATABASE: AHSearch, ATLA, PI, RI. TARGET AUDIENCE: AC, SP. SAMPLE COPIES.

This journal is not simply a journal on the history of religions; it also is aimed at a dialogue between different religions, at a discussion of man's ultimate concern as seen from the point of view of the world's religions. This results in a publication that is not drily academic, but attempts to relate the spirit of religion to mundane concerns. The editorial preceding the articles of each issue especially shows this concern as it reflects on the topic being considered in that issue. All the articles are signed and documented. Its "Book Review" section is simply a listing of books with imprint data. It is comparable to other "spiritualist" journals such as _Anima_, but it is much more down-to-earth; the reader is not overwhelmed by eastern religious technical terms.

25. _Journal of Religion_. DATE FOUNDED: 1921. MERGER: Formed by the union of _American Journal of Theology_ and _Biblical World_. FREQUENCY: q. PRICE: Institutions, $35.00/yr.; individuals, $22.00/yr.; students, $16.00/yr.; University of Chicago Divinity School, $16.00/yr. PUBLISHER: University of Chicago Press, Journals Division, P. O. Box 37005, Chicago, Illinois 60637. EDITOR: Robin W. Lorin, David Tracy, Anthony C. Yu. INDEX. ADVERTISEMENTS. CIRCULATION: 2,400. MICROFORMS: Microfilm, UMI; microfiche, KTO; MIM. REPRINTS: ISI Tear Service; UMI; from the publisher. BOOK REVIEWS. SPECIAL ISSUES. INDEXED/ABSTRACTED: AHCI, BRD, CC, GSScRel, HI, IZBG, OTA, RTA, RIO, SSCI. DATABASE: AHSearch, ATLA, HI, RI, SocScisearch. TARGET AUDIENCE: AC.

This journal is aimed at the scholar who studies religion from a purely objective, phenomenological point of view. The articles are written by scholars, are signed, and are amply documented. The book reviews are both short and long; the former average twenty per issue and comprise 150 to 500 words; the latter number about 25 and are composed on one page. The journal seeks to promote critical and systematic inquiry into religion. Contributions are encouraged from scholars in theology and other types of religious studies (literary, social, pscyhological, and philosophical). The articles have a Western slant and seem to assume that Christians or students of Christianity are its readers. Rarely if ever is there an article on the nature of religion from an Eastern perspective. The prose is dry. It is much like the Journal for the Scientific Study of Religion, except that it is more "academic," and its prose suffers by comparison.

26. Journal of the American Academy of Religion. DATE FOUNDED: 1933. TITLE CHANGES: Journal of Bible and Religion (1933-1966). FREQUENCY: q. PRICE: $50.00/yr. PUBLISHER: Scholars Press, P. O. Box 1608, Decatur, Georgia 30031. EDITOR: Robert Scharlemann. INDEX. ADVERTISEMENTS. CIRCULATION: 5,832. MANUSCRIPT SELECTION: Editor. MICROFORMS: UMI, publisher. REPRINTS: UMI; hard copy available from Scholars Press, Customer Services, P. O. Box 4869, Hampden Station, Baltimore, Maryland 21211. BOOK REVIEWS. INDEXED/ABSTRACTED: BullSig, CC, ElencBibBib, Elenchus, GSScRel, HI, IZBG, Magazines, NTA, RevHE, RIO, RPI, RTA, SSCI, Zdienst. DATABASE: ATLA, Francis, HI, RI, SocScisearch. TARGET AUDIENCE: AC. SAMPLE COPIES.

This journal includes scholarly articles on the full range of world religious traditions together with studies of the methodologies by which they are explored. Such fullness can include articles on Whitehead's ideas on the connection between theology and poetry and on the religious elements in Sartre's existential psychoanalysis. The other articles take up studies on the more usual topics of world religions. The book review section covers about thirty books, all of which are explicitly organized under subject headings for easy reference. Each review is signed and takes up one half to one page per review. The "Books Received" section is organized on the basis of whether the books are hardbound or paperbound.

27. Numen: International Review for the History of Religions. DATE FOUNDED: 1954. FREQUENCY: sa. PRICE: Dfl.93.80 or $34.50/yr.; Dfl.76.00 or $28.00/yr. for members of the International Association for the History of Religions or of affiliated societies. PUBLISHER: E. J. Brill, P. O. B. 9000, 2300 PA Leiden, The Netherlands. EDITOR: Heerman van Voss. ADVERTISEMENTS. CIRCULATION: 300. REPRINTS: Back issues from the publisher. BOOK REVIEWS. SPECIAL ISSUES. INDEXED/ABSTRACTED: CC, RIO, NTA. DATABASE: ATLA, RI. TARGET AUDIENCE: AC. SAMPLE COPIES.

As the organ of the International Association for the History of Religions, this journal investigates aspects of various religions, both dead and alive, and seeks to discover their meanings. This journal's articles are signed and are well documented. Most of the articles are in English although articles in Italian, French, and German are invited. Unlike some history of religion journals, the articles here are not permeated throughout by abstractions. It also investigates the history of religion such as

Mithraism or medieval Christianity's response to Buddhism. In contrast to History of Religions, the style of the articles is not dry at all. The book review section contains two or three signed book reviews that are of various lengths. There is also a section for books received. Occasionally an obituary of a famous scholar will be included. This journal is a must.

28. Orita: Ibadan Journal of Religious Studies. DATE FOUNDED: 1967. FREQUENCY: sa. PRICE: Nigeria, 8.00 naira/yr.; outside Nigeria, $16.00/yr., 12.00 pounds sterling/yr. PUBLISHER: University of Ibadan, Dept. of Religious Studies, Ibadan, Nigeria EDITOR: Amba Oduyoye. ILLUSTRATIONS. INDEX: Cumulated. CIRCULATION: 500. MANUSCRIPT SELECTION: Editor. REPRINTS: Back issues from the publisher. BOOK REVIEWS. INDEXED/ABSTRACTED: AfrAb. TARGET AUDIENCE: AC.

Orita seeks to promote the study and understanding of the implications of religion and particularly religion in Africa; this involves the study of Christianity, Islam, and traditional African religion. Every effort is given to providing equal space to each. The articles, in typescript, are written by scholars, primarily Nigerians. The articles are very objective covering such subjects as Yoruba sanctuary pottery, the Amarna letters, and religious movements in Nigeria. Each issue has an average of two signed book reviews consisting of three pages each. The style of writing tends to be rather dry, and typographical errors are numerous. Each issue is devoted to one particular topic.

29. Religion. DATE FOUNDED: 1971. FREQUENCY: q. PUBLISHER: Academic Press Inc. (London) Ltd., 24-28 Oval Road, London NW1 7DX, England. EDITOR: Stuart Mews. ILLUSTRATIONS. INDEX. ADVERTISEMENTS. CIRCULATION: 700. MANUSCRIPT SELECTION: Editor, after peer review. REPRINTS: Available from the authors; back issues from the publisher. BOOK REVIEWS. INDEXED/ABSTRACTED: AHCI, CC, NTA, OTA, RIO. DATABASE: AHSearch, ATLA, RI. TARGET AUDIENCE: AC, SP.

This is a British journal, but the editorial board draws on specialists in the study of religion from around the world. It is dedicated to the scientific, sociological, objective study of religion, religions, or aspects of religions. The journal's six articles do not reveal the authors' commitment or lack of it to the religion that they are studying. Each issue has five signed one page book reviews. The journal is definitely academic in tone.

30. Religion in Southern Africa. DATE FOUNDED: 1980. FREQUENCY: sa. PRICE: Individuals, R6.00/yr. in Southern

Africa; elsewhere R10.00/yr. or $12.00/yr.; libraries, R8.00/yr. in Southern Africa; elsewhere R10.00 or $12.00. PUBLISHER: Association for the Study of Religion (Southern Africa), University of Natal, P. O. Box 375, 3200 Pietermaritzburg, South Africa. EDITOR: Professor Martin H. Prozesky. INDEX: Every second year. CIRCULATION: 160. MANUSCRIPT SELECTION: Editorial board and referees. REPRINTS: Back issues from the Circulation Manager. BOOK REVIEWS. INDEXED/ABSTRACTED: ISAP, RIO, ZdienstTh. DATABASE: ATLA, RI. TARGET AUDIENCE: AC, SP. SAMPLE COPIES.

As a purely academic non-theological journal dealing with religious studies in South Africa, this publication contains very objective, somewhat dry articles on facets of religion in South Africa, and not necessarily on Christianity. There are several articles on the native religions of the area; the book reviews tend to have the same emphasis. Four signed 1,200 word book reviews are published in each issue. All of the articles and reviews are signed and are published photographically from typewritten pages. While other journals from South Africa deal with Christianity, this journal discusses religion in general in South Africa, especially as it is expressed by the native peoples.

31. Religious Studies. DATE FOUNDED: 1965. FREQUENCY: q. PRICE: Institutions, 44.00 pounds/yr. ($105.00/yr. in Canada and the United States); individuals, 22.00 pounds/yr. ($50.00/yr. in the United States and Canada). PUBLISHER: Cambridge University Press, the Edinburgh Building, Shaftesbury Road, Cambridge CB2 2RU, England; Cambridge University Press, 32 East 57th Street, New York, New York 10022. EDITOR: Professor S. R. Sutherland. INDEX. ADVERTISEMENTS. CIRCULATION: 1,200. MANUSCRIPT SELECTION: Editor and/or editorial Board. MICROFORMS: UMI. REPRINTS: ISI Tear Service, 3501 Market Street, Philadelphia, Pennsylvania 19104; each issue also available for 14.00 pounds or $32.00. BOOK REVIEWS. INDEXED/ABSTRACTED: AHCI, BHI, CC, HI, NTA, RIO, RTA. DATABASE: AHSearch, ATLA, HI, RI. TARGET AUDIENCE: AC.

This is a very academic journal that wishes to concern itself with the various fields of religious study, whether they be the psychological, philosophical, comparative, historical, or sociological aspects of the field. The journal's articles, however, have a very philosophical and objective quality about them. The six or seven articles are written primarily by American, British, and Irish academics. The prose is usually clear; at times it becomes very remote through the frequent use of the pronoun, "one." Western philosophical religion or Christianity is assumed; in the journal reviewed, the emphasis was on Western theism with no indication of discussing its Eastern counterpart. The reader will discover that the book reviews average twenty per issue, are signed, and comprise one to three pages apiece.

32. Religious Studies News. DATE FOUNDED: 1986. TITLE CHANGES: Council on the Study of Religion Bulletin, 1970-1986. FREQUENCY: bm. PRICE: $20.00/yr. Subscribers to journals of the constituent societies receive issues free. PUBLISHER: Scholars Press, 819 Houston Mill Rd., Atlanta, Georgia. EDITOR: Sherrie Hollis. ADVERTISEMENTS. CIRCULATION: 13,500. MANUSCRIPT SELECTION: Editor. MICROFORMS: UMI. INDEXED/ABSTRACTED: NTA, RIO. DATABASE: ATLA, RI. TARGET AUDIENCE: AC, SP. SAMPLE COPIES.

For those wishing to know about what is happening in the field of religion, this is an important publication since it has news, and announcements about the field of religious studies and about the constituent societies such as the American Academy of Religion and the Society of Biblical Literature. It is written by and for academics. Most of the journal is composed of news and announcements. One noteworthy feature is "Offline" which is dedicated to the use of computers in the study of religious texts; it is notable for its discussion of printer fonts for specialized languages such as Hebrew, Greek, and Arabic. It is the academic version of a denominational or sectarian news bulletin. If a library has a publication of one of the constituent societies, it should have this publication; in fact, it is probably a part of the subscription to that society's journal.

33. The Scottish Journal of Religious Studies. DATE FOUNDED: 1980. FREQUENCY: sa. PRICE: $10.00/yr., individuals; $20.00/yr., libraries. PUBLISHER: University of Stirling, Stirling FK9 4LA, Scotland. EDITOR: Glyn Richards. INDEX. ADVERTISEMENTS. CIRCULATION: 200. MANUSCRIPT SELECTION: Editorial Board and the International Advisory Board. REPRINTS: Back issues from the editor. BOOK REVIEWS. SPECIAL ISSUES. INDEXED/ABSTRACTED: RIO. DATABASE: ATLA, RI. TARGET AUDIENCE: AC, SP, UndSt. SAMPLE COPIES.

This journal seeks to promote the study of all the major religious traditions from a variety of standpoints and advocates a critical investigation of all those traditions. The articles encompass a wide range of subjects, from the theological dimensions of ecology to a study of Islamic mosques. The four or five signed articles and reviews are more relevant to the twentieth century than the articles in History of Religions which tends to be more phenomenological in its approach. The articles are sometimes difficult to read because of the layout and type-face, but they are worth the effort. The six signed 1,000 word reviews, written in a very lively style, are especially good.

34. Studies in Comparative Religion. DATE FOUNDED: 1967. TITLE CHANGES: Tomorrow, 1941-1966. FREQUENCY: q. PRICE: 8.80 pounds/yr.; United States, $19.50/yr. PUBLISHER: Perennial Books Ltd., Pates Manor, Bedfont, Middlesex TW14 8JP, England. EDITOR: Peter Hobson, Ralph Smith, Olive Clive-Ross. INDEX. ADVERTISEMENTS. CIRCULATION: Controlled. MANUSCRIPT SELECTION: Editors. MICROFORMS: UMI. REPRINTS: UMI; single and double issues available from the publisher for a price. BOOK REVIEWS. INDEXED/ABSTRACTED: CC, HI, AHCI. DATABASE: AHSearch, HI. TARGET AUDIENCE: AC, SP.

This periodical is devoted to the exposition of the teachings, spiritual methods, symbolism, and other facets of the world of religion. Traditional themes of religions of both East and West are explored in about fourteen articles per double issue, written by academics; many of the articles are documented, but the authors' credentials are not noted. The prose is somewhat difficult to read; it becomes abstract and very distant at times. The articles are very ecumenical; the exclusivistic emphasis in religion is not high-lighted. The books reviewed are also criticized from the same point of view; each issue has six signed one to three page of this type. Scattered throughout are quotations from famous religious people such as Augustine and Plotinus. For collections that view comparative religion from a Western point of view, this is a good corrective.

35. Studies in Religion/Sciences religieuses. DATE FOUNDED: 1971. TITLE CHANGES: Supersedes Canadian Journal of Theology, 1955-1971. FREQUENCY: q. PRICE: $20.00/yr., individuals; $30.00/yr., libraries; $10.00/yr., students. PUBLISHER: Wilfrid Laurier University Press, Waterloo, Ontario, Canada N2L 3C5. EDITOR: Tom Sinclair-Faulkner, Roland Chagnon. ILLUSTRATIONS. INDEX: For vols. 1-10, in vol. 10. ADVERTISEMENTS. CIRCULATION: 1,300. MANUSCRIPT SELECTION: Decision based on evaluation by two external readers. REPRINTS: Back issues available from the publisher. BOOK REVIEWS. SPECIAL ISSUES. INDEXED/ABSTRACTED: AHCI, Bullsig, NTA, OTA, RIO, RTA. DATABASE: AHSearch, ATLA, RI. TARGET AUDIENCE: AC, SP.

This journal is not concerned with the history of religion. Instead, it publishes about eight articles per issue on various topics within the Christian tradition. These signed articles not only deal with the New Testament but with rabbinic and Old Testament writings as well. The books reviewed are on other topics, however, that come closer to the study of the history of religion. The journal is sponsored by the Canadian Corporation for Studies in Religion, which, in turn, publishes supplements and special monographs. The articles may be written in French or English; they are clearly written. Twenty signed 500 word reviews are found in each issue. The issues are usually dedicated to one theme; the journal is comparable, in many ways, to Interpretation.

Primal Religions

36. Journal of Religion in Africa/Religion en Afrique. DATE FOUNDED: 1967. TITLE CHANGES: African Religious Research. FREQUENCY: 3/yr. PRICE: Gld.84.60. PUBLISHER: E. J. Brill, P. O. Box 9000, 2300 PA Leiden, The Netherlands. EDITOR: A. F. Walls, Lamin Sanneh. ILLUSTRATIONS: Occasionally. INDEX. ADVERTISEMENTS: In-house. CIRCULATION: 500. BOOK REVIEWS. INDEXED/ABSTRACTED: AHCI, CC, RIO. DATABASE: AHSearch, ATLA, RI. TARGET AUDIENCE: AC, SP.

Focusing on the scientific study of the forms and history of religion within Africa, with a special emphasis on sub-Saharan Africa, approximately four articles per issue contain research on African religion, its worship and ethics. Some articles reflect on the effect of mission on African religion. All articles are signed, and the authors are drawn from around the world; while the articles may be in French or English, most are written in English. There are two book reviews per year; each is signed and takes up two pages. The prose is engaging; it is proof that literary style does not have to be burdened by the weight of the content of the article. It is objective; that makes it different from other journals such as the Africa Theological Journal on African religion.

37. Latin American Indian Literatures Journal. DATE FOUNDED: July 1984. TITLE CHANGES: Latin American Indian Literatures (1977-1984). The current journal starts at vol. 1, but continues the tradition of the former journal. FREQUENCY: sa. PRICE: $13.00, individuals; $23.00, libraries; $28.00 and up for sponsors. PUBLISHER: Geneva College, Beaver Falls, Pennsylvania 15010. EDITOR:

Dr. Mary H. Preuss. ILLUSTRATIONS. INDEX. ADVERTISEMENTS. CIRCULATION: 200. MANUSCRIPT SELECTION: Editor and Board of Advisers. REPRINTS: Back issues available from the editor. BOOK REVIEWS. INDEXED/ABSTRACTED: Contact editor, too early to tell. DATABASE: Contact editor; too early to tell. TARGET AUDIENCE: AC, GP, SP, UndSt.

Each issue has two to four book reviews, each one signed and taking up three pages.

Spiritualism

38. Anima: An Experiential Journal. DATE FOUNDED: 1974. TITLE CHANGES: Anima: An Experimental Journal (1974-1976). FREQUENCY: sa. PRICE: $9.95/yr. PUBLISHER: Conococheague Associates, 1053 Wilson Avenue, Chambersburg, Pennsylvania 17201. EDITOR: Harry M. Buck. ILLUSTRATIONS. INDEX: Ten year index. ADVERTISEMENTS. CIRCULATION: 2,000. MANUSCRIPT SELECTION: Editorial board. INDEXED/ABSTRACTED: Dustbooks, PTLA, RIO. DATABASE: ATLA, RI. TARGET AUDIENCE: AC, GP, SP. SAMPLE COPIES.

This journal is very difficult to categorize. It contains essays, book reviews, fiction, and poetry; it is written by and for women. It focuses mainly on women in religion, not necessarily only in Christianity. It also discusses such ideas as Jungian psychology and Ying and Yang. It aims to promote a wholistic view of life. It is clear that many writers wish to expunge images that are contrary to that vision. The articles are controversial, but not strident. On occasion, there is a book review. This journal includes religious positions that are being heard more and more.

39. Creation. DATE FOUNDED: 1985. FREQUENCY: bm. PRICE: $17.00/yr., individuals; $29.00, libraries. PUBLISHER: Friends of Creation Spirituality, Inc., P. O. Box 19216, Oakland, California 94619. EDITOR: Jim Holland, Marcia Lovelace Tolva. ILLUSTRATIONS. ADVERTISEMENTS. CIRCULATION: 2,000. BOOK REVIEWS. TARGET AUDIENCE: GP.

This very new journal, containing about twelve articles per issue, is devoted to a creation-centered, historically-rooted, integrated, compassionate spirituality. The authors are theologians, scientists, biblical scholars, environmentalists, artists, economists, and psychologists. The authors, however, seem to be chosen for their views; judging by the first issue, there seem to be no opinions expressed that are contrary to the viewpoints of the Friends of Creation Spirituality. In addition to the regular articles, each issue is introduced with a letter from the editors, and "News and Notes." Each issue has an average of one book review, covering one page.

40. Healing Review. DATE FOUNDED: 1955. FREQUENCY: 3/yr. PRICE: Free, libraries; 2.80 pounds/yr., individuals. PUBLISHER: National Federation of Spiritual Healers, Old Manor Farm Studio, Church Street, Sunbury-on-Thames, Middlesex TW16 6RG England; printer: H. Doust, 1 Holmside, Gillingham, Kent ME7 4BQ, England. EDITOR: John Dreghorn. ILLUSTRATIONS. INDEX. ADVERTISEMENTS. CIRCULATION: 3,500. MANUSCRIPT SELECTION: Editorial panel. REPRINTS: From the printer; some back issues available from the publisher. BOOK REVIEWS. TARGET AUDIENCE: GP, HS, SP. SAMPLE COPIES.

This journal is dedicated to spiritual healing which is defined as healing of sick in body, mind, and spirit by means of laying of hands or by either prayer or meditation. Each issue has six to eight articles that are either original or from other publications. The journal advocates a view of health that is wholistic and that spiritual healing is the only true healing; it emphasizes true health and has training sessions advertised in its pages. Those who are put off by the idea of spiritual healing should give this journal a chance. The authors are drawn from all over the world and the articles are signed. In addition to the articles, there are two to three signed book reviews, each one occupying 300 words.

41. The Journal of Religion and Psychical Research. DATE FOUNDED: 1979. TITLE CHANGES: The Journal of the Academy of Religion and Psychical Research; name changed with January 1979 issue. FREQUENCY: q. PRICE: $15.00/yr., individuals (journal is a benefit of being a member of the academy); $8.00, libraries. PUBLISHER: The Academy of Religion and Psychical Research, P. O. Box 614, Bloomfield, Connecticut 06002. EDITOR: Mary Carman Rose. INDEX. CIRCULATION: 300. MANUSCRIPT SELECTION: Editor. REPRINTS: Back issues available from publisher at $2.00 each. BOOK REVIEWS. INDEXED/ABSTRACTED: RIO. DATABASE: ATLA, RI. TARGET AUDIENCE: AC, SP, UndSt. SAMPLE COPIES.

As a journal dedicated to be a forum for a dialogue and exchange of ideas in the areas in which religion and psychical research interface., this is a scholarly work containing articles not so much on things as seances, but on the non-tangible aspects of religion: dreams, life after death, intercession, witchcraft in the history of religion, and gnosticism. All of the articles are by scholars, mainly American, are documented, and are signed, as are the book reviews which number three, each one composed in two or three pages. One usual feature in this journal is the reporting of mystical and psychical experiences. The title may put people off, but the journal is a solid effort to explore the non-rational elements of religion

42. Studies in Formative Spirituality. DATE FOUNDED: 1979. TITLE CHANGES: Humanitas (1965-1979). FREQUENCY: 3/yr. PRICE: $16.00/yr. PUBLISHER: Institute of Formative Spirituality, Duquesne University, Pittsburgh, Pennsylvania 15282. EDITOR: Adrian van Kaam. INDEX. CIRCULATION: 2,000. MANUSCRIPT SELECTION: Editor. MICROFORMS: UMI. BOOK REVIEWS. INDEXED/ABSTRACTED: CC, CPLI, HI. DATABASE: HI. TARGET AUDIENCE: AC, SP.

In spite of the heavy jargon in the editorial on the meaning of formative spirituality and the glossary of the science of formative spirituality, the articles are written very clearly; they are written by experts in the field of religion and concentrate on various aspects of spirituality in many religions and aspects of life, e. g. education. The journal really deals not with spirituality so much as with the deepest possible ethics, whether religious or secular. Each issue has 100 book reviews, unsigned, written in only 100 words apiece. Besides the book review section, there are selected bibliographies on spirituality. This publication is very specialized; its approach seems to be unique, being a kind of cross between history of religions and the application of insights from that to daily life.

43. The Theosophist. DATE FOUNDED: 1879. FREQUENCY: m. PRICE: $8.00/yr; $16.00/yr., if mailed by airmail. PUBLISHER: The Theosophical Publishing House, Adyar, Madras-600020, India. EDITOR: Radha Burnier. ILLUSTRATIONS. INDEX. CIRCULATION: 2,000. MANUSCRIPT SELECTION: Editorial committee. REPRINTS: Vol. 1 from Wizards Bookshelf, Box 6600, San Diego, California 92106. BOOK REVIEWS. SPECIAL ISSUES: Rarely. TARGET AUDIENCE: AC, GP. SAMPLE COPIES.

As the publication of the Theosophical Society, both the articles, numbering about seven per issue, and the reviews seek to uphold the goals of the society: to remove conflict among people and religions. There is a general interest on the internal person as opposed to the external. All the articles and reviews are signed, and they are aimed at the theosophist as well as the layman. An average issue has two, signed, 250 word book reviews. This journal should be included in collections that do not have much on non-Western religions. While the articles are signed, neither the credentials nor the addresses of the authors are noted.

Religion and Society

44. Cross Currents. DATE FOUNDED: 1950. FREQUENCY: q. PRICE: Individuals: $8.00/yr.; 21.00/3 yrs.; outside of the United States and Canada, $8.50/yr., $22.50/3 yrs; libraries, $10.00/yr., $27.00/3 yrs., add $0.50 for postage for subscriptions outside the United States and Canada. PUBLISHER: Convergence, Inc., 1103 Van Houten Fields, West Nyack, New York 10994. EDITOR: Joseph Cunneen. ADVERTISEMENTS. CIRCULATION: 6,000. MICROFORMS: UMI. REPRINTS: UMI. BOOK REVIEWS. INDEXED/ABSTRACTED: CPLI, GSScRel, HI, OTA, RTA. DATABASE: HI. TARGET AUDIENCE: AC, SP, UndSt.

This journal, which describes itself as a quarterly review dedicated to exploring the implications of Christianity for our times, is a very inclusive journal, publishing articles not only on Christianity as it confronts social issues, but also philosophical issues such as the adequacy of existentialism, and the rise of Islam; it also contains an annual review of books in philosophy. At times, the focus is not on Christianity but on religion as it confronts society. This is especially evident in the book review section where books are selected for review for their discussion of values, whether they be books on religion or critical analyses of literature. Each issue, on the average, contains fifteen signed two to three page reviews. The journal is similar to Christianity and Crisis, but it is much more academic.

45. Journal for the Scientific Study of Religion. DATE FOUNDED: 1961. FREQUENCY: q. PRICE: $24.00/yr., $10.00/yr. for students and professors emeritus; outside the United States and Canada, $35.00/yr.; membership,

$20.00/yr., $10.00/yr. for students and professors emeritus, $23.00 outside of the United States and Canada. PUBLISHER: Society for the Scientific Study of Religion, University of Connecticut, Box U68A, Storrs, Connecticut 06268. EDITOR: Donald Capps. INDEX. ADVERTISEMENTS. CIRCULATION: 3,500. MICROFORMS: UMI. REPRINTS: UMI; back issues available from the publisher. BOOK REVIEWS. INDEXED/ABSTRACTED: AHCI, CC, GSScRel, HI, OTA, PA, RIO, SA, SSCI. DATABASE: AHSearch, ATLA, HI, RI, SA, SocScisearch. TARGET AUDIENCE: AC.

The journal is designed to be a forum for stimulating and communicating social scientific research on religious institutions and experience. The five or six articles are written mostly by American scholars and cover just about everything from state-church relationships to conversion experiences. The articles are objective and well documented. In addition to the articles there may be in each issue shorter articles designated as "Research Note," "Comment," or "Perspectives." The articles are objective, but the prose is not unengaging; at times many charts are used that employ theories of statistics. The books reviewed cover the same areas as the articles of the journal; each of the twelve reviews is signed and takes up one to twelve pages.

46. Journal of Feminist Studies in Religion. DATE FOUNDED: 1984. FREQUENCY: sa. PRICE: $12.00/yr., student; $15.00/yr., individual; $25.00/yr., institution; $50.00/yr., Contributing Subscriber; $100.00/yr., Sustaining Subscriber; $150.00, Founding Subscriber. PUBLISHER: Scholars Press, P. O. Box 1608, Decatur, Georgia 30031. EDITOR: Elisabeth Schussler Fiorenza; Judith Plaskow. ADVERTISEMENTS. CIRCULATION: Not yet determined. MANUSCRIPT SELECTION: Editors and editorial board. BOOK REVIEWS. INDEXED/ABSTRACTED: GSScRel, RIO, RTA. DATABASE: ATLA, RI. TARGET AUDIENCE: AC.

An average issue has one to two signed book reviews.

47. Journal of Religion and Health. DATE FOUNDED: 1961. FREQUENCY: q. PRICE: Institutions, $82.00/yr.; individuals, $33.00/yr. PUBLISHER: Institutes of Religion and Health, 3 West 29th Street, New York, New York 10001; printed by Human Sciences Press, Inc., 72 Fifth Avenue, New York, New York 10011. EDITOR: Harry C. Meserve. INDEX. ADVERTISEMENTS: In-house. CIRCULATION: 2,000. MANUSCRIPT SELECTION: Editor and editorial board. MICROFORMS: UMI. REPRINTS: UMI, ISI Tear Service. BOOK REVIEWS. INDEXED/ABSTRACTED: AHCI, CC, ExMed, GSScRel, PA, PCCA, RIO, RTA, SSCI. DATABASE: AHSearch, ATLA, RI, SocScisearch. TARGET AUDIENCE: SP.

This journal, founded by W. Clement Stone and having Norman Vincent Peal as one its life directors, has a very broad understanding of health and religion and is aimed at those who are interested in the indivisibility of human well-being in its physical, emotional, and spiritual aspects. In its seven or so articles, there is a heavy emphasis on a wholistic view of the individual, mankind, and the world. It approaches health from a broadly religious point of view; Jewish and Christian texts are cited but so are Freud and Jung. Each issue opens with a long editorial on the state of human health and ends with a book review. Each issue also has one signed two page book review. While this journal does not advocate faith healing, its wholistic viewpoint is not so far removed from that found in Healing Review.

48. The Journal of Religious Ethics. DATE FOUNDED: 1973. FREQUENCY: sa. PRICE: $12.00/yr., individuals; $18.00/yr., $34.00/2 yrs., $50.00/3 yrs. PUBLISHER: University of Notre Dame Press, Notre Dame, Indiana 46556. EDITOR: James T. Johnson. INDEX: In vol. 10, no. 2. ADVERTISEMENTS. CIRCULATION: 1,000. MANUSCRIPT SELECTION: Referees. MICROFORMS: UMI. REPRINTS: From the publisher for classroom use. BOOK REVIEWS. INDEXED/ABSTRACTED: AHCI, CC, HI, OTA, PI, RIO, RTA. DATABASE: AHSearch, ATLA, HI, PI, RI. TARGET AUDIENCE: AC, SP, UndSt. SAMPLE COPIES.

This publication is a scholarly journal investigating the area of religious ethics. The eight or so articles are divided into two parts; one is devoted to the topic of that issue while the other is concerned with other issues in religious ethics. Ethics is discussed from a Christian point of view; so a Buddhist view on an ethical problem would not appear in this journal while it might appear in the Journal of Dharma. The articles are documented and full references are given. The four to six one half page book reviews are signed, are rather short, and may be related exclusively to the main topic of that issue. The advertisements in each issue keep the reader up to date on new publications.

49. Review of Religious Research. DATE FOUNDED: 1959. FREQUENCY: q. PRICE: Individuals, $22.00/yr.; institutions, $30.00/yr. PUBLISHER: Religious Research Association, Box U-68A, Storrs, Connecticut 06268; printed by the Mennonite Press, Inc., 2505 North Main, North Newton, Kansas 67117. EDITOR: Edward C. Lehman, Jr. INDEX: Cumulated for v. 1-10. CIRCULATION: 1,200. MANUSCRIPT SELECTION: Editor. MICROFORMS: UMI. REPRINTS: UMI; single current copies $5.00 apiece; reprinted vols. 1-20 are

available from Hein. BOOK REVIEWS. INDEXED/ABSTRACTED: AHCI, CC, CERDIC, GSScRel, TLZ, RIO, RTA, SA, SCA, SSCI. DATABASE: AHSearch, ATLA, RI, SA, SocScisearch. TARGET AUDIENCE: AC, SP. SAMPLE COPIES:

This quarterly is devoted to furthering the understanding of the roles of religion in contemporary life. In fact, most of the articles apply the methods of sociology of religion to explain the place of religion in life. The writers are academics and are probably members of the Association since non-members have to pay $15.00 to have their submitted manuscripts reviewed. The issues explored are usually on how religion affects life and how life affects our religious choices. Each issue has seven signed book reviews, each one occupying one to two pages.

50. Social Compass: An International Review of Sociology of Religion/Revue internationale de sociologie de la religion. DATE FOUNDED: 1953. FREQUENCY: q. PRICE: Belgian francs 1,150.00/yr., individuals; 20% off for libraries; there are different prices for single, double, and reprint prices. PUBLISHER: Centre de Recherches Socio-religieuses, 1/21 Place Montesquieu, 1348 Louvain-la-Neuve, Belgium. EDITOR: A. Bastenier. ILLUSTRATIONS: Occasionally. INDEX. ADVERTISEMENTS. CIRCULATION: 1,500. MANUSCRIPT SELECTION: Editorial board. REPRINTS: Zwets; back issues available from the publisher for a price. BOOK REVIEWS. INDEXED/ABSTRACTED: AHCI, CC, RIO, RTA, SSCI. DATABASE: AHSearch, ATLA, RI, SocScisearch. TARGET AUDIENCE: AC.

This journal devotes its eight articles the study of the sociology of religion; some of the articles investigate meaning and power, the social forces that formed a Catholic regime, a sociological study of a cult, and divination in Zaire. The articles are written by scholars in the social sciences and are composed in English, French, or sometimes both. The authors' addresses are included in the journal. Each issue has one signed book review, written in three pages. Besides the book review section, there is a section for books reviewed. The advertisements keep this journal's readers aware of other journals and their contents that might be of interest to them.

51. Soundings: An Interdisciplinary Journal. DATE FOUNDED: 1917. TITLE CHANGES: Christian Scholar through 1967. FREQUENCY: q. PRICE: $12.00/yr., individuals; $18.00/yr., libraries; foreign subscribers, add $2.00. PUBLISHER: Soundings, University of Tennessee, 306 Alumni Hall, Station B, Knoxville, Tennessee 37996-0530. EDITOR: Ralph Norman. ILLUSTRATIONS: Occasionally. INDEX. ADVERTISEMENTS. CIRCULATION: 1,700. MANUSCRIPT SELECTION: Editor and editorial board. MICROFORMS: UMI, microfilm and

microfiche; KTO, microfiche. REPRINTS: UMI, ISI/OATS; back issues also from the publisher. SPECIAL ISSUES. INDEXED/ABSTRACTED: AHCI, AHI, America, CC, CDA, CIJE, FLI, HA, LLBA, OT/ANE, RIC, RIO, RTA, SA. DATABASE: AHSearch, America, ATLA, HA, RI, SA. TARGET AUDIENCE: AC. SAMPLE COPIES.

As an interdisciplinary journal, Soundings seeks to publish essays which use one discipline to probe the ideas of another or which connect two disciplines in order to provide a new perspective. The essays, written by scholars, do that by treating such subjects as Deconstruction or the morality of vengeance through an examination of Shakespeare. At times there are special sections such as one on the professions. In some ways many of the articles have a philosophical cast or an approach to literature that seeks religious values. That this is considered to be a religious journal can be seen by the advertisements in it.

Eastern Religions

52. The Divine Life. DATE FOUNDED: 1938. FREQUENCY: m. PRICE: $7.00/yr.; Rs20.00/yr. PUBLISHER: The Divine Life Society, The Swanda Publication League, P. O. Shwanandanagar, Distt. Tehri-Garhwal, U. P. Himalayas, India. EDITOR: Swami Krishnananda. INDEX. ADVERTISEMENTS. TARGET AUDIENCE: GP.

This is the official journal of the Divine Life Society which seeks to encourage Indian religion and philosophy, especially Yoga and Hinduism; there is a good deal of mention of mantras and the Bhagavad-gita. All of the five or so articles per issue are signed and written by various swamis. In addition to the articles, there is a section devoted to news about the Divine Life Society. Throughout each issue there are quotations from Swami Sivananda. This journal is especially important for those interested in Eastern religious thought patterns.

53. The Eastern Buddhist. DATE FOUNDED: 1921 (Old Series); 1965 (New Series). FREQUENCY: sa. PRICE: $15.00/yr. PUBLISHER: Scholars Press, P.O. Box 1608, Decatur, Georgia 30031. ILLUSTRATIONS. ADVERTISEMENTS: Advertisements only on an exchange basis. CIRCULATION: 1,500. MANUSCRIPT SELECTION: Editorial board. MICROFORMS: SP. REPRINTS: Hard copy from the publisher. BOOK REVIEWS. INDEXED/ABSTRACTED: AHCI, CC, RIO, RPI. DATABASE: AHSearch, ATLA, RI. TARGET AUDIENCE: AC, SP.

As a journal written by academics for scholars, it is a well laid out publication dedicated to the study of Mahayana Buddhism; it is non-sectarian. The authors are from East and West; the articles are in English, either originally or as translations. Although the journal is aimed at scholars and academics specializing in Buddhism will benefit most from it, non-specialists can also benefit from it since technical terms used in the articles are translated into English. Each issue has an average of four signed reviews covering three to four pages. The section, "Translations," contains translations and commentary on texts; "Views and Reviews" is a kind of Buddhist personal witness section.

54. Japanese Journal of Religious Studies. DATE FOUNDED: 1974. TITLE CHANGES: Contemporary Religions in Japan (1960-1970). FREQUENCY: q. PRICE: Individuals: 3,500 yen/yr., $15.00/yr. outside Japan; 6,000 yen/2 yrs., $25.00/2 yrs. outside Japan; institutions: 5,000 yen/yr., $20.00/yr. outside Japan; 8,500 yen/2 yrs., $35.00/2 yrs. outside Japan. PUBLISHER: Nanzan Institute for Religion and Culture, 18, Yamazato-cho, Showa-ku, Nagoya 466, Japan. EDITOR: Jan Swyngedouw. INDEX. CIRCULATION: 600. INDEXED/ABSTRACTED: CC, AHCI, RIO. DATABASE: AHSearch, ATLA, RIO. TARGET AUDIENCE: AC, SP.

Each issue of this journal begins with an "Editor's Page," followed by four articles, written by scholars from around the world, on some aspect of religion in Japan. It is difficult to categorize this journal; sometimes it is a history of religions journal; at others it is a history of religious ideas (wherever they may be found, e. g. in Japanese secular literature) journal. The journal itself wishes to advance interreligious understanding and further the pursuit of knowledge in the study of religion, especially Japanese religion; Japanese authors are especially invited to make contributions. There are no book reviews and no section for books received. The summer/fall issues are published together and are focused on one theme. This journal is definitely broader in scope than Japanese Religions; it is so broad in its approach, however, that it is difficult to compare it to another journal.

55. Japanese Religions. DATE FOUNDED: 1959. FREQUENCY: sa. PRICE: 3,600 yen/yr., $16.00/yr.(outside Japan)/volume (4 numbers in 2 years). PUBLISHER: Japanese Religions, NCC Center for the Study of Japanese Religions, c/o Kyoto Diocese of Japan, Episcopal Church, Karasuma Shimotachiuri, Kamikyo-ku, Kyoto 602, Japan. EDITOR: Yuki Hideo. CIRCULATION: 600. MANUSCRIPT SELECTION: Editors. REPRINTS: From the publisher; back issues available from the publisher. BOOK REVIEWS. INDEXED/ABSTRACTED: RIO, RTA, TA. DATABASE: ATLA, RI. TARGET AUDIENCE: AC, GP, SP.

The journal's title does not reveal the fact that, while all of Japan's religions are discussed, many of the articles discuss the relationship of Christianity to other religions and Japanese culture; other articles do discuss the other religions of Japan, but the emphasis surely seems to be on Christianity's place in the Japanese culture. All the articles are signed and documented and written by scholars or specialists; that does not mean that the general public would not gain from reading this journal; the English is very readable and technical terms do not get in the way. The articles are objective, but the enthusiasm for the subject at hand is apparent. Each issue has an average of five signed book reviews, each one taking up one to three pages. In appeal, it is much like the Japan Christian Quarterly, although more religions are treated here.

56. The Journal of the International Association of Buddhist Studies. DATE FOUNDED: 1978. FREQUENCY: sa. PRICE: individuals, $20.00/yr., institutions, $35.00/yr. PUBLISHER: The International Association of Buddhist Studies, Inc., c/o Dept. of South Asian Studies, 1258 Van Hise, 1220 Linden Drive, Madison, Wisconsin 53706. EDITOR: A. K. Narain. ILLUSTRATIONS. ADVERTISEMENTS. CIRCULATION: 600. MICROFORMS: UMI. REPRINTS: UMI; back issues also available. BOOK REVIEWS. TARGET AUDIENCE: AC, SP.

Dedicated to publishing articles on Buddhism from the point of view of all disciplines, including philosophy, history, sociology, religion, etc., this journal is divided into three sections. The first section contains five to six signed articles, written by scholars, from around the world on all aspects of Buddhism. The following book reviews are on books covering the same subjects in English. Finally, there is a section called "Notices," that reveals special collections, announcements of meetings and obituaries. This journal on Buddhism is not for the neophyte in the field who, without careful handling, could get lost by all the technical terminology. This is in contrast to the treatment in the Eastern Buddhist. All of the articles are documented, but the notes and the Chinese characters are placed at the end of the articles rather than at the bottom of the page. Five signed three page book reviews are found in each issue.

57. The Middle Way. DATE FOUNDED: 1926. FREQUENCY: q. PRICE: England, 6.00 pounds/yr.; foreign, 7.50 pounds/yr.; foreign air mail, 10.00 pounds/yr.; if payment is not made in pounds sterling, 2 pounds should be added to the price. PUBLISHER: The Buddhist Society, 58 Ecleston Square, London SW1V 1PH, England. EDITOR: John Snelling. ILLUSTRATIONS. INDEX. ADVERTISEMENTS. CIRCULATION: 2,500. MANUSCRIPT SELECTION: Editor. BOOK REVIEWS. TARGET AUDIENCE: AC, SP.

This journal exists to publish and make known the principles of Buddhism and to encourage their study and application. All material in sympathy with those goals will be considered for publication. The approximately eight articles are signed, but the authority of the author is not revealed. The essays can be formal studies on some aspect of Buddhism or interviews with a famous Buddhist. Its format, advertisements, and pictures may lead one to think of this journal as aimed at the general public, but technical terms are found in some articles and one not familiar with those terms may become lost; other articles will be of interest to the public and the historian of religions. In addition to the articles and nine signed, one to two page book reviews there is a section, "Newsround," reporting news of Buddhism in England and around the world; each issue also has an opening editorial on an aspect of Buddhism as it pertains to the modern world.

58. Philosophy East and West. DATE FOUNDED: 1951. FREQUENCY: q. PRICE: Individuals: $15.00/yr., $28.00/2 yrs.; institutions: $20.00/yr., $38.00/2 yrs.; air mail: $20.00/yr., $40.00/2 yrs. PUBLISHER: University of Hawaii Press, 2840 Kolowalu Street, Honolulu, Hawaii 96822. EDITOR: Eliot Deutsch. INDEX. ADVERTISEMENTS. CIRCULATION: 1,500. MANUSCRIPT SELECTION: Editor and editorial board. MICROFORMS: UMI. REPRINTS: Back issues also available from the publisher. BOOK REVIEWS. SPECIAL ISSUES. INDEXED/ABSTRACTED: AHCI, CC, PI, RTA, SA, SSCI. DATABASE: AHSearch, PI, SA, SocScisearch. TARGET AUDIENCE: AC, SP.

The book review section does not cover many books, but the five or six books examined require four to six pages.

59. The Sikh Courier. DATE FOUNDED: 1960. FREQUENCY: q. PRICE: 3.50 pounds/yr.; 30.00 pounds, life membership. PUBLISHER: The Sikh Cultural Society of Great Britain, 88 Mollison Way, Edgware, Middlesex HA8 5QW, England. EDITOR: Dr. S. S. Kapur; Amar Sing Chhatwal, Managing Editor. INDEX. ADVERTISEMENTS. CIRCULATION: 3,000. MANUSCRIPT SELECTION: Editors. REPRINTS: Back issues from the publisher. BOOK REVIEWS. SPECIAL ISSUES. TARGET AUDIENCE: AC, GP, SP, UndSt. SAMPLE COPIES.

This journal is devoted to the study of Sikh religion, history, art, and culture. The six or eight articles study religion comparatively, usually with the Sikh religion being compared to another major religion such as Christianity or Islam. A good deal of space is given to explaining the thoughts of Guru Nanak, the authoritative figure in Sikhism. The articles are signed but the authority of the writers is not noted. While each issue may average two or four reviews, not every issue will have them. It is the only leading and widely circulated Sikh religious magazine in English outside of India. The editing and proofreading could be improved since in the sample issue seen some words are spelled differently in the same article. It should be noted that the more recent issues have been published with better quality paper and printing than was true of earlier issues of this publication.

60. Spectrum. DATE FOUNDED: 1962. TITLE CHANGES: British Wheel of Yoga Journal, 1979. FREQUENCY: q. PRICE: Individuals, members only, 8.00 pounds/yr.; free to selected libraries. PUBLISHER: British Wheel of Yoga, 27 Hillcrest, Westdene, Brighton BN1 5FP, England. EDITOR: Lindy Randall. ILLUSTRATIONS. ADVERTISEMENTS. CIRCULATION: 4,200. MANUSCRIPT SELECTION: Editor. REPRINTS: Back issues from the editor. BOOK REVIEWS. TARGET AUDIENCE: GP, SP. SAMPLE COPIES: Back numbers available is postage is paid.

As the journal of the British Wheel of Yoga, Spectrum appeals to the layman interested in Yoga as well as those who teach it. The articles not only explain the exercises and postures of Yoga that lead to inner peace, but the other articles explain the more philosophical nature of Yoga. What is important to the neophyte are the articles on the nature and history of Yoga written in very simple language. There are also news items, official reports, poems, and meditations as well as four 250 word book reviews in each issue. The articles and reviews are signed. There is also a section for letters.

Near Eastern Religions

61. Institute of Archaeology Publications, Assyriological Series. DATE FOUNDED: 1984. FREQUENCY: irr. PRICE: Variable. PUBLISHER: Andrews University Press, Berrien Springs, Michigan 49104. EDITOR: Dr. Lawrence T. Geraty. ILLUSTRATIONS. INDEX. CIRCULATION: Variable. MANUSCRIPT SELECTION: Selections made by the Horn Archaeological Museum/Institute of Archaeology at Andrews University. REPRINTS: Back issues available from the publisher. TARGET AUDIENCE: AC, SP.

62. Iraq. DATE FOUNDED: 1934; suspended 1941-1945. FREQUENCY: sa until 1984; a from 1985. PRICE: 15.00 pounds/yr. PUBLISHER: British School of Archaeology in Iraq, 31-34 Gordon Square, London WC1H OPY, England. EDITOR: Mr. J. D. Hawkins. ILLUSTRATIONS. ADVERTISEMENTS: In house. INDEX: For vols. 1-30. CIRCULATION: 700. MANUSCRIPT SELECTION: Editor and editorial committee. REPRINTS: From the publisher; back issues from the publisher. SPECIAL ISSUES. INDEXED/ABSTRACTED: AATechAbs, Avery, BHI, OTA, RIO. DATABASE: ATLA, RI. TARGET AUDIENCE: AC, SP.

This journal is devoted to studies of the history, art, archaeology, religion, and economic and social life of Iraq, and to a lesser degree to the study of the countries around it. The time span covered is from the beginning of the culture in Iraq to 1700. Articles of a purely philological nature will not be found. The six articles per issue are signed. Each issue is introduced with an editorial which usually covers news relating to the British School of Archaeology in Iraq.

63. Journal of Near Eastern Studies. DATE FOUNDED: 1884. TITLE CHANGES: Hebraica, (1884-1895); American Journal of Semitic Languages and Literatures, (1895-1941). FREQUENCY: q. PRICE: $27.00/yr., individuals; $20.00/yr., students; $50.00/yr., libraries. PUBLISHER: University of Chicago Press, 5801 S. Ellis Ave., Chicago, Illinois 60637. EDITOR: Robert D. Biggs. ILLUSTRATIONS. ADVERTISEMENTS. CIRCULATION: 2,200. MANUSCRIPT SELECTION: Editor in consultation with referees. MICROFORMS: Canner; Johnson ; UMI. REPRINTS: Walther J. Johnson; back issues available from the publisher in hard copy. BOOK REVIEWS. INDEXED/ABSTRACTED: AFS, AHCI, CC, HI, IZBG, LLBA, MLA, NTA, OTA, RIO, RTA, SSCI. DATABASE: AHSearch, ATLA, HI, RI, SocScisearch. TARGET AUDIENCE: AC, SP. SAMPLE COPIES: To libraries.

This journal is dedicated to the scientific study of the texts and archaeology of the ancient Near East. Not all of the articles are directly related to the Old Testament, but they do illuminate the cultural milieu of the biblical period as well as discuss the ancient religions of the period. In an average issue there are eight to twelve book reviews, each one signed and taking up one to two pages. It complements in a more detailed way the contents of such journals as the Journal of Biblical Literature and Vetus Testamentum. No axes are ground in the six to eight articles published. It does advertize journals that might be of interest to the readers of the journal.

64. Journal of Northwest Semitic Languages. DATE FOUNDED: 1971. FREQUENCY: a. PRICE: Not fixed. PUBLISHER: Department of Semitic Languages, University of Stellenbosch, Stellenbosch 7600, Stellenbosch, South Africa. EDITOR: F. Charles Fensham. INDEX: Vol. 6 and vol. 11 have indexes to the previous five volumes. CIRCULATION: 350. MANUSCRIPT SELECTION: Editor. REPRINTS: Back issues are available. BOOK REVIEWS. INDEXED/ABSTRACTED: OTA. TARGET AUDIENCE: AC.

This journal is comparable to the Journal of Semitic Studies. It concentrates on the literature of the Old Testament and Ugarit. Some of the languages studied are Arabic, Hebrew, Ugaritic, Sumerian, Akkadian, Aramaic, and Phoenician. The articles are signed, as are the short reviews; each issue has seven such signed reviews, written in 500 words. Notable are the very complete five year indexes; items indexed are citations from the Bible, authors and authors cited, Akkadian and Sumerian texts quoted; and Ugaritic literature cited; the same is done for languages and literatures from other countries and peoples. The authors' addresses are cited at the back of each issue.

65. Journal of Semitic Studies. DATE FOUNDED: 1956. FREQUENCY: sa. PRICE: $45.00/yr. PUBLISHER: Oxford University Press, Walton Street, Oxford OX2 6DP, England. EDITOR: C. E. Bosworth and M. E. J. Richardson. INDEX. ADVERTISEMENTS. CIRCULATION: 700. MANUSCRIPT SELECTION: Editors. MICROFORMS: UMI. REPRINTS: Swets. BOOK REVIEWS. INDEXED/ABSTRACTED: AHCI, CC, MLA, NTA, OTA, RIO, RTA. DATABASE: AHSearch, ATLA, RI. TARGET AUDIENCE: AC, SP, UndSt. SAMPLE COPIES.

Comparable to the Journal of Near Eastern Studies, this journal is dedicated to research into the languages and literature of the Near East, both ancient and modern. Most of the articles are in English, but occasionally, there will be essays in other languages, such as French. In most cases, Near Eastern words are transliterated, but occasionally the actual words are printed. All of the articles are signed with the academic residence of each author given. The publisher maintains that the journal is aimed at undergraduate students; however, few undergraduates would read this journal because of its technical nature and the requirement that the reader be familiar with languages and literatures of the Near East. In each issue there are thirty five signed critical essays on books; each review takes one page.

66. The Journal of the Ancient Near Eastern Society. DATE FOUNDED: 1968. TITLE CHANGES: The Journal of the Ancient Near Eastern Society of Columbia University, (1968-1984). FREQUENCY: a. PRICE: $10.00/yr., individuals; $15.00/yr., libraries. PUBLISHER: Ancient Near Eastern Society, Jewish Theological Seminary, Broadway and 122nd St., New York, New York 10027. EDITOR: Edward L. Greenstein and David Marcus. ILLUSTRATIONS. INDEX. ADVERTISEMENTS. CIRCULATION: 400. MANUSCRIPT SELECTION: Editors and editorial committee. MICROFORMS: CIS. REPRINTS: From AMS Press. SPECIAL ISSUES. INDEXED/ABSTRACTED: OTA, RTA. TARGET AUDIENCE: AC, SP, UndSt. SAMPLE COPIES.

Like the Journal of Cuneiform Studies and the Journal of Near East Studies, this publication publishes articles on all facets of the ancient Near East. It has especially strong offerings that combine Mesopotamian and Northwest Semitic studies, as well as articles that discuss biblical problems in light of the ancient Near East. The essays are quite technical; the texts being discussed may be reproduced or they may be transliterated. About every five or six issues there is a cumulative index.

67. Palestine Exploration Quarterly. DATE FOUNDED: 1869. TITLE CHANGES: Palestine Exploration Fund Quarterly Statement, (1869-1936). FREQUENCY: sa. PRICE: 12.50

pounds/yr. or $25.00/yr. PUBLISHER: The Palestine Exploration Fund, 2 Hinde Mews, Marylebone Lane, London W1M 5RR, England. EDITOR: The Rev. Prof. P. R. Ackroyd. ILLUSTRATIONS. INDEX. ADVERTISEMENTS. CIRCULATION: 800. MANUSCRIPT SELECTION: Editor. REPRINTS: Dawson; back issues available from the publisher. BOOK REVIEWS. INDEXED/ABSTRACTED: BHI, NTA, OTA, RIO, RTA. DATABASE: ATLA, RI. TARGET AUDIENCE: AC, SP.

Each issue has an average of five to ten signed book reviews, comprising 200 words.

68. Sources from the Ancient Near East. DATE FOUNDED: 1974. FREQUENCY: irregular. PRICE: $24.00/yr. PUBLISHER: Undena Publications, P. O. Box 97, Malibu, California 90265. EDITOR: Giorgio Buccellati, Marilyn Kelly-Buccellati. ILLUSTRATIONS. INDEX. CIRCULATION: 500. MANUSCRIPT SELECTION: Editorial board. REPRINTS: Back issues are available. INDEXED/ABSTRACTED: OTA. TARGET AUDIENCE: AC, SP.

This series provides contributions to the study of the history, religion, literature, art, and archaeology of the Ancient Near East. Each fascicle is devoted to one aspect of the literature of that area. There are other serials like this one, but in this bibliography, the Bulletin of the American Schools of Oriental Research and the Biblical Archaeology Review deal with the same material, the first being more scholarly, the second more popular. For those who want to review the primary sources upon which conclusions are made, this series is valuable.

Judaism

69. Conservative Judaism. DATE FOUNDED: 1945. FREQUENCY: q. PRICE: $23.00/yr., individuals; $50.00/yr., libraries. PUBLISHER: The Rabbinical Assembly and the Jewish Theological Seminary of America, 3080 Broadway, New York, New York 10027. EDITOR: Rabbi David Wolf Silverman. INDEX. ADVERTISEMENTS. CIRCULATION: 1,800. MANUSCRIPT SELECTION: Editorial board. MICROFORMS: UMI. BOOK REVIEWS. SPECIAL ISSUES. INDEXED/ABSTRACTED: IJP. TARGET AUDIENCE: AC, SP.

This journal has three to five signed book reviews that run two to three pages each.

70. The Jewish Quarterly Review. DATE FOUNDED: 1910. TITLE CHANGES: Jewish Quarterly Review (London), (1888-1908). FREQUENCY: q. (volume starts in July). PRICE: $25.00/yr.; institutions, $35.00/yr. PUBLISHER: The Jewish Quarterly Review, 250 N. Highland Ave., Merion Station, Pennsylvania 19066; Dropsie University, Broad and York Streets, Philadelphia, Pennsylvania 19132. EDITOR: Leon Nemoy. ILLUSTRATIONS: Sometimes. INDEX. ADVERTISEMENTS. CIRCULATION: 1,000. MANUSCRIPT SELECTION: Editor. MICROFORMS: UMI. REPRINTS: UMI. BOOK REVIEWS. INDEXED/ABSTRACTED: AHCI, CC, IJP, NTA, OTA, RIO, RTA. DATABASE: AHSearch, ATLA, RI. TARGET AUDIENCE: AC, SP.

This journal, besides book reviews and books received, contains four to six articles on the history and interpretation of Jewish texts. These texts include not only the Old Testament, but also more modern discussions; but the emphasis is on the Old Testament, Haggadah, and the Halakhah. When Hebrew is cited, the citation is unpointed.

The articles, signed and written by scholars, are of interest to New Testament scholars as well since some of the essays attempt to relate the discussion of the Old Testament to the meaning of the New Testament. In some issues there are "Critical Notes," which usually discuss some minute detail of Judaism. There are approximately six signed reviews per year that are about two pages long. This journal is really very much like the Journal of Biblical Literature in its approach.

71. Journal for the Study of Judaism. DATE FOUNDED: 1970. FREQUENCY: sa. PRICE: Dfl.88.00/yr. PUBLISHER: E. J. Brill, Oude Ryn 33a-35, Leiden, The Netherlands. EDITOR: Prof. Dr. A. S. van der Woude. ILLUSTRATIONS. CIRCULATION: 650. MANUSCRIPT SELECTION: Editorial board. REPRINTS: Back issues available from the publisher. BOOK REVIEWS. INDEXED/ABSTRACTED: NTA, OTA, RIO, ZAW. DATABASE: ATLA, RI. TARGET AUDIENCE: AC, SP. SAMPLE COPIES: From the publisher.

As the qualifier to the title, "in the Persian, Hellenistic and Roman Period," suggests, this journal is devoted to the academic study of Judaism in the Persian, Hellenistic, and Roman periods. While all the articles in the reviewed issue were in English, contributions are invited in French and German as well; the reviews are in all three languages. The articles are written by scholars from around the world, are highly documented, and objective. Besides the signed book reviews, which number thirty or forty covering two to three pages each, there are also listings of other books (unreviewed), and of currently published articles in the field of early Judaism. It is very comparable to the Jewish Quarterly Review, except that it does not relate its studies as explicitly to the New Testament. However, anyone wishing to study the milieu in which early Christianity arose, will need to consult this journal.

72. Journal of Jewish Studies. DATE FOUNDED: 1948. FREQUENCY: sa. PRICE: 13.00 pounds ($27.50)/yr.; students: 8.00 pounds ($17.50)/yr.; singe issues: 7.50 pounds ($16.00). PUBLISHER: Oxford Centre for Postgraduate Hebrew Studies, 45 St. Giles', Oxford OX1 2LP, England. EDITOR: Geza Vermes. INDEX. CIRCULATION: 1,000. MICROFORMS: UMI. REPRINTS: Back issues available from the publisher. BOOK REVIEWS. INDEXED/ABSTRACTED: AHCI, AMHA, BHI, CC, IJP, NTA, OTA, RIO, RTA. DATABASE: AHSearch, ATLA, RI. TARGET AUDIENCE: AC, SP.

The approximately eight articles of this academic journal are centered on the history of the Jews and their literature; the articles focus primarily on early Jewish history, although the Centre wishes to foster studies on the period from the biblical era to the present time; the essays are signed and documented. The books reviewed cover the period that the Centre wishes to cover in its articles. The twenty signed reviews may be short but the nature of each book is revealed through the succinct criticism. In addition to the reviews, there are nine one half page book notes. It is comparable to the Jewish Quarterly Review and the Journal for the Study of Judaism except that it has a wider scope than those two do.

73. Journal of Reform Judaism. DATE FOUNDED: 1953. TITLE CHANGES: CCAR Journal. FREQUENCY: q. PRICE: $12.00/yr., $20.00/2 yrs., $28.00/3 yrs.; overseas subscriptions add $2.00 for air mail. PUBLISHER: Central Conference of American Rabbis, 21 East 40th St., New York, New York 10016. EDITOR: Samuel M. Stahl. INDEX: Every twenty-five years. ADVERTISEMENTS. CIRCULATION: 2,200. MICROFORMS: UMI. REPRINTS: UMI. BOOK REVIEWS. INDEXED/ABSTRACTED: IAJS, IJP, RTA. TARGET AUDIENCE: GP, SP.

Each issue of this quarterly devotes about four articles to a particular theme, whether it be on practical problems in the rabbinate, the holocaust years, or a famous Jew. The remainder of the journal is consists of four, signed, two page book reviews, letters to the editor, other sections on the Jewish liturgy, traditions and on how Jews should relate with the culture around them. The journal's tone is irenic and down to earth; it is aimed at the practicing rabbi and members of his congregation. Its point of view seems to be that it is possible to be a faithful Jew while assimilating some of the ideals of a non-Jewish culture or environment.

74. Judaism. DATE FOUNDED: 1952. FREQUENCY: q. PRICE: United States and Canada, $12.00/yr., $20.00/2 yrs., $28.00/3 yrs.; foreign, $13.00/yr., $22.00/2 yrs., $31.00/3 yrs.; students, $8.00/yr. PUBLISHER: American Jewish Congress, 15 East 84th St., New York, New York 10028. EDITOR: Robert Gordis. INDEX. ADVERTISEMENTS. CIRCULATION: 5,000. MICROFORMS: UMI. REPRINTS: UMI; back issues from the publisher. BOOK REVIEWS. INDEXED/ABSTRACTED: AHCI, CC, GSScRel, IJP, NTA, RIO, RTA, SSCI. DATABASE: AHSearch, ATLA, RI, SocScisearch. TARGET AUDIENCE: GP, SP. SAMPLE COPIES.

As a "Quarterly Journal of Jewish Life and Thought," Judaism is devoted to the discussion of religious, moral, and philosophical concepts of Judaism and their relevance to problems in modern society. Many of the issues are partly or wholly devoted to one subject, whether it be Martin Buber or American Judaism; the ten articles written by academics and rabbis, drawn from the United States and Canada, are signed and documented. The articles are very far-ranging, extending from exegesis on biblical texts to modern concerns about genetics. The articles cover the same types of subjects as Theology Today, except that they are seen from a Jewish perspective. The journal begins with an essay, "The First Reader," that introduces the basic ideas of each article. Occasionally there is a poem. The reviews, numbering about two to four may run from two to five pages, with the five page reviews usually being review articles. The section for books received is arranged by subject.

75. Modern Judaism. DATE FOUNDED: 1981. FREQUENCY: 3/yr. PRICE: Individuals, $17.00/yr., $32.00/2 yrs.; institutions, $31.00/yr., $54.00/2 yrs.; postage for foreign orders, add $3.25 per year. PUBLISHER: The Johns Hopkins University Press, Journals Division, Baltimore, Maryland 21218. EDITOR: Steven T. Katz. INDEX. ADVERTISEMENTS. CIRCULATION: 1,000. MANUSCRIPT SELECTION: Editor. BOOK REVIEWS. INDEXED/ABSTRACTED: AHCI, CC, IJP, RIO. DATABASE: AHSearch, ATLA, RI. TARGET AUDIENCE: AC, SP.

This journal seeks to offer perspectives on the concerns and events in modern Jewish experience since the eighteenth century Jewish Enlightenment. Hailed in 1984 by the Association of American Publishers as the best new journal published in the United States in the last three years, this periodical publishes about six articles per issue on the history of Judaism and Jewish thought from the eighteenth century; it is usually related to the current scene. The articles are signed, documented, and written in a lively style with a definite absence of jargon. Each of the two to four signed reviews averages three pages; there is an occasional review article. It is not connected with any branch of Judaism.

76. Newsletter for Targumic and Cognate Studies. DATE FOUNDED: 1974. FREQUENCY: sa. PUBLISHER: Department of Near Eastern Studies, University of Toronto, Ontario M5S 1A1, Canada. EDITOR: E. G. Clarke. CIRCULATION: 200. REPRINTS: Back issues available. SPECIAL ISSUES. TARGET AUDIENCE: AC, SP.

As the title suggests, this newsletter is aimed at those pursuing the academic study of the Targums and related fields. The publication may have news about meetings, but its main function is to produce a bibliography of materials recently published in the field. The bibliography is divided into three sections: books, articles, and reviews. There may also be abstracts of articles written in Arabic.

77. Reconstructionist. DATE FOUNDED: 1935. FREQUENCY: 8/yr. PRICE: $20.00/yr.; foreign subscribers, add $3.00; membership to the Jewish Reconstructionist is $50.00/yr. and

includes the journal. PUBLISHER: Federation of Reconstructionist Congregations and Havurot, 270 W. 89th St., New York, New York 10024. EDITOR: Jacob J. Staub. INDEX. ADVERTISEMENTS. CIRCULATION: 8,200. MANUSCRIPT SELECTION: Editor. MICROFORMS: UMI. REPRINTS: UMI; single copies from publisher at $3.00 apiece. BOOK REVIEWS. INDEXED/ABSTRACTED: IJP. TARGET AUDIENCE: GP, SP.

The Reconstructionist addresses the religious, political, social and moral issues of contemporary Jewish life and does so energetically. It attempts to be innovative, and where necessary, controversial. Each issue begins with an editorial followed by several features including prayers, poetry, explanations of the Torah, and issues in synagogue life. While there are no special issues, each issue devotes the bulk of its articles to one subject, be it lay-rabbinic relations, or homosexuality. Not all issues have book reviews, but the ones that do contain them usually have two that are signed and run one to one and a half pages. In format and in approach, it is very much like Christian Century or Christianity Today.

78. Tradition: A Journal of Orthodox Thought. DATE FOUNDED: 1958. FREQUENCY: q. PRICE: Members, $18.00/yr., $32.00/2 yrs., $45.00/3 yrs.; non-members, $20.00/yr., $36.00/2 yrs., $51.00/3 yrs.; library, $25.00/yr.; Canada: library, $31.00/yr., individual, $24.00/yr.; foreign countries: library, $54.00/yr., individual, $28.00/yr. PUBLISHER: Rabbinical Council of America, 275 Seventh Ave., New York, New York 10001. EDITOR: Walter S. Wurzburger. INDEX: Cumulated. CIRCULATION: 3,500. MANUSCRIPT SELECTION: Editor. MICROFORMS: UMI. BOOK REVIEWS: INDEXED/ABSTRACTED: AHCI, IAJS, IJP, OTA, RTA. DATABASE: AHSearch. TARGET AUDIENCE: AC, SP.

This journal focuses on the interpretation of Judaism through the orthodox prism. This does not mean that the four signed articles are only over points of the Torah; other articles address the problem of how an Orthodox Jew should interact with modern secular culture. A helpful section is the survey of recent halakhic periodical literature. This journal does not have the usual section for book reviews; instead, it has two or three signed book review essays, each one averaging seven pages. Scholars and those wishing to understand their Orthodox Jewish faith more fully will find the articles attractive; Christians also will discover something of value here since occasionally the relationship between Christianity and Judaism is discussed.

Christianity

Bible Studies

79. American Bible Society Record. DATE FOUNDED: 1843. TITLE CHANGES: Bible Society Record (1843-1855). FREQUENCY: 10/yr. PRICE: Free to all donors to the American Bible Society; free to libraries. PUBLISHER: American Bible Society, 1865 Broadway, New York, New York 10023. EDITOR: Clifford P. Macdonald. ILLUSTRATIONS. INDEX. ADVERTISEMENTS: Only in-house. CIRCULATION: 450,000. MANUSCRIPT SELECTION: The editor. REPRINTS. TARGET AUDIENCE: GP. SAMPLE COPIES: To libraries and individuals.

Like the Trinitarian Bible Society Quarterly Record, this journal is dedicated to reporting the translation and transmission of the Bible in foreign lands. In contrast to the same journal, the American Bible Society Record does not strongly push one point of view. The reader also gains much information on the lands for which the Bible is being translated. It has several reports. In the May issue the reports on the distribution of the Bible are presented regionally while the "Good News Updates" gives reports on the distribution of the Bible both nationally and internationally. The articles are written in-house and the color illustrations make the journal very attractive.

80. American Schools of Oriental Research Newsletter. DATE FOUNDED: 1939. TITLE CHANGES: Archaeological Newsletter, 1971. FREQUENCY: q. PRICE: U. S. and Canada: $15.00/yr.; $11.00/yr., students and retired faculty; overseas: $17.00/yr.; $13.00/yr., students and retired overseas faculty. PUBLISHER: American Schools of Oriental

Research, 4243 Spruce Street, Philadelphia, Pennsylvania 19104. EDITOR: James A. Sauer. ILLUSTRATIONS. CIRCULATION: 3,000. MICROFORMS: UMI. REPRINTS: UMI. INDEXED/ABSTRACTED: RIO. DATABASE: ATLA, RI. TARGET AUDIENCE: AC, SP.

This is a newsletter of one of the most renowned archaeological societies. Within its sixteen pages there is news of such things as new library acquisitions, letters to the editor, lists of ASOR approved archaeological projects, news from the field, announcements of meetings, notices to readers for subscriptions to pertinent information, and announcements of fellowships and professorships. For those doing or wishing to do professional archaeological work or study in the Middle East, this journal is essential.

81. Australian Biblical Review. DATE FOUNDED: 1951. FREQUENCY: a. PRICE: A$6.00/yr.; US$7.00/yr.; 4.00 pounds sterling/yr. PUBLISHER: Fellowship for Biblical Studies, Queen's College, Parkville, Victoria 3052, Australia. EDITOR: Professor N. M. Watson. INDEX: Every five years. CIRCULATION: 500. MANUSCRIPT SELECTION: Editorial Committee. REPRINTS: Most back issues are available from Mrs. H. M. Lade, 38 Uvadale Grove, Kew, 3101, Australia. BOOK REVIEWS. INDEXED/ABSTRACTED: NTA, OTA, RIO. DATABASE: ATLA, RI. TARGET AUDIENCE: AC, SP, UndSt. SAMPLE COPIES.

This annual is a kind of a cross between the Journal of Biblical Literature and Interpretation. Containing approximately four articles written primarily by Australians, the typescript journal contains not only objective biblical studies, but theological applications as well. In addition, the articles occasionally concentrate on the use of the Scripture in one of the early Fathers, such as Tertullian. In some ways then the scope of study is broader than the two other journals mentioned above, but one does not feel that the articles are as deep and analytical. All the articles are documented and signed and the authors' addresses are listed on the last page of the journal, on the inside of the back cover. Occasionally there will be a book review article covering a major publication, but in general the book reviews are short, numbering fourteen to sixteen, signed, 500 word essays; at times, they are only descriptive of the contents of the books being reviewed.

82. Bible Advocate. DATE FOUNDED: 1863. TITLE CHANGES: The Hope of Israel, originally; The Advent and Sabbath Advocate and Hope of Israel, 1872; The Advent and Sabbath Advocate, 1874; Sabbath Advocate and Herald of the Advent, 1888; The Bible Advocate and Herald of the Coming Kingdom, 1900; Bible Advocate, 1972. FREQUENCY: m. (except for August). PRICE: No charge. PUBLISHER: Bible

Advocate Press, P. O. Box 33677, Denver, Colorado 80233. EDITOR: Jerry Griffin. ILLUSTRATIONS. INDEX. CIRCULATION: 11,500. MANUSCRIPT SELECTION: Editorial staff. REPRINTS: Recent back issues available from the publisher. REPRINTS: Publisher. BOOK REVIEWS. SPECIAL ISSUES: Rarely. TARGET AUDIENCE: GP. SAMPLE COPIES.

This journal does not have a regular section for book reviews; generally speaking there are one to two reviews per quarter, unsigned and using 300 words.

83. Bible and Spade. DATE FOUNDED: 1972. FREQUENCY: q. PRICE: $10.00/yr. to individuals and libraries. PUBLISHER: Word of Truth Productions, Box 288, Ballston Spa, New York 12020. EDITOR: Bryant G. Wood. ILLUSTRATIONS. INDEX. CIRCULATION: 1,000. MANUSCRIPT SELECTION: Articles selected if they have material on archaeology and the Bible. INDEXED/ABSTRACTED: CPI. TARGET AUDIENCE: GP, UndSt.

This journal, dedicated to the authentication and illumination of the Bible, should not be considered as conservative. It is supposedly aimed at the general public and undergraduate students, but the articles would also appeal to beginning graduate students or to scholars who are experts in other fields. The articles may be written specifically for the journal or are reprinted from other journals. In terms of appeal, it stands between the Biblical Archaeologist and the Biblical Archaeology Review. It is not as dry as the former or as flashy as the latter. The indexes are particularly complete; the first is general and includes people and documents discussed; the second is an index of biblical passages cited.

84. Bible Collectors' World. DATE FOUNDED: 1985. FREQUENCY: q. MERGER: Successor to The Bible Collector, 1985. PRICE: $6.00/yr., domestic; $10.00/yr., foreign PUBLISHER: Bible Collectors' World, Box 311, Oak Creek, Wisconsin 53154 in association with the International Society of Bible Collectors, P. O. Box 2485, El Cajon, California 92021. EDITOR: Carl Johnson. ILLUSTRATIONS. ADVERTISEMENTS. MANUSCRIPT SELECTION: Editor. BOOK REVIEWS. TARGET AUDIENCE: AC, SP.

This journal is associated with the International Society of Bible Collectors and is the successor to The Bible Collector. Each issue has about four articles or features. The articles and reviews are signed, but the authority of the author is not noted. The journal carries news about the translation of the Bible as well as answers to questions to such things as where one can obtain biographical information on translators. There is usually one main article on a translation or a text of the Bible. On the average, there will be three unsigned book reviews, each one consisting to one half to three quarters of a page. Of interest to collectors will be the advertisements of Bibles for sale.

85. The Bible Friend. DATE FOUNDED: 1903. TITLE CHANGES: Bibel Vennen (Norse for Bible Friend). FREQUENCY: m. PRICE: $3.00/yr. for both libraries and individuals. PUBLISHER: Osterhus Publishing House, Inc., 4500 W. Broadway, Minneapolis, Minnesota 55422. EDITOR: Mrs. Cyrus Osterhus. ILLUSTRATIONS. CIRCULATION: 17,000. MANUSCRIPT SELECTION: Editor. REPRINTS: Back issues are available from the publisher. REPRINTS. TARGET AUDIENCE: SP. SAMPLE COPIES.

The Bible Friend is a monthly that is openly conservative, stressing conservative Christianity and American patriotism. The twenty five or thirty articles are written mainly by American Christians from various denominations. Some of the articles appear to be written in-house, while others are composed by outside authors, or are extracted from other journals. The journal is aimed at missionaries, pastors, and the general public. The tone of the journal may offend some, but those who do not agree with its clearly conservative stance will meet some challenging arguments.

86. Bible Review. DATE FOUNDED: 1985. FREQUENCY: q. PRICE: $15.00/yr., United States; $17.00/yr., foreign. PUBLISHER: Biblical Archaeology Society, 3000 Connecticut Ave., N.W., Washington, D. C. 20008. EDITOR: Hershel Shanks. ILLUSTRATIONS. ADVERTISEMENTS. MANUSCRIPT SELECTION: Editor. BOOK REVIEWS. INDEXED/ABSTRACTED: NTA, OTA, RIO, RTA. DATABASE: ATLA, RI. TARGET AUDIENCE: AC, GP, SP.

As the editor points out in the first issue, it is difficult to describe this journal's contents. It is not a technical journal on biblical studies; instead it contains about four articles on biblical topics written by scholars in the field for the educated general public. Articles on the Song of Solomon, the stories of the birth of Jesus, and on the Qumran scrolls are some of the subjects covered. In addition, each issue contains two, two page, signed book reviews. It fills a valuable role in translating modern biblical research to the general reader who may use it for personal knowledge or for use in teaching in the church. Some of the advertisements, however, are aimed at the scholar. The color illustrations and photographs make this journal very attractive.

87. The Bible Today. DATE FOUNDED: October, 1962. FREQUENCY: bm. PRICE: $10.00/yr.; $11.50/yr. for those outside the U. S. PUBLISHER: The Liturgical Press, St.

John's Abbey, Collegeville, Minnesota, 56321. EDITOR: The Rev. Carroll Stuhlmueller, C. P. ILLUSTRATIONS. INDEX. ADVERTISEMENTS. CIRCULATION: 10,500. MANUSCRIPT SELECTION: Editor assigns articles to various associate editors or himself; unsolicited articles are reviewed by the editor. MICROFORMS: UMI; back issues also from the publisher. REPRINTS. BOOK REVIEWS. SPECIAL ISSUES: Occasionally. INDEXED/ABSTRACTED: CPLI, NTA, OTA. TARGET AUDIENCE: GP, HS, UndSt. SAMPLE COPIES.

This is a popularly written journal that deals with the Bible and its meaning for modern life. The articles are mainly written by experts in the field who are generally Roman Catholic and American, and not always academics. Each issue focuses on one book of the Bible and its interpretation. It also has a "Seer's Corner" which has photographs of parts of the ancient world that relate to the Bible; "Jacob's Well" where questions about the Bible are answered; "Bible Terms Today," a column for readers' comments; announcements of special Bible study sessions; on editorial; and a book review section which contains twenty five to thirty signed reviews along with fifteen to twenty book notices of about one or two sentences apiece. This is a responsible journal for lay people who are not specialists in biblical studies but yet want to know what the Bible means, both then and now. In some ways, this is a more popular version of Interpretation.

88. The Bible Translator: Practical Papers. DATE FOUNDED: 1950. TITLE CHANGES: The Bible Translator, 1972. FREQUENCY: sa.; in April and October, alternating with The Bible Translator: Technical Papers. PRICE: $12.00/yr. or 6.00 pounds/yr. PUBLISHER: United Bible Societies, University of Aberdeen, Dept. of Religious Studies, Aberdeen AB9 2UB, Scotland. EDITOR: The Rev. E. McG. Fry. INDEX. ADVERTISEMENTS. CIRCULATION: 2,900. MANUSCRIPT SELECTION: Editor after consultation with the editorial committee. MICROFORMS: UMI. BOOK REVIEWS: Not usually; signed; 500 words-1 page. INDEXED/ABSTRACTED: CPI, NTA, OTA, RIO, RTA, RPTA. DATABASE: ATLA, RI. TARGET AUDIENCE: AC, SP. SAMPLE COPIES.

89. The Bible Translator: Technical Papers. DATE FOUNDED: 1950. TITLE CHANGES: The Bible Translator until 1972. FREQUENCY: q; published twice a year, alternatively with The Bible Translator: Practical Papers PRICE: $12.00/yr. or 6.00 pounds/yr. PUBLISHER: United Bible Societies, University of Aberdeen, Dept. of Religious Studies, Aberdeen AB9 2UB, Scotland. EDITOR: Dr. P. Ellingworth. INDEX. ADVERTISEMENTS: Occasionally. CIRCULATION: 2,900. MANUSCRIPT SELECTION: By the editor after consultation with the editorial committee.

MICROFORMS: UMI. BOOK REVIEWS. INDEXED/ABSTRACTED: CPI, NTA, OTA, RIO, RTA. DATABASE: ATLA, RI. TARGET AUDIENCE: AC, SP. SAMPLE COPIES: Available as long as they are in print.

The articles, written by scholars, are devoted to translating the Bible and the exegesis of it. Its emphasis is literary and philological. It has a book review and short notes section. This journal should not be considered only as a publication devoted to translation techniques; its articles will attract scholars and readers of such journals as the Journal of Biblical Literature and Interpretation. It also advertises its own translation aids and handbooks.

90. Biblebhashyam. DATE FOUNDED: 1975. FREQUENCY: q. PRICE: $8.00/yr., surface mail; $10.00/yr., air mail. PUBLISHER: St. Thomas Apostolic Seminary, Post Box No. 1, Vadavathoor, Kottayam 686010, India. EDITOR: Dr. Matthew Vellanickal. INDEX. CIRCULATION: 4,000, in two languages. MANUSCRIPT SELECTION: Editorial board. REPRINTS: Back issues from the publisher. BOOK REVIEWS. SPECIAL ISSUES. INDEXED/ABSTRACTED: NTA, OTA. TARGET AUDIENCE: UndSt. SAMPLE COPIES.

Each issue has two to five signed book reviews taking up one to two pages.

91. BibleWorld. DATE FOUNDED: November 1908. TITLE CHANGES: The Bible in New York until 1972; current title since then. FREQUENCY: 8/yr. PRICE: Free. PUBLISHER: International Bible Society, 144 Tices Lane, East Brunswick, New Jersey 08816. EDITOR: Richard Kevin Barnard. ILLUSTRATIONS: CIRCULATION: 100,000. MANUSCRIPT SELECTION: Editor. TARGET AUDIENCE: GP. SAMPLE COPIES.

This eight page publication, printed in a newspaper-like tabloid format, is a popular publication aimed at the general evangelical Christian public and ministers, and gives news of Bible translations and translators throughout the world. It has many illustrations and uses a good deal of color. Its main focus the New International Version of the Bible. It is not as objective as the publications of the American Bible Society, but it is not as doctrinaire as the Trinitarian Bible Society Quarterly Record. It focuses on both current and past translations of the Bible. Occasionally there is an article on good methods of translation. One of the by-products of reading such a journal is an increased knowledge of foreign languages and lands. Since this journal is free, churches should have it. Back issues are available as xerox copies from the publisher.

92. Biblica. DATE FOUNDED: 1920. FREQUENCY: q. PRICE: Italy, 35,000 lire/yr.; $35.00/yr., elsewhere. PUBLISHER: Biblical Institute Press, Piazza della Pilotta 35, 00187 Rome, Italy. EDITOR: Horacío Simian-Yofre. INDEX: Yes; also cumulative indexes for vols. 1-25, and 26-50. ADVERTISEMENTS: In house. CIRCULATION: 1,900. MANUSCRIPT SELECTION: Editor. BOOK REVIEWS. INDEXED/ABSTRACTED: AHCI, CC, NTA, OTA, RIO, RTA DATABASE: AHSearch, ATLA, RI. TARGET AUDIENCE: AC, SP.

As the title of the journal suggests, this publication is devoted to biblical studies and is very comparable to the other academic journals in the field such as the Journal of Biblical Literature. In contrast to the latter, however, the one under review publishes articles in French, Italian, German, and English; it is included here since many articles are in English and for those that are not, English summaries are given at the end of the essay. The six or so articles are signed and documented by academics from around the world. Roman Catholic bias does not seem to be evident. The English prose is a bit more lively than found in some other academic journals. Besides the fifteen, signed, one to six book reviews which are divided into the categories of Old Testament, New Testament, and other interests, there is a books received section. This journal is important since it is published by one of the leading, if not the leading, Roman Catholic schools devoted to biblical studies.

93. Biblical Archaeologist. DATE FOUNDED: 1938. FREQUENCY: q. PRICE: $16.00/yr., U. S. and Canada; $18.00/yr., foreign; students and retired faculty: $10.00/yr., U. S. and Canada; $12.00/yr., foreign. PUBLISHER: American Schools of Oriental Research, 4243 Spruce Street, Philadelphia, Pennsylvania 19104. EDITOR: Eric M. Meyers. ILLUSTRATIONS. INDEX: ADVERTISEMENTS. CIRCULATION: MANUSCRIPT SELECTION: Editor. BOOK REVIEWS. SPECIAL ISSUES: INDEXED/ABSTRACTED: AI, CA, CPI, CPLI, HI, NTA, RIO, RTA. DATABASE: ATLA, HI, RI. TARGET AUDIENCE: AC, GP, SP.

Like the Biblical Archaeology Review this journal appeals to the general public, but the contents tend to be a little bit more scholarly, containing about eight articles written by scholars in the field who are introduced in a section called "Introducing the Authors." The articles relate archaeology to the Bible, not necessarily "proving" the Bible but giving the historical context in which the culture of the Bible arose. The articles have bibliographies or lists for suggested reading. Besides the book review section, containing three signed two page essays, there is also a section for books received. Some of the advertisements announce new archaeology activity seeking people to help.

94. Biblical Archaeology Review. DATE FOUNDED: 1975. FREQUENCY: bm. PRICE: $22.50/yr. for libraries and individuals. PUBLISHER: Hershel Shanks, 1317 F Street, NW, Washington, D. C. 20004. EDITOR: Hershel Shanks. ILLUSTRATIONS. INDEX. ADVERTISEMENTS. CIRCULATION: 115,000. MANUSCRIPT SELECTION: Editor. REPRINTS: No, but permission can be sought to reprint articles; back issues available from the publisher. BOOK REVIEWS. INDEXED/ABSTRACTED: GSScRel, NTA, OTA, RIO, RTA. DATABASE: ATLA, RI. TARGET AUDIENCE: GP. SAMPLE COPIES: To libraries only.

This journal is a very attractive publication about archaeology as it relates to the Old and New Testaments. It has the largest circulation for an archaeology magazine dedicated to the Bible and the only one written for the layman. The photographs accompanying the articles written by American and Israeli scholars are striking and bring the articles to life. Many of the photographs are in color. In addition to the five articles, which are signed and have bibliographies, there are two or three signed book reviews and a section for letters. The Biblical Archaeology Review supports various publication contests and awards prizes for the best books in the field of biblical studies. This journal is a good counterpart for scholar and layman alike who might be put off by the more scholarly Biblical Archaeologist.

95. Biblical Research. DATE FOUNDED: 1955. FREQUENCY: a. PRICE: $4.20. PUBLISHER: Leslie Hoppe, 5401 S. Cornell Ave., Chicago, Illinois 60615. EDITOR: Robert Boling, 5555 S. Woodlawn Ave., Chicago, Illinois 60637. CIRCULATION: 875. MANUSCRIPT SELECTION: Articles are selected papers presented by members of the Chicago Society of Biblical Literature at its three annual meetings. INDEXED/ABSTRACTED: IZBG, OTA, ElencBibBib, NTA, RIO. DATABASE: ATLA, RI. TARGET AUDIENCE: AC, SP.

Like the Journal of Biblical Literature this annual is dedicated to the scientific study of the Bible, but each issue takes a topical approach such as an examination of structuralism as it relates to biblical studies. The articles are drawn from the papers presented by the members of the Chicago Society of Biblical Research at its three annual meetings. An attractive feature of the journal is that the authors are local, from the Chicago area in general; it permits the reader to get an idea of the state of biblical research in Chicago. All the articles are written by scholars and are documented; back issues are available from the circulation manager.

96. Biblical Theology Bulletin. DATE FOUNDED: 1971. FREQUENCY: q. PRICE: $12.00/yr. (USA); $14.00/yr. (International); $16.00/yr. for libraries. PUBLISHER: Business Office: Biblical Theology Bulletin, Theology Dept., St. John's University, Jamaica, New York 11439. EDITOR: Co-editors: David M. Bossman, Leland J. White, Editorial Office: Biblical Theology Bulletin, Box BD, St. Bonaventure, New York 14778. ILLUSTRATIONS: INDEX: ADVERTISEMENTS: CIRCULATION: 1,700. MANUSCRIPT SELECTION: By review by the editorial board. MICROFORMS: UMI. REPRINTS: Back issues also available from the Business Office. BOOK REVIEWS. INDEXED/ABSTRACTED: NTA, OTA, RIO, RTA. DATABASE: ATLA, RI. TARGET AUDIENCE: AC, GP, SP, UndSt. SAMPLE COPIES: Libraries only.

This journal is dedicated to the task of relating biblical scholarship to the general public interested in the subject. This journal is very similar in interest and format to Interpretation. The authors are mainly Roman Catholic although it is difficult to label the theology expressed as strictly Roman Catholic. Instead of having the footnotes at the end of the articles, authorities are cited within the article and a list of "Source Materials" is added at the end of the piece. The eight, signed, half page book reviews cover all books written by all types of authors, whether Roman Catholic or not. Occasionally an artistic piece, such as a poem is included.

97. Bulletin of the John Rylands University Library of Manchester. DATE FOUNDED: 1903. TITLE CHANGES: Bulletin of the John Rylands Library until 1972. FREQUENCY: 2/yr. PRICE: vol. 67, 1984/1985, 20 pounds sterling; vol. 68, 1985/1986, 25 pounds sterling. PUBLISHER: Dr. Frank Taylor, The John Rylands University Library, Deansgate, Manchester M3 3EH, England. EDITOR: Dr. Frank Taylor. ILLUSTRATIONS: INDEX: Cumulative indexes for volumes 1-25, 26-50, 51-60. REPRINTS: Back issues are available from Kraus Reprint (vols. 1-52); vols. 53-, from the library. INDEXED/ABSTRACTED: AES, BHI, CC, HA, Infodex, LISA, OTA, RIO, RTA TRI. DATABASE: ATLA, HA, RI. TARGET AUDIENCE: AC, SP.

This journal, dedicated to publications on theology, the humanities, bibliography, and manuscripts, is aimed primarily at academics. The authors of the articles are from all over the world; the journal is objective and is devoted the scientific, intellectual study of theology.

98. Bulletin of the United Bible Societies. DATE FOUNDED: 1949. FREQUENCY: sa. PRICE: $3.00/yr. PUBLISHER: United Bible Societies, P. O. Box 810340, 7000 Stuttgart 80,

West Germany. EDITOR: The General Secretary. ILLUSTRATIONS. CIRCULATION: 5,000. MANUSCRIPT SELECTION: Articles chosen or commissioned by the society's information officer in consultation with the editor. REPRINTS: Back issues available from the editor. TARGET AUDIENCE: AC, SP, UndSt. SAMPLE COPIES.

This is the most comprehensive of the journals dedicated to the translation of the Bible. Like the Bible Translator and BibleWorld, it reports on the availability of translations of the of the Bible and the techniques and philosophy behind translating effectively. Each issue, containing two "quarters," is devoted to one subject, each issue having about six signed articles written by international clerics and scholars. The issue covering the first and second quarters contains the annual report, part of which covers the activities of the constituent members of the United Bible Societies.

99. Buried History. DATE FOUNDED: March, 1984 (in the present format) MERGER: With Ancient Times in 1964. FREQUENCY: q. PRICE: A$10.00/yr.; A$11.00/yr. overseas. PUBLISHER: The Australian Institute of Archaeology, 174 Collins Street, Melbourne, Victoria, Australia 3000. EDITOR: Gordon G. Garner. ILLUSTRATIONS. INDEX. CIRCULATION: 1,000. MANUSCRIPT SELECTION: Editor. MICROFORMS: MIM. BOOK REVIEWS. INDEXED/ABSTRACTED: NTA, OTA. TARGET AUDIENCE: GP, SP. SAMPLE COPIES.

This small but informative quarterly seeks to understand the Bible in its historical and cultural setting. This may include reports on Israeli sites or on sites in the Near East generally. The articles, usually written in-house, use reliable sources. The one or two articles are generally written in non-technical prose so that those who are not professional archaeologists will be able to glean some helpful information from the articles. There is an occasional signed book review taking up one page. This journal is much like the Bulletin of the American Schools of Oriental Research, but is much smaller and less technical. In terms of audience, it aims at the same one as the Biblical Archaelogy Review, but the latter's format is much more attractive.

100. Catholic Biblical Quarterly. DATE FOUNDED: 1939. FREQUENCY: q. PRICE: $15.00/yr. to individuals and libraries. PUBLISHER: Catholic Biblical Association, Catholic University, Washington, D. C. 20064. EDITOR: Joseph A. Fitzmyer, S. J., Catholic University, Washington, D. C. 20064. INDEX: Printed in the October issue; also a decennial index. ADVERTISEMENTS: CIRCULATION: 4,000. MANUSCRIPT SELECTION: By the editorial board. MICROFORMS:

UMI. REPRINTS: Back issues available from the Catholic Biblical Association. BOOK REVIEWS. SPECIAL ISSUES: Supplement of members, published every five years. INDEXED/ABSTRACTED: CC, CPLI, ElencBibBib, HI, NTA, OTA, RIO, RTA. DATABASE: ATLA, HI, RI. TARGET AUDIENCE: AC, SP. SAMPLE COPIES.

Dedicated to the study of the Bible, its culture, language, and theology, this journal is edited by Roman Catholics, but the articles in the journal are not limited to a Catholic understanding of Scripture; scholars from non-Catholic backgrounds and even secular schools contribute to this journal. The seven or so signed articles are arranged in a sequence that starts with the Old Testament and progresses to studies on the New Testament. The book review section covers about 60 or 70 pages covering fifty books in signed essays; it may include reviews of collected essays. Like other scholarly journals on the Bible, such as the Journal of Biblical Literature and Interpretation, it has a "books received" section.

101. Expository Times. DATE FOUNDED: 1889. FREQUENCY: m. PRICE: United Kingdom, 10.95 pounds/yr.; United States, $19.95/yr.; Canada, 24.95/yr. PUBLISHER: T. and T. Clark, 36 George Street, Edinburgh, EH2 2LQ, Scotland. EDITOR: Dr. C. S. Rodd. INDEX. ADVERTISEMENTS. CIRCULATION: 8,000. MANUSCRIPT SELECTION: Editor. REPRINTS: Back issues are available. BOOK REVIEWS. INDEXED/ABSTRACTED: BHI, CC, IZBG, NTA, OTA, RIO, RTA. DATABASE: ATLA, RI. TARGET AUDIENCE: AC, SP. SAMPLE COPIES: Only to libraries.

This journal, aimed at the clergy, scholars, and the educated laity, fulfills its role well by keeping the clergy and laity informed about books that are of scholarly interest. The short sermons are clear and helpful although some of the exegesis leading to the little sermons is not very detailed. Besides articles on the Bible, there are some that discuss pastoral care. The section, "Talking Points from Books," offers reflection on current literature; there is also an editorial written by "Presbuteros." An average issue contains twenty, signed 300 word book reviews. All of the documented articles and reviews are written by academics or clerics. This journal does not quite carry the academic depth of Interpretation, but like the Quarterly Review, it is aimed at educating and maintaining a well-educated clergy.

102. Holy Land. DATE FOUNDED: 1975. FREQUENCY: q. PRICE: $6.00/yr. to libraries and individuals. PUBLISHER: Fr. Benjamin Celli, OFM, Franciscan Printing Press, P. O. B. 186, 91001-Jerusalem, Israel. EDITOR: Fr. Raphael Bonanno,

OFM. ILLUSTRATIONS. INDEX. ADVERTISEMENTS. CIRCULATION: 18,400. MANUSCRIPT SELECTION: Editor. REPRINTS: Back issues are available. BOOK REVIEWS. SPECIAL ISSUES. TARGET AUDIENCE: AC, GP, UndSt. SAMPLE COPIES.

Holy Land is a journal that is dedicated to exploring in a popular way the religious aspects of Palestine, including archaeology and devotion. It has a Franciscan ecumenical emphasis which includes dialogue with Moslems and emphasizes the need for peace in the Middle East. Not only will the general public gain from this journal, but also scholars will learn something from the ten or so articles in this periodical. Each issue has a theme for many of of its articles, such as evangelization and the holy name. Two, signed, one page book reviews are published. It is comparable to Bible and Spade so far as its appeal is concerned. However, this seems to be one of the few biblical archaeology journals that is concerned for the present concerns of the Middle East as well as for the past.

103. Horizons. DATE FOUNDED: 1888. FREQUENCY: a. PUBLISHER: Scripture Gift Mission, Incorporated, Radstock House, 3 Eccleston Street, London SW1W 9LZ, England. ILLUSTRATIONS. TARGET AUDIENCE: GP, SP.

This fifteen page journal, published by the Scripture Gift Mission, is an annual summary of the translation and delivery of Scripture throughout the world. It is similar to other publications like the Bulletin of the United Bible Societies. This small journal does not discuss the methods of translation; the articles, however, do note the difficulties in translating a language or in translating Scripture for an illiterate population. All the articles are unsigned and are written in-house.

104. Horizons in Biblical Theology: An International Dialogue. DATE FOUNDED: 1979. FREQUENCY: sa. PRICE: Institutions: $15.00, U.S.A. and Canada; $17.00, other countries; individuals: $12.00, U.S.A. and Canada; $12.50, other countries; students: $8.00. PUBLISHER: Pittsburgh Theological Seminary, 616 North Highland Avenue, Pittsburgh, Pennsylvania 15206. EDITOR: Ulrich Mauser. CIRCULATION: 800. MANUSCRIPT SELECTION: Editors. BOOK REVIEWS. INDEXED/ABSTRACTED: NTA, OTA, RIO. DATABASE: ATLA, RI. TARGET AUDIENCE: AC, SP.

This journal contains three to five articles that interpret various parts of the Bible as well as discuss the methods of its interpretation. The authors are concerned not only with the historical and philological aspects of the passages studied but also with their theology. All of the authors are scholars; their articles are clearly documented. In addition to the articles, there may be two to four book reviews in some issues; each review runs about a page and a half and is signed. This journal is similar to Interepretation.

105. Interpretation: A Journal of Bible and Theology. DATE FOUNDED: 1947. FREQUENCY: q. PRICE: Domestic: $11.00/yr., $27.00/3 yrs.; foreign: $12.50/yr.; $30.00/3 yrs. PUBLISHER: Union Theological Seminary in Virginia, 3401 Brook Road, Richmond, Virginia 23227. EDITOR: Dr. Paul J. Achtemeier. INDEX. ADVERTISEMENTS. CIRCULATION: 12,000. MANUSCRIPT SELECTION: Articles are commissioned, mostly; occasional freelance articles accepted; themes of of the issues decided by Advisory Council and Board. MICROFORMS: UMI. REPRINTS: UMI. BOOK REVIEWS. SPECIAL ISSUES. INDEXED/ABSTRACTED: BRI, CPI, HI, IZBG, NTA, RIO, RTA, SSI. DATABASE: ATLA, HI, RI, SSI. TARGET AUDIENCE: AC, SP.

Dedicated to the task of connecting biblical studies and theology, this journal tries to relate current scholarly opinions to the life of the church. Each issue usually focuses on one topic, such as a book of the Bible. The articles are scholarly and documented, containing little or no jargon. The authors do offer opinions, but the tone is not strident. Each issue also has a section of expository articles, written by either scholars or ministers. This journal is as scholarly as the Journal of Biblical Literature but not as dry; it relates scholarly studies to the contemporary world as do Christianity Today and Christian Century but is more related to the movements taking place in the academic world. A typical issue includes four scholarly articles, book reviews, and a "books received" section. In each issue there are four major and eleven minor reviews, all signed; the former are 900-1,200 words long while the latter average 200 to 400 words.

106. Israel Exploration Journal. DATE FOUNDED: 1950. FREQUENCY: q. PRICE: $26.00/yr. including postage by surface mail. PUBLISHER: Israel Exploration Society, P. O. Box 7041, Jerusalem, Israel. EDITOR: Prof. J. Greenfield. ILLUSTRATIONS. INDEX: Decennially. CIRCULATION: 2,700. MANUSCRIPT SELECTION: On the basis of interest to readers and academic soundness. MICROFORMS: UMI. REPRINTS: UMI; back issues are available. BOOK REVIEWS. INDEXED/ABSTRACTED: CA, CC, OTA, RAA, RIO, RTA, SSCI. DATABASE: ATLA, RI, SocScisearch. TARGET AUDIENCE: AC, SP.

This journal is devoted to the archaeology of the Middle East. It is very technical, and while the publisher holds that the journal is aimed at the general audience as well as more specialized audiences, it is definitely aimed more at the latter than the former. Libraries that hold such journals as the Journal of Biblical Literature or Vetus Testamentum that scientifically examine Scripture should have this journal; libraries that have journals on the scientific study of the Middle East should also have this journal. The eight articles are signed and illustrated with drawings or photographs. Five signed reviews are in an average issue, covering one and a half pages each. One notable feature is a special section containing short reviews of books in Hebrew. Most of the authors are Israeli; a "Notes and News" section gives preliminary reports from most excavations in Israel.

107. Journal for the Study of the New Testament. DATE FOUNDED: 1978. FREQUENCY: 3/yr. PRICE: Individuals: 10.50 pounds or $19.50; institutions: 30 pounds or $50.00. PUBLISHER: JSOT Press, 343 Fulwood Rd., University of Sheffield, Sheffild S10 3BP, England. EDITOR: Christopher Tuckett. INDEX. ADVERTISEMENTS: In-house. CIRCULATION: 850. MANUSCRIPT SELECTION: Editorial board. MICROFORMS: UMI. BOOK REVIEWS. INDEXED/ABSTRACTED: NTA, RIO, RTA. DATABASE: ATLA, RI. TARGET AUDIENCE: AC.

Each 128 page issue contains six documented articles written by scholars from around the world. The authors interpret passages from the New Testament historically, philologically, and theologically. While no particular emphasis seems evident, it is noteworthy that many of the articles attempt to relate the New Testament to its Jewish background. Citations in Hebrew and allusions to the targums are found. In addition, each issue has ten to twelve signed, one to two page book reviews. Finally, there is a section of books received; this section will be changed to look more like the "Booklist" of the Journal for the Study of the Old Testament.

108. Journal for the Study of the Old Testament. DATE FOUNDED: 1976. FREQUENCY: 3/yr. PRICE: $17.50/yr., individuals; $44.00/yr., libraries. PUBLISHER: JSOT Press, Dept. of Biblical Studies, University of Sheffield, Sheffield S10 2TN, England. EDITOR: David J. A. Clines, Philip R. Davies. INDEX. ADVERTISEMENTS. CIRCULATION: 1,200. MANUSCRIPT SELECTION: Editorial board. REPRINTS: UMI; from the publisher. BOOK REVIEWS. INDEXED/ABSTRACTED: BullSig, IZBG, OTA, RIO, RTA. DATABASE: ATLA, Francis, RI. TARGET AUDIENCE: AC, SP, UndSt. SAMPLE COPIES: Upon request for libraries.

This journal publishes six to eight articles per issue on Old Testament or on the state of Old Testament research; the articles are written by scholars from around the world in a very objective style; little or no theological reflection is evident. Such a style is also found in a journal like the Journal of Biblical Literature. Usually each issue contains twenty to fifty review notes which are signed and written in 100 words. Only occasionally is there a true book review, and that is a review article of about three pages. The other reviews are short comments on books listed topically.

109. Journal of Biblical Literature. DATE FOUNDED: 1881. FREQUENCY: q. PRICE: $50.00/yr. to libraries and individuals; price based on annual income of individual subscriber. PUBLISHER: Scholars Press, P. O. Box 1608, Decatur, Georgia 30031. EDITOR: Victor P. Furnish. INDEX. ADVERTISEMENTS. CIRCULATION: 7,143. MANUSCRIPT SELECTION: Editor, assisted by outside readers. MICROFORMS: Publisher. REPRINTS: Hard copy back issues available from: Scholars Press, Customer Service, P. O. Box 4869, Hampden Station, Baltimore, Maryland 21211. BOOK REVIEWS. INDEXED/ABSTRACTED: BRI, CC, ElencBibBib, HI, IJP, IZBG, MPI, NTA, OTA, RIO, RTA. DATABASE: ATLA, HI, RI. TARGET AUDIENCE: AC. SAMPLE COPIES.

This quarterly is dedicated to the philological and historical study of the literature of the Bible. This means that some articles will also study aspects of religion in the ancient Near East, such as that at Ebla. Short "Critical Notes" are also included. The book review section, besides containing about twenty signed, two page reviews, is also supplemented in one issue per year by reviews of books of collected essays; those reviews usually just list the contents of the book; there is also a "Books Received" section. This journal is very much like the Journal of New Testament Studies. Interpretation also covers some of the same topics, but the latter is aimed at a broader audience--the well-educated clerics and laymen as well as scholars.

110. The Journal of Theological Studies. DATE FOUNDED: 1899. FREQUENCY: sa. PRICE: United Kingdom, 32 pounds/yr.; United States and Canada, $75.00/yr.; elsewhere 37 pounds/yr. PUBLISHER: Oxford University Press, Walton Street, Oxford OX2 6DP, England. EDITOR: Professor M. D. Hooker and the Rev. Professor M. F. Wiles. INDEX. CIRCULATION: 1,200. MANUSCRIPT SELECTION: Editors. MICROFORMS: UMI. BOOK REVIEWS. INDEXED/ABSTRACTED: BHI, CC, NTA, OTA, RIO, RTA. DATABASE: ATLA, RI. TARGET AUDIENCE: AC. SAMPLE COPIES:

This semiannual journal is devoted to the study of theology and biblical studies. The articles, written by academics drawn from around the world, are documented and signed. It also has a section, "Notes and Studies," which comprises short studies or comments on other academic works, such as are found in the Journal of Biblical Literature. The rather large book review section containing fifty signed two page essays is followed by shorter reviews, followed again by a books received section. This journal covers all aspects of biblical and theological studies, from the Old Testament to the modern period, including history. It is very much like the Journal of Biblical Literature but its scope is much larger.

111. Levant. DATE FOUNDED: 1969. FREQUENCY: a. PRICE: 12.50 pounds/yr., $25.00/yr., individuals; 15.00 pounds/yr., $30.00/yr., shelf price. PUBLISHER: British School of Archaeology in Jerusalem and British Institute at Amman for Archaeology and History, c/o British Academy, 20-21 Cornwall Terrace, London NW1 4QP, England. EDITOR: Dr. P. R. S. Moorey. ILLUSTRATIONS. ADVERTISEMENTS: Only from sponsoring bodies. CIRCULATION: 650. MANUSCRIPT SELECTION: Editorial committee and assessors. REPRINTS: Back issues available from Dawson. SPECIAL ISSUES: A supplementary series is being planned. INDEXED/ABSTRACTED: RILA, NTA, RIO. DATABASE: ATLA, RI. TARGET AUDIENCE: AC, SP, UndSt.

112. New Testament Studies. DATE FOUNDED: 1954. FREQUENCY: q. PRICE: 28.00 pounds/yr.; United States and Canada, $69.00/yr.; students, 14.00 pounds ($30.00)/yr.; members have different rates. PUBLISHER: Cambridge University Press, The Edinburgh Building, Shaftesbury Road, Cambridge CB2 2RU, England; 32 East 57th Street, New York, New York 10022. EDITOR: G. N. Stanton. CIRCULATION: 2,600. MANUSCRIPT SELECTION: Editor. MICROFORMS: UMI. REPRINTS: ISI Tear Service; UMI. INDEXED/ABSTRACTED: AHCI, CC, HI, NTA, RIO, RTA. DATABASE: AHSearch, ATLA, HI, RI. TARGET AUDIENCE: AC, SP.

This journal, published under the auspices of the Studiorum Novi Testamenti Societas, prints articles in the field of New Testament studies; the articles are written by scholars from around the world; the articles are mostly in English although articles in French or German are accepted. The articles not only cover the theology of a particular portion of the New Testament, but also its versions, e. g. Old Latin, and its sources, e. g. quotations found in the Fathers. The authors' styles are quite engaging. In one of the issues every year, a summary of the annual meeting is produced along with list of its members and committees. Its strength is its international scope.

113. Novum Testamentum. DATE FOUNDED: 1956. FREQUENCY: q. PRICE: Gld100.00/yr. ($37.00). PUBLISHER: E. J.

Brill, Postbus 9000, 2300 PA Leiden, The Netherlands. EDITOR: Dr. H. J. de Jonge. ADVERTISEMENTS: In-house only. MANUSCRIPT SELECTION: Editor and editorial staff. REPRINTS: Back issues only available as complete volumes; missing issues must be claimed in ten months. BOOK REVIEWS. INDEXED/ABSTRACTED: AHCI, CC, NTA, RIO, RTA. DATABASE: AHSearch, ATLA, RI. TARGET AUDIENCE: AC.

Like New Testament Studies this journal is dedicated to publishing essays on the the New Testament. All the articles are written by scholars in the field and are signed. Most of them are in English. This journal also covers the theology, structure, and sources of the New Testament books. In contrast to New Testament Studies, however, there is a book review section containing one to three signed, one page essays and a listing of books received. The writing styles are quite lively.

114. Restoration Quarterly. DATE FOUNDED: 1957. FREQUENCY: q. PRICE: $11.00/yr. PUBLISHER: Restoration Quarterly Journal, Inc., ACU Box 8227, Abilene, Texas 79699. EDITOR: Thomas H. Olbricht. INDEX: Every 10 years. ADVERTISEMENTS: Occasionally. CIRCULATION: 1,400. MANUSCRIPT SELECTION: Editors and readers. REPRINTS: Only specific quarterly issues, not articles; back issues available from the publisher. BOOK REVIEWS. INDEXED/ABSTRACTED: BibIntern, Biblica, NTA, OTA, RIO. DATABASE: ATLA, RI. TARGET AUDIENCE: AC, GP. SAMPLE COPIES.

An average issue contains ten signed, one-page book reviews.

115. Scriptura: Tydskrif vir Bybelkunde/Journal of Biblical Studies. DATE FOUNDED: July, 1980. FREQUENCY: 3/yr at the minimum. PRICE: R10.00/yr. for libraries and individuals. PUBLISHER: University of Stellenbosch, Dept. of Biblical Studies, Stellenbosch 7600, Republic of South Africa. EDITOR: B. C. Lategan. INDEX. CIRCULATION: 400-450. MANUSCRIPT SELECTION: Editorial Board. REPRINTS. BOOK REVIEWS. SPECIAL ISSUES. INDEXED/ABSTRACTED: NTA, RIO. DATABASE: ATLA, RI. TARGET AUDIENCE: AC, SP, UndSt. SAMPLE COPIES.

This journal began with the ambition to publish biblical studies in non-technical language, appealing to a variety of prospective audiences whether it be the specialist, the teacher of religion or the well-educated layman, something which Interpretation does now. The journal has evolved into the above, but appears to have fewer articles, most of which are in Afrikaans with English abstracts; the book reviews are mostly in English, and while few, are quite extensive, usually 1,000 to 1,200 words in length; the journal is printed in typescript, and the bibliographies are listed at the end of the articles. At times the typescript pages are not easy to read. Most of the writers are from South Africa and are related to the University of Stellenbosch.

116. Scripture Bulletin. DATE FOUNDED: January 1969. TITLE CHANGES: Scripture, changed to current title in January 1969. FREQUENCY: sa. PRICE: 3.00 pounds/yr. in England, Ireland, Africa, Asia, Latin America; 3.50 pounds/yr. in other European countries; $10.00 or equivalent in other overseas countries. PUBLISHER: The Catholic Biblical Association of Great Britain, in collaboration with the Bible Reading Fellowship. EDITOR: Michael Prior. INDEX. CIRCULATION: 900. MANUSCRIPT SELECTION: Editor with the advice from the editorial board and editorial advisors. REPRINTS: Back issues from the editor. BOOK REVIEWS. INDEXED/ABSTRACTED: CPLI, ElencBibBib, IZBG, NTA, OTA. TARGET AUDIENCE: AC, SP. SAMPLE COPIES.

In keeping with the purpose of the Association, this journal aims to promote the knowledge and use of the Scriptures. This is accomplished by publishing articles on meetings of biblical organizations such as the World Catholic Federation for the Biblical Apostolate, as well as others' experiences in Israel or various interpretations of the Bible. Some of the latter may include studies of the place of women in the Bible or the history of the Douay version of the Bible, or a biography of a famous interpreter of Scripture. The journal contains notices of upcoming meetings of interest to the members and concludes with a book review section arranged by subject and devoted to books on the Bible. Most of the articles are written by people connected with the Association and are written in a style that will attract the laity. Its book review section usually contains fifteen to twenty signed 600 word essays.

117. Semeia. DATE FOUNDED: 1974. FREQUENCY: q. PRICE: $35.00/yr., individuals; $25.00/yr., libraries. PUBLISHER: Scholars Press, P. O. Box 1608, Decatur, Georgia 30031. EDITOR: John Dominic Crossan. ADVERTISEMENTS. CIRCULATION: 1,324. MANUSCRIPT SELECTION: Editorial Board. MICROFORMS: Publisher. REPRINTS: UMI; hard copies from Scholars Press, Customer Services P. O. Box 4869, Hampden Station, Baltimore, Maryland 21211. SPECIAL ISSUES: Semeia Studies, formerly Semeia Supplements, published irregularly, not available by subscription. INDEXED/ABSTRACTED: ElencBibBib, NTA, RIO, RTA. DATABASE: ATLA, RI. TARGET AUDIENCE: AC. SAMPLE COPIES.

This experimental journal, which started irregularly, has now become a quarterly and is dedicated to using the methods, models, and findings of linguistics, folklore studies, contemporary literary criticism, structuralism, social anthropology, and other modern disciplines to explore new areas of biblical criticism. The articles, numbering about eight and written by scholars, are either original or reprinted from other sources. There are occasional responses to the articles of a previous issue; each issue is dedicated to a specific subject. Sometimes an issue is edited by a specially appointed editor.

118. Society of Biblical Literature Seminar Paper Series. DATE FOUNDED: 1880. FREQUENCY: a. PRICE: Changes annually. PUBLISHER: Scholars Press, P. O. Box 1608, Decatur, Georgia 30031. EDITOR: Kent H. Richards. CIRCULATION: 1,500. MANUSCRIPT SELECTION: REPRINTS: Back issues from Scholars Press Customer Service, P. O. Box 4869, Hampden Station, Baltimore, Maryland, 21211. INDEXED/ABSTRACTED: RIO. DATABASE: ATLA, RI. TARGET AUDIENCE: AC.

This annual publication is both the summation and indication of work in progress in biblical studies. The forty articles are seminar papers that were delivered at the annual meeting. The articles, written by scholars in their fields, are aimed at similarly trained scholars. The articles are historical and philological in nature; there is no hint of sectarian interest in the articles. The subjects covered are everything from the life, culture, and religion of the periods of the Old Testament, intertestamental literature, and the New Testament. The methods of investigation are literary, sociological and historical.

119. Studia Theologica: Scandinavian Journal of Theology. DATE FOUNDED: 1948. FREQUENCY: sa. PRICE: $25.00/yr. for 1985. PUBLISHER: Universitetsforlaget, P. O. Box 2959 Toyen, 0608 Oslo 6, Norway. EDITOR: Arvid S. Kapelrud. INDEX. ADVERTISEMENTS. CIRCULATION: 700. MICROFORMS: UMI. INDEXED/ABSTRACTED: CC, NTA, RIO. DATABASE: ATLA, RI. TARGET AUDIENCE: AC, SP. SAMPLE COPIES.

This journal is devoted to the exegesis and study of Scripture and is very very similar to such other publications as the Journal of Biblical Literature and the Catholic Biblical Quarterly. All the articles are documented and signed, although the reader does not know the authority of the writer in the field. However, the authors, who are mainly Scandinavian, are very familiar with the literature. Most of the articles are written in English; a few are written in French or German. Unlike the other journals in this field, there is no book review section. This journal will allow an English reader to understand the trends in Scandinavian biblical scholarship.

120. Trinitarian Bible Society Quarterly Record. DATE FOUNDED: 1859. FREQUENCY: q PRICE: Depends on the type of membership. PUBLISHER: The Trinitarian Bible Society, 217 Kingston Road, London SW19 3NN, England. EDITOR: The same as the publisher. CIRCULATION: 12,000. BOOK REVIEWS. TARGET AUDIENCE: GP, SP.

The journal is aimed primarily at evangelical, conservative Christians and concentrates on information about the Bible, its translation and distribution. Those wishing for a scientific study of scripture will not find it here where the topic of the Bible and its distribution dictate the the nature of the articles. It is enlightening to know to what lengths and dangers Christians experience to translate and distribute the Bible. The articles are written in-house or are reprints of addresses made by members of the society or by those who have the same interests. On occasion there is a book review. The journal is really closer to being a newsletter.

121. Vetus Testamentum. DATE FOUNDED: 1951. FREQUENCY: q. PRICE: 126 guilders ($57.25). PUBLISHER: E. J. Brill, P.O. Box 9000, 2300 PA Leiden, The Netherlands. EDITOR: J. A. Emerton, W. L. Holladay. ILLUSTRATIONS: Occasionally. INDEX. ADVERTISEMENTS: In-house. CIRCULATION: 2,650. MANUSCRIPT SELECTION: Editorial board. BOOK REVIEWS. INDEXED/ABSTRACTED: NTA, OTA, RIO. DATABASE: ATLA, RI. TARGET AUDIENCE: AC.

Sponsored by the International Organization for the Study of the Old Testament, each 128 page issue contains about six scholarly, documented articles on various aspects of the Old Testament. Most of the articles are philological and historical in nature. Following the articles are several "Short Notes" on some technical aspects of Old Testament interpretation. Each issue has one very thorough book review which is signed and covers four to seven pages. Following the book review, there is a fourteen page "Book List" section which contains half page, signed reviews of other books in the field. This serial is very similar to the Journal of Biblical Literature in both emphasis and organization.

122. Word in Action: The Bible in the World. DATE FOUNDED: 1972. TITLE CHANGES: Bible Society Monthly Reporter (1817-1904), superseded by Bible in the World (1905-1972) which was superseded by the current tile. FREQUENCY: 3/yr. PRICE: Free to supporters; free to libraries. PUBLISHER: Bible Society, 146 Queen Victoria Street, London EC4V 4BX, England. EDITOR: Gill Woodward. ILLUSTRATIONS. CIRCULATION: 200,000. MANUSCRIPT SELECTION: Stories selected worldwide from news of the Bible societies.

REPRINTS: Back issues available from the publisher. TARGET AUDIENCE: GP. SAMPLE COPIES.

Like *BibleWorld*, this journal in tabloid newspaper format reports on the spread of the Bible throughout the world as well as on translating and study aids. It also reports on church membership. The goal of the Bible Society is to make sure everyone has a Bible. The journal has several monochrome photographs which may not be related to any story, but the captions themselves give meaning to the pictures. The journal is in an attractive format, clearly printed and organized; its tight focus gives this tabloid journal a better organization than other serials in the same format.

History of Christianity

123. The American Historical Review. DATE FOUNDED: 1895. FREQUENCY: 5/yr. PRICE: Based on the income of the members; $43.00/yr., United States; $47.00/yr., foreign subscribers. PUBLISHER: American Historical Association, 400 A Street, S. E., Washington, D. C. 20003. EDITOR: Otto Pflanze. ILLUSTRATIONS. INDEX. ADVERTISEMENTS. CIRCULATION: 15,600. MANUSCRIPT SELECTION: Editors; book reviews are solicited. MICROFORMS: UMI. BOOK REVIEWS. INDEXED/ABSTRACTED: BRD, HI, RG, CC, RIO, SSCI. DATABASE: ATLA, HI, RG, RI, SocScisearch. TARGET AUDIENCE: AC, SP.

This journal contains about three articles per issue dealing with various historical subjects in any time period; it definitely is not limited to American history; it is an American journal dedicated to the study of history, usually western history, It has a huge book review section which is divided by subject; there is an average of 180 reviews per issue, all signed and composed on half a page; its index is very detailed. Those studying religion will find this journal helpful in understanding the cultural forces surrounding the rise and history of Christianity. There is also a section on bibliographies and documents.

124. American Journal of Archaeology. DATE FOUNDED: 1897. TITLE CHANGES: American Journal of Archaeology and of the History of the Fine Arts, (1885-1896). FREQUENCY: q. PRICE: $35.00/yr. PUBLISHER: Archaeological Institute of America, Box 1901, Kenmore Station, Boston, Massachusetts 02215. EDITOR: Brunilde S. Ridgway. ILLUSTRATIONS. CIRCULATION: 4,000. MICROFORMS: UMI. REPRINTS: Johnson

Reprint Corporation. BOOK REVIEWS. INDEXED/ABSTRACTED: ABS, AI, BRI, BRD, BRISSP, CC, HI, OTA, SSCI, SSI. DATABASE: HI, SocScisearch, SSI. TARGET AUDIENCE: AC.

This quarterly is devoted to the archaeological study of the ancient world. The authors are mainly American; the journal has about fifteen articles per issue, all signed. In one of the issues there is usually a review of American work in classical archaeology. In addition to the plates and drawings for each article, there are also reports from the field and announcements of grant money available. In each issue there are generally fifteen signed book reviews, each one composed in one or two pages. Those in the field of religion will find it helpful since it sometimes discusses such topics as sacrifice and funerary urns. It will help students of religion to place classical religion in its social context.

125. Archives and History. DATE FOUNDED: 1945. FREQUENCY: Biennially. PRICE: $6.00/yr. PUBLISHER: Dr. Aug. R. Suelflow, Concordia Historical Institute, 801 DeMun Avenue, St. Louis, Missouri 63105. EDITOR: Dr. Aug. R. Suelflow. CIRCULATION: 150. MANUSCRIPT SELECTION: Printing of the Minutes and Reports delivered at the biennial meetings of the Archivists' and Historians' Conference. REPRINTS: Back issues available from the Concordia Historical Institute. TARGET AUDIENCE: AC, SP, UndSt. SAMPLE COPIES: Only to libraries; occasionally to individuals.

This biennial publication, printed from camera ready copy, contains twenty to twenty five articles of addresses delivered at the meetings of the Archivists' and Historians' Conference. The articles cover the technical aspects of being an archivist; there are also some historical studies. It also contains the usual reports of a conference as well as devotional materials. The technical papers are definitely aimed at the professional and may be of some interest to archivists in fields other than religion. This journal will also appeal to those interested in local history.

126. Catholic Historical Review. DATE FOUNDED: 1915. FREQUENCY: q. PRICE: $20.00/yr.; memberships: $25.00/yr.; students: $17.50/yr.; retirees: $10.00/yr. PUBLISHER: The Catholic University of America Press, Washington, D. C. 20064. EDITOR: The Rev. Prof. Robert Trisco. ILLUSTRATIONS. INDEX. ADVERTISEMENTS. CIRCULATION: 2,150. MANUSCRIPT SELECTION: Editor, associate editors, or advisory editors. MICROFORMS: Publisher. REPRINTS: Kraus. BOOK REVIEWS. INDEXED/ABSTRACTED: AHCI, America, BRI, BullSig, CC, CPLI,

HA, HI, IBRevHum, IntMedBib, OTA, RTA. DATABASE: AHSearch, America, Francis, HA, HI. TARGET AUDIENCE: AC. SP.

The bulk of this journal is devoted to book reviews, which are divided into sections "Modern European," "American," "Canadian," and "Latin American." In addition to the fifty, signed, 500 word reviews, the three or four signed articles are devoted to investigations into the history of Catholics and Roman Catholicism. The articles seem to be on obscure points in Catholic history, but by relating them to the cultural events around them, the articles are made more interesting; the authors know how to engage the readers by writing engaging prose; the article on George Mivart, for instance, was rivetting. While the books reviewed do occasionally deal with non-Catholic subjects, books on Roman Catholicism do predominate. In addition there are two other sections, one devoted to news, "Notes and Comments," and the other containing a bibliography of academic articles appearing in other journals devoted to Christianity ; this bibliography is topically divided. Following that listing there is a books received section.

127. Church History. DATE FOUNDED: 1932. FREQUENCY: q. PRICE: $20.00/yr. PUBLISHER: American Society of Church History, 305 E. Country Club Lane, Wallingford, Pennsylvania 19086. EDITOR: Martin E. Marty, Jerold C. Brauer, Robert Grant. INDEX. ADVERTISEMENTS. CIRCULATION: 3,400. MANUSCRIPT SELECTION: Editors. MICROFORMS: Publisher; vol. 1-17, ATLA Preservation Board; vols. 18-, UMI. BOOK REVIEWS. INDEXED/ABSTRACTED: AHCI, CPI, HI, OTA, RIO, RILA, RTA. DATABASE: AHSearch, ATLA, HI, RI. TARGET AUDIENCE: AC, GP, SP.

As a journal written by academics for academics, it contains about six articles on various aspects of church history which are written in a very objective style and are heavily documented; at times this objectivity leads to ponderous prose and long introductions to articles before the thesis is stated. Not all aspects of church history are studied, however; a review of articles published shows that they primarily deal with the period of the Renaissance to the present. About one third of the journal is given over to book reviews; generally, there are sixty to sixty five reviews, each one signed and covering one page; in addition to those reviews, there are "Booknotes" which number fifteen and are half the size of the regular reviews. The reviews appear to be arranged chronologically, that is books on the early church are reviewed first, and books on the modern period are reviewed last. The articles and the book reviews discuss little-known but important aspects of the history of the church.

128. Early American Literature. DATE FOUNDED: 1966. TITLE CHANGES: Current title varies with Early American Literature Newsletter. FREQUENCY: 3/yr. PRICE: $9.00/yr., individuals; $10.00/yr., libraries; $12.00/yr., foreign. PUBLISHER: University of North Carolina Press, Box 2288, Chapel Hill, North Carolina 27514. EDITOR: Everett Emerson. INDEX: Apparently appearing every ten years. ADVERTISEMENTS. CIRCULATION: 800. MANUSCRIPT SELECTION: Editor. REPRINTS: Back issues from the publisher. BOOK REVIEWS. SPECIAL ISSUES. INDEXED/ABSTRACTED: CC, MLAInt, RIO. DATABASE: ATLA, RIO. TARGET AUDIENCE: AC, SP, UndSt.

While this journal is not primarily devoted to articles on religion, many of its articles pertain to religion, especially as it was expressed in early American literature or as it is related to the treatment of certain authors by church authorities; such an interest is also displayed in the book reviews. All of the four or five articles are signed and short biographical sketches of the authors are given at the end of each issue. The book review section has four long, signed essays. Also at the end of each issue is news about the people and societies of interest to this journal's normal readers: specialists, scholars, and undergraduate students. This journal would be of interest to scholars specializing in early American culture and that would include those interested in religion in early America.

129. The English Historical Review. DATE FOUNDED: 1886. FREQUENCY: q. PRICE: 29.00 pounds/yr.; $55.00/yr. PUBLISHER: Longman Group, Ltd., Longman House, Harlow, Essex CM20 2JE, United Kingdom. EDITOR: Dr. A. D. Macintyre. INDEX. ADVERTISEMENTS. CIRCULATION: 3,000. MANUSCRIPT SELECTION: Editor, after consulting with specialist readers. MICROFORMS: UMI. BOOK REVIEWS. INDEXED/ABSTRACTED: BHI, CC, HI, RIO. DATABASE: ATLA, HI, RI. TARGET AUDIENCE: AC, GP, SP, UndSt. SAMPLE COPIES.

This journal, dedicated to the study of all aspects of English history, does not really relate to the study of religion, unless some aspect of religion as it pertains to English history is studied. The five articles are divided between longer articles, short notes, and documents. The articles as well as the book reviews are signed; the articles are documented. The book review section is rather substantial, numbering about 120 essays, signed, and occupying more than two pages apiece. In addition to the book reviews proper, there is a section of short notices of other books and a listing of other publications in the general field of history.

130. The Innes Review. DATE FOUNDED: 1950. FREQUENCY:

sa. PRICE: $10.00/yr. PUBLISHER: Scottish Catholic Historical Association, John S. Burns and Sons, 25 Finlas St., Glasgow GWW 5DS, Scotland. EDITOR: Dr. M. Lynch. ILLUSTRATIONS. INDEX. ADVERTISEMENTS. CIRCULATION: 500. BOOK REVIEWS. INDEXED/ABSTRACTED: BHI. TARGET AUDIENCE: AC, SP.

Dedicated to the study of Catholicism in Scotland, especially during the time of the Reformation, this journal contains about three well documented historical articles written by Scottish scholars on some phase of Scottish Catholicism, whether in its political or religious ramifications. While there is no book review section *per se*, books are reviewed in the section called "Miscellany." In some issues, whole articles become review articles. In general, each issue has two to three reviews, each one signed and composed in one or two pages. The journal is very objective, but given the stated reason for the title of the journal, the covert emphasis in some of the articles is that the Scottish Catholicism of the sixteenth and seventeenth centuries was not all that bad. At times, when documents are quoted, especially poetry, they are cited in the original; those not familiar with Old or Middle English may find the reading difficult.

131. *The Journal of Ecclesiastical History*. DATE FOUNDED: 1950. FREQUENCY: q. PRICE: 45.00 pounds/yr.; $105.00/yr. in the United States and Canada; individuals: 25.00 pounds/yr., $55.00/yr. in the United States and Canada. PUBLISHER: Cambridge University Press, The Edinburgh Building, Shaftesbury Road, Cambridge CB2 2RU, England; 32 East 57th St., New York, New York 10022. EDITOR: P. A. Linehan, B. I. Bradshaw. INDEX. ADVERTISEMENTS. CIRCULATION: 1,100. MICROFORMS: UMI. REPRINTS: ISI Tear Service, 3501 Market Street, Philadelphia, Pennsylvania 19104. BOOK REVIEWS. INDEXED/ABSTRACTED: BHI, CC, HA, HI, RIO, GSScRel, IZBG, NTA, RTA. DATABASE: ATLA, HA, HI, RI. TARGET AUDIENCE: AC, SP.

The five main articles of each issue are written by authors primarily drawn from English-speaking countries. The topics covered include discussions about the early church down to nineteenth century Anglicanism. There is little or no discussion of contemporary church history. Ten to twenty signed full reviews are included as well as fifteen to twenty shorter notices. Besides the numerous book reviews, there may be a review article or an article under the rubric, "Notes and Documents." The articles are well documented.

132. *The Journal of Religious History*. DATE FOUNDED: 1960. FREQUENCY: 2/yr.; 4 issues per volume. PRICE: Individuals, $18.50/yr. (United States), 10.00 pounds/yr.

(England), $A16.00/yr. (Australia); libraries, $33.40/yr. (United States), 18.00 pounds/yr. (England), $A29.00/yr. (Australia). PUBLISHER: Sydney University Press for the Association for the Journal of Religious History, School of History, Philosophy and Politics, Macquarie University, North Ryde, NSW, 2113 Australia. EDITOR: Professor Bruce E. Mansfield. INDEX: biennially (4 numbers per volume covering two years). ADVERTISEMENTS. CIRCULATION: 600. MANUSCRIPT SELECTION: Editor with advice from specialist readers. MICROFORMS: KTO. REPRINTS: UMI. BOOK REVIEWS. SPECIAL ISSUES: Occasionally. INDEXED/ABSTRACTED: AHCI, APAIS, CC, NTA, RIO, RPI, RTA. DATABASE: AHSearch, ATLA, RI. TARGET AUDIENCE: AC, SP, UndSt. SAMPLE COPIES.

This journal is devoted to the study of Christianity in Australia and England. The articles are very scholarly and are written primarily by Australian academics. The articles are meticulously documented and are signed. In addition to the five to fifteen signed, 650 word regular book reviews, there are short notices of books which are really short book reviews. The index is arranged by author. The journal is comparable to Church History, but it is more focused on Australasian religion. This journal would be a good addition to those collections that specialize in Australian church history and to libraries that wish to balance a collection top-heavy with European and American scholarship.

133. Journal of the Canadian Church Historical Society. DATE FOUNDED: 1950. FREQUENCY: 2/yr. PRICE: $12.00/yr.; US$12.00/yr. for non-Canadian subscriptions. PUBLISHER: Canadian Church Historical Society, c/o General Synod Archives, 600 Jarvis Street, Toronto, Ontario, Canada M4Y 2J6. EDITOR: Professor Elwood Jones. INDEX: Just one covering 1950-1979. CIRCULATION: 300-350. MANUSCRIPT SELECTION: Editor and editorial board. MICROFORMS: Entire run on Micromedia; MIM. REPRINTS: Back issues from the publisher. BOOK REVIEWS. SPECIAL ISSUES. INDEXED/ABSTRACTED: America, Can, CHR, HA, RIO. DATABASE: ATLA, America, HA, RI. TARGET AUDIENCE: AC. SAMPLE COPIES.

This semiannual is similar to the Journal of Religious History (Australia) in that just as the the latter covers religious movements in Australia, this one covers religious movements in Canada, mostly those that are related to Anglicanism. Each issue has a theme, whether it be the role of the laity, ethnohistory, women and religion, etc. Both of the articles in each issue are usually by Canadian academics or clerics. In addition to the four to ten, 500 word signed reviews, starting in 1985 the journal will begin a feature on recent publications. Its "Notes and Comments" announces meetings, articles of interest in other journals, and publication ventures. The journal is attractively printed and easy to read. All of the footnotes are at the end of each article.

134. Newsletter. DATE FOUNDED: 1968. TITLE CHANGES: Foundation for Reformation. Newsletter (1968-1974). FREQUENCY: q. PRICE: free. PUBLISHER: Center for Reformation Research, 6477 San Bonita Ave., St. Louis, Missouri 63105. CIRCULATION: 2,800. MICROFORMS: UMI. REPRINTS: UMI. TARGET AUDIENCE: AC, SP.

For those interested in Reformation and Renaissance research, this is a valuable newsletter. It contains news of people, new publications, conferences, calls for papers, and most importantly for some, a listing of those who have won fellowships and grants; such a list provides readers with sources for their own studies. In content, it is very similar to the now defunct Council on the Study of Religion Bulletin; in size it is similar to the latter's successor, Religious Studies News.

135. Recusant History: A Journal of Research in Post-Reformation Catholic History in the British Isles. DATE FOUNDED: 1957. FREQUENCY: sa; one volume equals four issues. PRICE: 12.00 pounds/yr.; foreign, add 1 pound to the price. PUBLISHER: Catholic Record Society, Mr. L. Gooch, MA, 12 Melbourne Place, Wolsingham, Co. Durham DL13 3EH, England. EDITOR: A. F. Allison, D. M. Rogers, and Michael Hadgetts. INDEX. ADVERTISEMENTS: On the back page only. CIRCULATION: 800. MANUSCRIPT SELECTION: Editors. REPRINTS: Back issues available from William Dawson and Sons Ltd. INDEXED/ABSTRACTED: BHI. TARGET AUDIENCE: AC, SP.

This periodical contains about eight studies on Catholicism in the post-Reformation period. Most of the articles are historical in nature, but those interested in the study of literature may find something here as well since there are occasional articles on such literary figures as Robert Southwell and Alexander Pope. In each May issue there is the annual report of the Catholic Record Society as well as a newsletter and bibliography which is comprised of articles from other periodicals, theses, and migrations and accessions of manuscripts. The Catholic Record Society was founded to make material accessible for the study of post-Reformation Catholicism; its emphasis is definitely on the study of primary sources.

136. The Second Century: A Journal of Early Christian Studies. DATE FOUNDED: 1981. FREQUENCY: q. PRICE: $10.00/yr.; $19.00/2 yrs.; $28.00/3 yrs. PUBLISHER: Mercer University, Macon, Georgia 31207. EDITOR: Everett

Ferguson. ILLUSTRATIONS. INDEX. ADVERTISEMENTS: Not as yet; they are being accepted. CIRCULATION: 550. MANUSCRIPT SELECTION: Manuscripts are recommended by readers; final decision by editor. REPRINTS. BOOK REVIEWS. INDEXED/ABSTRACTED: BP, RevHE, RIO, RTA. DATABASE: ATLA, RI. TARGET AUDIENCE: AC, SP, UndSt. SAMPLE COPIES.

This journal does for the second century Christian literature what Vigiliae Christianae does for the study of early Christian literature in general. As the title indicates, the emphasis is basically on the second century although articles on the literature and religion of the surrounding centuries are accepted if they bring the second century into focus. The three articles per issue are signed, well printed, and well organized. The four, two page book reviews are signed; it appears that the inclusion of the index in the fourth issue excludes the book review section in that issue. Other notable features are abstracts from foreign journals and the listing in the first number of research groups in North America studying early Christianity.

137. The Sixteenth Century Journal. DATE FOUNDED: 1970. TITLE CHANGES: Sixteenth Century Essays and Studies (1970-1972). FREQUENCY: q. PRICE: $25.00/yr., individuals; $28.00/yr, domestic libraries; $32.00/yr., foreign libraries. PUBLISHER: The Sixteenth Century Journal Publishers, Inc., c/o R. V. Schnucker, Northeast Missouri State University LB 115, Kirksville, Missouri 63501. EDITOR: Robert M. Kingdon. ILLUSTRATIONS. INDEX. ADVERTISEMENTS. CIRCULATION: 1,400. MANUSCRIPT SELECTION: Blind referee system with the editors having the final decision. MICROFORMS: Microfiche from the publisher. REPRINTS. BOOK REVIEWS. SPECIAL ISSUES. INDEXED/ABSTRACTED: ABC, CC, CERDIC, MLA, RILA, RIO, RTA. DATABASE: ATLA, RI. TARGET AUDIENCE: AC, SP, UndSt. SAMPLE COPIES: Free to libraries; individuals, at cost.

While this journal may publish anything that pertains to early modern times (1450-1648), it would be fair to say that most of the articles deal with the place of religion, and specifically, the Reformation, in Europe during that period. All the articles are signed and written by experts in the field. Art and dance are also examined in some articles. The articles are documented. Occasionally, the editorial control could be tighter, e. g. providing names under pictures. Books are reviewed in twenty to twenty five signed essays written in 500 to 700 words. In addition there is a section for books received so that one knows the current literature in the field.

Denominations

138. *American Baptist Quarterly*. DATE FOUNDED: 1982. TITLE CHANGES: *Foundations* until vol. 25, 1982. FREQUENCY: q. PRICE: United States, $15.00/yr.; foreign, $20.00/yr. PUBLISHER: American Baptist Historical Society, 1106 Goodman Street, Rochester, New York 14620. EDITOR: William R. Millar. ILLUSTRATIONS. CIRCULATION: 1,200. MANUSCRIPT SELECTION: Editor. MICROFORMS: UMI. REPRINTS: UMI; back issues available from the publisher for $5.00 apiece. BOOK REVIEWS. INDEXED/ABSTRACTED: America, HA, RIO, RTA. DATABASE: America, ATLA, HA, RI. TARGET AUDIENCE: AC, SP.

This journal is dedicated to the investigation of the history of the Baptists in the United States. That does not mean, however, that there will not be occasional articles of theological interest or an investigation of the history of Baptists in Canada; there will be, but the journal is aimed primarily at the history of Baptists in the United States in its five to ten articles, written by scholars who document their articles in detail. While there are book reviews, not every issue has such a section; the issues that do have reviews, average six signed reviews per issue, occupying three pages each. There are "jubilee" issues that publish articles that do not fit into regular thematic issues. Such thematic issues focus on ecumenism and racial justice. The journal is very objective.

139. *The American Benedictine Review*. DATE FOUNDED: 1950. FREQUENCY: q. PRICE: $10.00/yr., United States and Canada; $10.50/yr. other countries. PUBLISHER: *The*

American Benedictine Review, Assumption Abbey, Richardton, North Dakota 58652. EDITOR: Fr. Terrence Kardong, O. S. B. ILLUSTRATIONS: Occasionally. INDEX. CIRCULATION: 1,100. MANUSCRIPT SELECTION: Editor does the first screening and then sends manuscripts to three readers. MICROFORMS: UMI. REPRINTS: From the editor. SPECIAL ISSUES: Occasionally. INDEXED/ABSTRACTED: America, CPI, MLA, NTA. DATABASE: America. TARGET AUDIENCE: AC. SAMPLE COPIES: Upon request.

Dedicated to the academic study of monasticism, especially the American Benedictine version of it, its articles are very wide ranging, including not only historical surveys, but also essays on current monastic practices such as the reading of a Protestant novel at a monastery in Minnesota and a subsequent analysis of that novel. The seven to nine articles are documented. Even though there is no book review section, there is an occasional review essay. The articles are well written and engage the reader.

140. The Australasian Catholic Record. DATE FOUNDED: January 1895-1913; new series, 1924. FREQUENCY: q. PRICE: A$15.00/yr. PUBLISHER: Editorial Board, ACR, St. Patrick's College, Manly, New South Wales 2095, Australia. EDITOR: Editorial board. INDEX. ADVERTISEMENTS. CIRCULATION: 2,500. MANUSCRIPT SELECTION: Editorial board. REPRINTS: Back issues from the manager, at the publisher. BOOK REVIEWS. INDEXED/ABSTRACTED: CPLI, NTA. TARGET AUDIENCE: GP, SP. SAMPLE COPIES.

This Roman Catholic quarterly contains about eight articles per issue, some of which are dedicated to one particular theme, such as the last things. Other articles are chosen from free-lance submissions to the editor. The articles are documented and support the Roman Catholic position on such issues as Heaven, Hell, and Purgatory. Besides the book review section, this journal has two sections which are helpful to the Roman Catholic, whether layman or cleric. The first is a set of homilies for the Sundays and feast days in the following quarter. The second is called "The Australasian Scene" which is a discussion of religious or social events that reflect on the state understanding of Australasian religion. There are six signed reviews, averaging 500 words or one page apiece. This journal sees itself as the only Roman Catholic journal in Australia in the fields of both theology and church history.

141. Baptist History and Heritage. DATE FOUNDED: August 1965. FREQUENCY: q. PRICE: $8.50/yr., domestic; $11.00/yr., foreign. PUBLISHER: Historical Commission of the Southern Baptist Convention, 901 Commerce St., Suite 400, Nashville, Tennessee 37203. EDITOR: Lynn E. May, Jr.

INDEX: Cumulated indexes are prepared; the latest is a twenty year cumulation. CIRCULATION: 2,250. MANUSCRIPT SELECTION: Editor. BOOK REVIEWS. INDEXED/ABSTRACTED: America, RIO. DATABASE: America, ATLA, RI. TARGET AUDIENCE: AC, SP.

This journal began as an organ that would contain articles on the history of Baptism to enable Baptists to understand themselves, their history, and to discover a historical perspective on the future. The current journal does this by devoting each issue to a particular subject such as stewardship among Southern Baptists or church music. In addition to the articles and book reviews, each issue has a bibliography on the subject discussed as well as news notes about Southern Baptists. Each issue has five, one page, signed reviews. The eight or so articles are documented and signed although the authority of each writer is not noted.

142. The Baptist Quarterly. DATE FOUNDED: 1908; new series, 1922. TITLE CHANGES: Transactions of the Baptist Historical Society until 1921. FREQUENCY: q. PRICE: 9.00 pounds/yr.; 1/2 price for ministers, students in the British Isles and missionaries; 11.00 pounds/yr. for libraries. PUBLISHER: Baptist Historical Society, Baptist Church House, 4 Southampton Row, London WC1B 4AB, England. Orders to: The Rev. T. S. H. Elwyn, 148 Greenvale Road, Eltham, London SE9 1PQ, England. EDITOR: The Rev. K. W. Clements, MA, Bristol Baptist College, Woodland Road, Bristol BS8 1UN, England. INDEX: At the end of each two year volume. ADVERTISEMENTS: Very few; most are in-house. CIRCULATION: 700. MANUSCRIPT SELECTION: Editor. MICROFORMS: UMI. REPRINTS. BOOK REVIEWS. INDEXED/ABSTRACTED: ABC, BHI, IZBG, RIC, RIO, SIPBL. DATABASE: ATLA, RI. TARGET AUDIENCE: AC, GP, SP, UndSt. SAMPLE COPIES: Upon consideration of each request.

This journal is the only British serial dealing with Baptist history. The signed articles deal with aspects of the history of the Baptist movement in England. Generally, those with an interest in the radical reformation will find this journal interesting. There is also a kind of special piece at the end of each issue, such as "in the study" which contains several reviews, combined in one article, of books that might be of interest to those studying the Bible or theology. Some articles are so long that they are continued in later issues. Each issue has two or three, one page, signed book reviews. The yearly index is very complete, not only listing the articles, authors, and reviews, but even the names, conferences, other journals, denominations, and places that were mentioned in the articles in that particular volume.

143. The Baptist World. DATE FOUNDED: 1954. FREQUENCY: m. (except for July-August which is combined in one issue.). PRICE: $4.00/yr., $10.00/3 yrs. PUBLISHER: Baptist World Alliance, 1628 Sixteenth St., NW, Washington, D. C. 20009. EDITOR: Cyril E. Bryant. ILLUSTRATIONS. ADVERTISEMENTS. CIRCULATION: 8,000. MICROFORMS: UMI. REPRINTS: UMI. TARGET AUDIENCE: GP.

This newsletter publishes news about the activities of Baptists from all over the world. It not only reports news of individual Baptists but also of Baptist conventions and their goals for the coming years. The tone of the newsletter is very objective and irenic. Emphasis is laid upon the brotherhood of all Baptists and not on their differences. Ecumenical concerns are mentioned objectively. This is a good newsletter and will appeal to the more moderate and liberal Baptists.

144. Brethren Life and Thought. DATE FOUNDED: 1955. FREQUENCY: q. PRICE: $12.00/yr. PUBLISHER: Brethren Press, 1451 Dundee Avenue, Elgin, Illinois 60120. EDITOR: Dr. Warren S. Kissinger. INDEX. CIRCULATION: 800. MANUSCRIPT SELECTION: Editor. MICROFORMS: UMI. REPRINTS: Back issues more than a year old available from the publisher. BOOK REVIEWS. INDEXED/ABSTRACTED: BRM, RIO, RPI, RTA. DATABASE: ATLA, RI. TARGET AUDIENCE: AC, GP, SP. SAMPLE COPIES.

As the title suggests, this journal is devoted to studying the faith, history, and life of the Brethren. At times an issue will be devoted to one subject; at others, an issue will have articles devoted to several topics; the editor has attempted to alternate between the two. The writers, mainly American Brethren, compose their articles in a straightforward manner. Some use footnotes; others do not. Each issue has six to eight, one page, signed book reviews. Compared to other Brethren journals, like Christian Brethren Review, this journal is general in scope, covering many subjects in one issue. Occasionally, the typographical errors are prevalent enough to cause a sentence to be contradictory or confusing.

145. Calvin Theological Journal. DATE FOUNDED: 1966. FREQUENCY: sa. PRICE: $10.00/yr., $16.00/2 yrs., $21.00/3yrs.; through agents, $7.00/yr., $11.25/ 2yrs., $14.25/3 yrs. PUBLISHER: Board of Publications (Christian Reformed Church), 2850 Kalamazoo, SE, Grand Rapids, Michigan 49560. EDITOR: Dr. Cornelius Plantinga, Jr. INDEX. CIRCULATION: 1,020. MANUSCRIPT SELECTION: Editorial staff. REPINTS: Back issues available from Calvin Theological Seminary, 3233 Burton Street, SE, Grand Rapids, Michigan 49506. REPRINTS: UMI. BOOK REVIEWS.

INDEXED/ABSTRACTED: CPI, ElencBibBib, NTA, OTA, RIO, RTA. DATABASE: ATLA, RI. TARGET AUDIENCE: AC, SP. SAMPLE COPIES: To libraries.

This semiannual of about 100 pages, while printed by a conservative organization, includes articles that do not stridently urge that point of view. It may also deal with conservative doctrinal issues which some might have thought to be dead, but indeed are not. Those who have read only liberal or mainstream journals should read this one. The articles are signed with biographical details at the end of the journal. It not only has book reviews and a books received section but also book notes which are short reviews of current books; there are about ten to fifteen signed book reviews, each comprising two to four pages apiece.

146. The Canadian Catholic Review. DATE FOUNDED: 1983 FREQUENCY: m. (11/yr). PRICE: Canada, $25.00/yr.; foreign, $40.00/2 yrs.; U. S., US$25.00/yr., US$40.00/2 yrs. PUBLISHER: Canadian Catholic Review Corporation, St. Thomas More College, 1437 College Drive, Saskatoon, Saskatchewan S7N OW6, Canada. EDITOR: Daniel Callam. ILLUSTRATIONS. INDEX. ADVERTISEMENTS. CIRCULATION: 2,100. MANUSCRIPT SELECTION: Editor. BOOK REVIEWS. TARGET AUDIENCE: GP, SP.

This monthly is aimed at the Catholic who is very interested in his church, both historically and in the current applications of its teachings. It contains about five signed articles per issue, in addition to the special features such as movie and television reviews. Each issue highlights a famous Catholic such as Henry Newman. An average issue contains nine, half page, signed reviews. The language is direct and not patronizing. Actually this journal is probably aimed at the cleric, but it is the type of journal that should be read by the person in the pew. It is attractively printed; and the contents are varied so that there will probably be something for every reader's interest.

147. Catena. FREQUENCY: m. PRICE: 4.56 pounds/yr. PUBLISHER: Catenian Association, 8 Chesham Place, London, England SW1 8HP. EDITOR: L. T. Simmonds. ILLUSTRATIONS. ADVERTISEMENTS. CIRCULATION: 13,000. MANUSCRIPT SELECTION: Editor. BOOK REVIEWS. SPECIAL ISSUES. TARGET AUDIENCE: GP, SP.

Each issue has about two or three book reviews comprising 200 to 250 words; they are not always signed.

148. Catholic Digest. DATE FOUNDED: 1936. FREQUENCY: m. PRICE: $11.97/yr.; $4.00 extra for Canada; $8.00 extra for subscriptions from other countries. PUBLISHER: The College

of St. Thomas, St. Paul's Square, P. O. Box 64090, St. Paul, Minnesota 55164. EDITOR: Henry Lexau. ILLUSTRATIONS. ADVERTISEMENTS. CIRCULATION: 5,000. MANUSCRIPT SELECTION: Selected from other periodicals. MICROFORMS: UMI. REPRINTS: UMI. INDEXED/ABSTRACTED: CPLI. TARGET AUDIENCE: GP.

This periodical has the same format as the Readers' Digest. It edits articles from other journals and then publishes them. It includes articles from secular as well as religious magazines on such topics as health, faith, and tradition. Interspersed among the articles are short items recounting true stories or humor derived from life which have been submitted by readers. For those who cannot subscribe to popular religious journals this is a substitute.

149. Catholic Theological Society of America. Proceedings. DATE FOUNDED: 1946. FREQUENCY: a. PRICE: $7.50/yr. PUBLISHER: The Catholic Theological Society of America, Bellarmine College, Louisville, Kentucky 40205. EDITOR: George Kilcourse. INDEX. CIRCULATION: 1,500. MICROFORMS: UMI. REPRINTS: UMI. INDEXED/ABSTRACTED: CPLI, NTA. TARGET AUDIENCE: AC, SP.

This annual publishes the reports and papers given at the annual convention of the society. Each annual meeting is devoted to one theme. The authors of the papers are world-class scholars including such people as Johann Baptist Metz and James M. Gustafson. In addition to the papers and reports there are several appendices, one listing the new members and their doctoral dissertations.

150. Christ to the World. DATE FOUNDED: 1955. FREQUENCY: bm. PRICE: $14.00/yr. PUBLISHER: Christ to the World, Via di Propaganda 1-c, 00187 Rome, Italy. INDEX. CIRCULATION: 12,000. BOOK REVIEWS. INDEXED/ABSTRACTED: CPLI. TARGET AUDIENCE: GP.

This Roman Catholic journal is dedicated to "promoting the apostolate among non-Christian and dechristianized people." The articles contained in it may be translated speeches from the pope as well as other articles translated from other journals. They are heavily weighted toward the missionary task of the church. Following the articles is a section for letters, followed by sections of news and views from around the world that impinge upon missionary work. An average issue contains two unsigned half page book reviews which are scattered throughout the journal, usually at the end of an article. The journal is issued with the "cum approbatione ecclesiastica vicariatus."

151. Christian Brethren Review. DATE FOUNDED: May, 1963. TITLE CHANGES: The Journal of the Christian Brethren Research Fellowship; changed February, 1982. FREQUENCY: sa, on the average. PRICE: A benefit of membership at 7.50 pounds per year; nonmembers, up to 3.50 pounds per issue. PUBLISHER: The Paternoster Press, Ltd., 3 Mount Radford Crescent, Exeter EX2 4JW, England. EDITOR: G. John Polkinghorne. ADVERTISEMENTS: In-house publications only. CIRCULATION: Above 500. MANUSCRIPT SELECTION: Executive Committee. REPRINTS: Back issues from the publisher. BOOK REVIEWS. TARGET AUDIENCE: AC, GP, SP. SAMPLE COPIES: By arrangement.

This journal, which is published irregularly, dedicates each issue to one subject which may be of interest to non-Brethren. Due to the occasional nature of publication, some issue numbers are combined in one physical issue. All the articles are signed by authors who are mainly academics and English-speaking. Occasionally there will be book reviews, each one being 500 to 1,00 words. Like Interpretation, this journal is not only aimed at the scholar and cleric, but also at the educated layman. The articles are written from the point of view of faith and are mildly conservative. The journal is a good companion to Brethren Life and Thought. Each issue has a different editor.

152. Cistercian Studies. DATE FOUNDED: 1966. FREQUENCY: q. PRICE: Belgium, 650 Belgian francs/yr.; United States and Canada, $15.00/yr.; United Kingdom, 8.50 pounds/yr.; Australasia, A$16.00/yr. PUBLISHER: Cisterciensia, Abbaye N. D. de la Paix, B-6460 Chimay, Belgium. EDITOR: Brother Patrick Hart. INDEX: decennial. MICROFORMS: UMI. BOOK REVIEWS. INDEXED/ABSTRACTED: CPLI. TARGET AUDIENCE: AC, SP.

This journal is dedicated to the study of the Cistercians; its emphasis is mostly historical although there may be a meditative piece. In spite of this emphasis, however, articles on other monastic traditions are published, e. g. the Benedictine tradition and Thomas Merton. Thomas Merton, in fact, is the center of attention of many issues as can be seen by the translation and publication of several of his manuscripts. Interpretations of the parables of Bernard of Clairvaux are also produced. The seven or so articles are signed and documented; they are objective in nature, though the enthusiasm for the Cistercian tradition is evident. The thirty three signed one page book reviews are arranged by subject, and each review has a separate number. This is a solid journal for those interested in monasticism and the medieval church as it is reflected in the monastic movement.

153. Concordia Historical Institute Quarterly. DATE

FOUNDED: 1928. FREQUENCY: q. PRICE: $15.00/yr. PUBLISHER: Concordia Historical Institute, 801 De Mun Avenue, St. Louis, Missouri 63105. EDITOR: Dr. Hilton Oswald. ILLUSTRATIONS. INDEX: Every four years. ADVERTISEMENTS. CIRCULATION: 2,000. MANUSCRIPT SELECTION: Editor and associate editors. REPRINTS: Photocopies from the publisher. BOOK REVIEWS. INDEXED/ABSTRACTED: America, HA, RIO. DATABASE: America, ATLA, HA, RI. TARGET AUDIENCE: AC, GP, SP, UndSt. SAMPLE COPIES.

Published by the Concordia Historical Institute which is affiliated with the Lutheran Church-Missouri Synod, this journal is dedicated to publishing articles on the history of the Lutheran Church-Missouri Synod in America. It may also include articles on the history of Lutheranism in other countries, such as China. It is the oldest journal on the history of Lutheranism in America. The articles are signed and there is an inset box containing a short biography of the author at the beginning of each article. It has a section, "From the Field," which pertains to the Lutheran mission in the United States; there is also a section on Institute news. An average issue contains two signed one page book reviews. Of the journals and publications from the Concordia Historical Institute, it should be noted that only the Concordia Journal is strongly slanted; the other two, Concordia Historical Institute Quarterly and The Lutheran Historical Conference: Essays and Reports are quite objective.

154. Concordia Journal. DATE FOUNDED: 1975. TITLE CHANGES: Concordia Theological Monthly through 1974. MERGER: Lehre und Wehre (1855-1929) absorbed by Concordia Theological Monthly (1930-1972). FREQUENCY: bm. PRICE: $8.00/yr. United States; $9.00/yr., Canada; $12.00/yr., foreign. PUBLISHER: The Ovid Bell Press, Inc., Fulton, Missouri 65251; Concordia Seminary, 801 De Mun Avenue, St. Louis, Missouri 63105. EDITOR: Quentin F. Wesselschmidt. CIRCULATION: 8,500. MANUSCRIPT SELECTION: Editorial committee. BOOK REVIEWS. INDEXED/ABSTRACTED: IZBG, NTA, OTA, RBIC, RIO, RTA. DATABASE: ATLA, RI. TARGET AUDIENCE: AC, SP, UndSt. SAMPLE COPIES: Libraries, on a limited basis; yes, individuals.

Dedicated to the furthering the theological stance of the Lutheran Church-Missouri Synod, this attractively published journal carries two or three articles per issue on topics with a Missouri Synod bias. The twelve to fourteen signed book reviews, occupying one page each, are also written from the same bias. The journal is quite apologetic and does not have the less argumentative tone of the Lutheran Theological Journal. In addition to the articles and book reviews, there are also homiletic aids. In spite of its bias, the journal is helpful in informing people about a conservative, American Lutheran viewpoint.

155. Downside Review. DATE FOUNDED: 1880. FREQUENCY: q. PRICE: 12.00 pounds/yr. or $22.00/yr. PUBLISHER: Downside Review, Stratton-on-the Fosse, Bath BA3 4RH, England. INDEX. CIRCULATION: 600. MICROFORMS: UMI. BOOK REVIEWS. INDEXED/ABSTRACTED: CPI, RIO, NTA, OTA, RTA. DATABASE: ATLA, RI. TARGET AUDIENCE: AC, SP.

This Roman Catholic journal devotes many of its articles to studying the history of English Catholicism. It also includes exegetical articles as well as essays on non-English Catholicism. Its interest is primarily in the modern period, especially in the nineteenth century; however, articles on medieval Catholicism are occasionally printed. The five articles are signed, but no mention of the authority of the writers is revealed. Not every issue has book reviews, but those that do average about four such essays, signed, and occupying about one page each. The journal definitely appeals to the educated English Catholic.

156. The Furrow. DATE FOUNDED: 1950. FREQUENCY: m. PRICE: 19.00 pounds/yr., Republic of Ireland; 16.00 pounds/yr. or $26.00/yr., elsewhere; 22.00 pounds/yr. or $35.00/yr., airmail; 12.50 pounds/yr. or $15.00/yr., seminarians. PUBLISHER: The Furrow Trust, St. Patrick's College, Maynooth, County Kildare, Ireland. EDITOR: The Reverend Ronan Drury. ILLUSTRATIONS: Seldom. INDEX. ADVERTISEMENTS. CIRCULATION: 8,000. MANUSCRIPT SELECTION: Editor. MICROFORMS: UMI. REPRINTS: UMI; copy also available from publisher. BOOK REVIEWS. SPECIAL ISSUES: Sometimes. INDEXED/ABSTRACTED: CPLI, NTA, OTA. TARGET AUDIENCE: AC, GP, HS, UndSt. SAMPLE COPIES.

The Furrow is a very wide ranging journal exploring the meaning of Christianity, especially Roman Catholicism, from the point of view of Vatican II. The articles range from a contemporary definition of God to the place of sports as viewed from the perspective of Vatican II. Each issue has a "Chronicle" in which plays and movies are reviewed. There may also be a "News and Views" section in some issues along with eight signed book reviews, each one composed with 450 words. The journal is very free from jargon and wishes to appeal to all audiences, including high school students.

157. The Greek Orthodox Theological Review. DATE FOUNDED: 1954. FREQUENCY: q. PRICE: $14.00/yr., individuals; $13.00/yr., libraries. PUBLISHER: Holy Cross Orthodox Press, Holy Cross Greek Orthodox School of Theology, 50 Goddard Ave., Brookline, Massachusetts 02146. EDITOR: The Very Reverend Nomikos Michael Vaporis. CIRCULATION: 1,500.

MANUSCRIPT SELECTION: Editor; previously published articles not accepted. MICROFORMS: UMI. REPRINTS: From the publisher. BOOK REVIEWS. SPECIAL ISSUES: Occasionally. INDEXED/ABSTRACTED: BABH, HA, RIO, RTA, DATABASE: ATLA, HA, RI. TARGET AUDIENCE: AC, GP, SP, UndSt. SAMPLE COPIES.

This quarterly, which was once a semiannual, draws its authors mainly from Greece and the United States who are clerics, academics, and theologians. It focuses mainly on the theology and history of the Orthodox Church, but the point of view is not obvious and the scholarly tone of the articles will appeal to Christians of any denomination. The articles are signed and occasionally documented. Each one of the four to five book reviews is signed and composed in two pages. They appeal to the same groups as those who write them: clerics, academics, and theologians, although the educated lay public would also be attracted to some of the articles. Occasionally, the writers will write in Ecclesiastical Greek which does not appear to be too different from Koine Greek. It is quite comparable to the Sobornost; the latter, however, with its illustrations and and a more even inclusion of authors from the church and academia, may have a wider appeal.

158. Historical Magazine of the Protestant Episcopal Church. DATE FOUNDED: 1932. FREQUENCY: q. PRICE: $15.00/yr.; $4.25/issue. PUBLISHER: Historical Society of the Episcopal Church, P. O. Box 2247, Austin, Texas 78768. EDITOR: John F. Woolverton. ILLUSTRATIONS. INDEX. CIRCULATION: 1,500. MICROFORMS: UMI. REPRINTS: UMI. BOOK REVIEWS. INDEXED/ABSTRACTED: America, HA, RIO. DATABASE: America, ATLA, HA, RI. TARGET AUDIENCE: AC, SP.

The approximately four signed articles fulfill the purpose implied in the title of the journal: to investigate the history of the Episcopal Church, beginning with tis foundation in England, otherwise known as the the Anglican Church. About two of the articles concentrate on the history of the church, in its movements or its important people. Other articles may focus on the current membership of the Protestant Episcopal Church or on religious ideas found in current fiction writers. The articles are well documented; and though aimed at academics and specialists in the field, well-educated lay people will also find the articles interesting. Nine to ten signed one page book reviews are written in each issue. The books reviewed are not limited to those on the Episcopal Church; reviews of books on biblical studies, however, do not seem to be included.

159. Horizons: The Journal of the College Theology

Society. DATE FOUNDED: 1974. FREQUENCY: sa. PRICE: $12.00/yr., individual; $16.00/yr., institutional. PUBLISHER: Walter E. Conn, Horizons, Villanova University, Villanova, Pennsylvania 19085. EDITOR: Walter E. Conn. INDEX. ADVERTISEMENTS. CIRCULATION: 1,350. MANUSCRIPT SELECTION: Blind peer review by board of critical readers. MICROFORMS: UMI. REPRINTS: From the Institute for Scientific Information. BOOK REVIEWS. INDEXED/ABSTRACTED: CPLI, GSScRel, NTA, RIO, RTA, SSCI. DATABASE: ATLA, RI, SocScisearch. TARGET AUDIENCE: AC, SP. SAMPLE COPIES: Only to libraries.

This semiannual, 240 page journal, averaging seven to nine articles, is dedicated to theological and religious studies; that apparently does not include biblical studies like those found in the Bulletin of the John Rylands University Library, which also describes itself as devoted to theology, among other things. Although this journal is Roman Catholic in its publication, the editorial board is quite ecumenical and the tone of the articles does not reveal a Catholic bias. One special feature of this journal is a special book review section devoted to one book. Another is the huge book review section, covering sixty books; each one page review is signed. The authors are scholars who begin each of the articles with an abstract of the argument to be made.

160. The Journal of the Interdenominational Theological Center. DATE FOUNDED: 1973. FREQUENCY: sa; vol. covers fall issue one year and the spring issue of next. PRICE: $6.00/yr., individuals; $8.00/yr., institutions. PUBLISHER: Faculty of the Interdenominational Theological Center, 671 Beckwith St., S. W., Atlanta, Georgia 30314. EDITOR: Dr. John C. Diamond, Jr. INDEX. CIRCULATION: 1,000. MANUSCRIPT SELECTION: Board of editors. REPRINTS: From the publisher. BOOK REVIEWS. SPECIAL ISSUES. INDEXED/ABSTRACTED: RIO, RTA. DATABASE: ATLA, RI. TARGET AUDIENCE: AC, SP, UndSt. SAMPLE COPIES: Yes, libraries; on a limited basis to individuals.

While the title of the journal implies that this publication is devoted to ecumenism and is supported by various black denominational schools, this periodical is, in fact, one of the few, if not only, academic journal to focus on the history Christianity among Afro-Americans. Sometimes there is an article on the black religious experience that does not involve Christianity. The seven or so articles, even the heaviest, are written in clear, energetic prose. The writers may be drawn from around the world, but in fact, most of them are Americans. The authors' authority is noted; most of the articles are documented. The articles not only cover historical figures, but also concepts, such as liberation theology. The number of book reviews in each issue is variable; they are unsigned and composed in 500 words. This journal should appeal to Christians of all backgrounds.

161. The Journal of the Moscow Patriarchate. DATE FOUNDED: 1971. FREQUENCY: m. PRICE: 6.00/yr. PUBLISHER: Moskovskaya Patriarkhiya Novodevichii pr, 1, Moscow G-35, Russian S.F.S.K., USSR. EDITOR: Archbishop Pitirim of Volokolamsk. ILLUSTRATIONS. INDEX. INDEXED/ABSTRACTED: RIO. DATABASE: ATLA, RI. TARGET AUDIENCE: GP, SP.

This journal's many articles are written by authorities in the Russian Eastern Orthodox Church, with several addresses and reports from the Patriarch of Moscow and all Russia. There are sermons on church life, on the peace movement, on Orthodox sister churches, on the ecumenical movement, and on theology. The journal's writers make sure that they do not say anything contrary to Soviet policy; there is a great deal of emphasis on patriotism to the Motherland.

162. The Journal of the United Reformed Church History Society. DATE FOUNDED: 1973. MERGER: Transactions of the Congregational Historical Society and Presbyterian Church History Society Journal to 1972. FREQUENCY: sa. PRICE: 3.75 pounds/yr. PUBLISHER: United Reformed Church History Society, 86 Tavistock Place, London WC1H 9RT, England. EDITOR: Dr. Clyde Binfield. INDEX: At the end of each volume. ADVERTISEMENTS. CIRCULATION: 600. MANUSCRIPT SELECTION: Editor. REPRINTS: Transactions of the Congregational Historical Society available as a Kraus reprint; back issues available in hard copy. BOOK REVIEWS. INDEXED/ABSTRACTED: America, BRI, HA. DATABASE: America, HA. TARGET AUDIENCE: AC, SP, UndSt. SAMPLE COPIES: At the discretion of the Society.

This semiannual thirty five page journal is dedicated to the study of Congregational and Presbyterian history. The articles are not limited to the British scene but also include those denominations' history in the United States. The three articles are signed and are written by Britons with an occasional American contribution. Each issue has six 500 word book reviews. Subscription to the journal includes membership to the society and access to its library and study events.

163. Louvain Studies. DATE FOUNDED: 1966. FREQUENCY: sa. PRICE: BF400.00/yr., $8.00/yr., 5.00 pounds/yr.; BF700.00/2 yrs., $15.00/2 yrs., 8.00 pounds/2 yrs.; BF1,000.00/3 yrs., $21.00/3 yrs., 11.50 pounds/3 yrs. PUBLISHER: Faculty of Theology, University of Louvain (K. U. L.), Leuven, Belgium. EDITOR: Marc Alexander, Carlos Medina. INDEX: Every two years. CIRCULATION: 2,000.

MICROFORMS: UMI. REPRINTS: UMI. BOOK REVIEWS. INDEXED/ABSTRACTED: CLA, CPLI, NTA, OTA, RTA. TARGET AUDIENCE: AC, SP.

This Roman Catholic journal discusses theological and ecclesiastical issues with the Roman Catholic position assumed but not articulated. The articles are written by authors drawn from around the world; with few exceptions they are all Roman Catholic, and many of them either have connections with or graduated from the University of Leuven. biblical exegesis is employed only in the explication of a position held; it is not done for its own sake. The book reviews are divided into two sections; one containing longer essays, and the other shorter notices. Both types are signed; the former takes up two pages while the latter uses half that amount of space. In some issues there is a section called "Chronicles" detailing news of Roman Catholics and Roman Catholic activities, guest lecturers, and doctoral dissertations presented to the faculty. The journal concludes with a section on books received.

164. Lutheran Historical Conference: Essays and Reports. DATE FOUNDED: 1966. FREQUENCY: biennially. PRICE: $75.00/yr. PUBLISHER: Lutheran Historical Conference, 801 De Mun Avenue, St. Louis, Missouri 63105. EDITOR: Dr. August R. Sueflow. CIRCULATION: 200. MANUSCRIPT SELECTION: Prints essays and reports delivered at the biennial meetings of the Lutheran Historical Conference. REPRINTS: Back issues from the Concordia Historical Institute. SPECIAL ISSUES: Biennially in alternate years with "Essays and Reports." INDEXED/ABSTRACTED: RIO. DATABASE: ATLA, RI. TARGET AUDIENCE: AC, SP, UndSt. SAMPLE COPIES: Only to libraries.

This biennial publication of the only pan-Lutheran, interdisciplinary organization in North America, contains approximately twelve to fourteen articles that were delivered at the meeting of the Lutheran Historical Conference. The authors are usually from the United States; at times an author may be from Canada. The journal is photographed from typescript. The publication will appeal to archivists, librarians, and historians.

165. Lutheran Theological Journal. DATE FOUNDED: 1967. FREQUENCY: 3/yr. PRICE: $10.00/yr. PUBLISHER: Lutheran Publishing House, 205 Halifax Street, Adelaide, South Australia, 5006, Australia. EDITOR: Dr. H. P. Hamann. INDEX. ADVERTISEMENTS: In-house only. CIRCULATION: 650. MANUSCRIPT SELECTION: Editor, with the help of an editorial group. REPRINTS: Some hard copy, especially from recent years, from the publisher. BOOK REVIEWS. INDEXED/ABSTRACTED: NTA, OTA, RIC, RIO. DATABASE: ATLA,

RI. TARGET AUDIENCE: SP. SAMPLE COPIES: Upon request.

This Australian journal, approximating 100 pages, promotes the confessional position of the Lutheran Church. Each issue has about four articles, plus a special section or two, an occasional theological comment or a printing of a document relating to a Lutheran position. The articles, while supporting the Lutheran confession, are not calls to arms; this is also seen in the reviews which are evenhanded. On the average, each issue has four to five signed book reviews, averaging one page per review; however, the number of reviews per issue varies widely. The journal is very informative about the Lutheran position on issues.

166. LWF Documentation. DATE FOUNDED: 1978. TITLE CHANGES: Lutheran World, 1954-1977. FREQUENCY: irr. (about six times a year.). PUBLISHER: The Lutheran World Federation, Department of Communication, Publication Office, 150 Rte. de Ferney, CH 1211 Geneva 20, Switzerland. EDITOR: Frances Maher. ILLUSTRATIONS: Occasionally. INDEXED/ABSTRACTED: RIO. DATABASE: ATLA, RI. TARGET AUDIENCE: SP.

As the other part of the continuation of Lutheran World, this serial, in contrast to the LWF Report, was originally conceived to include essays on various topics; but recent issues reveal that each issue of the Documentation is also devoted to one subject such as the ordination of women or Christian communication. This publication has more of the format of a typical journal than the Report does. Some of the articles may be signed, especially those that are materials preparatory to one of the assemblies. Here again, Christians of all persuasions will find food for thought as one denomination deals with the issues both inside and outside the church.

167. LWF Report. DATE FOUNDED: 1978. TITLE CHANGES: Lutheran World, 1954-1977. FREQUENCY: irr. PUBLISHER: Lutheran World Federation, 150 Rte. de Ferney, 1211 Geneva 20, Switzerland. EDITOR: Frances Maher. INDEXED/ABSTRACTED: RIO. DATABASE: ATLA, RI. TARGET AUDIENCE: SP.

As the title suggests, these are reports to the Lutheran World Federation about various theological, social, and ecclesiastical issues facing the church; these include the charismatic movement, human rights, and communion, to name a few. In earlier issues, there were disclaimers that the reports did not reflect the views of the federation; in later issues such disclaimers are not found. Included in the reports are the proceedings of the assemblies of the Lutheran World Federation. In spite of the rather documentary format, these reports are interesting.

168. Mennonite Life. DATE FOUNDED: 1946. FREQUENCY: q. PRICE: $8.00/yr.; $14.00/2 yrs. PUBLISHER: David A. Haury, Bethel College, North Newton, Kansas 67117. EDITOR: David A. Haury. ILLUSTRATIONS. INDEX: Every five years. CIRCULATION: 1,000. MANUSCRIPT SELECTION: Editor, with advice from editors and outside readers. REPRINTS: Back issues from the editor. BOOK REVIEWS. INDEXED/ABSTRACTED: HA, RIO. DATABASE: ATLA, HA, RI. TARGET AUDIENCE: AC, GP, HS, SP, UndSt. SAMPLE COPIES.

This is a very attractively published journal dedicated to study of Mennonite life and culture. In addition, some articles pertain to American religion in general and its relationship to American culture. The articles are signed and the addresses of the authors, mostly North American, are given. In addition to the three signed 500 word book reviews, there is a yearly bibliography on the radical reformation that usually appears in the June issue. The journal's format appears to be aimed at the popular audience, but the four or five articles are scholarly and documented. The publication is a good companion and supplement to the Mennonite Quarterly Review.

169. The Mennonite Quarterly Review. DATE FOUNDED: 1927. FREQUENCY: q. PRICE: $17.00/yr., United States and Canada; $18.00/yr. abroad. PUBLISHER: Mennonite Historical Society, Goshen College, Goshen, Indiana 46526. EDITOR: John S. Oyer. ILLUSTRATIONS. INDEX. CIRCULATION: 1,000. MANUSCRIPT SELECTION: 20% solicited for special issues for which authors are selected by editorial committee; 80% are unsolicited; decisions made by reader evaluators and editorial staff. MICROFORMS: AMS. REPRINTS. BOOK REVIEWS. SPECIAL ISSUES. INDEXED/ABSTRACTED: America, HA, RIO, RP, RTA. DATABASE: America, ATLA, HA, RI. TARGET AUDIENCE: AC, GP, SP, UndSt. SAMPLE COPIES.

This journal is dedicated to promoting interest in and dissemination of information about Anabaptist-Mennonite history, thought, life, and current affairs. It advocates the idea that the free church is a viable alternative in today's world, although it has long abandoned any attempt at an "orthodox" interpretation of Anabaptist or Mennonite tradition. The four articles per issue are written by academics and researchers as are the reviews. The articles are also supplemented by research notes which are discussions of documents and meetings of the Mennonites. In addition, each issue contains about eight signed book reviews, comprising 800 words apiece. This journal is a good companion to Mennonite Life.

170. *Methodist History*. DATE FOUNDED: 1962. TITLE CHANGES: Supersedes in part *World Parish* (1948-1962). FREQUENCY: q. PRICE: $10.00/yr. PUBLISHER: General Commission on Archives and History of the United Methodist Church, P. O. Box 127, Madison, New Jersey 07940. EDITOR: Charles Yrigoyen. INDEX. ADVERTISEMENTS. CIRCULATION: 850. MANUSCRIPT SELECTION: Editor. MICROFORMS: UMI. BOOK REVIEWS. INDEXED/ABSTRACTED: America, HA, RIO, RTA. DATABASE: America, ATLA, HA, RI. TARGET AUDIENCE: AC, SP.

Containing about three articles per issue written by academics, this journal explores the history of Methodism in England and the United States; the studies are mostly on the social movements in the history of Methodism; even the few articles on individuals are sociological in nature. The articles are well documented; the English used is correct if not a bit dry and unexciting. The nine books reviewed in each issue are also concerned mostly with Methodist history; those that are not, deal with famous Americans; each review is signed and consists of one page. Notable features of this journal are a section called "Discovery," which discusses personal finds pertaining to Methodist history, and a "Current Register of Historical Sites," that lists places considered historic by Methodists.

171. *Network*. DATE FOUNDED: 1976 (new series) FREQUENCY: q. PRICE: 1.75 pounds/yr. PUBLISHER: United Society for the Propagation of the Gospel, 15 Tufton Street, London SW1P 3QQ, England. EDITOR: Anthony Richmond. ILLUSTRATIONS. CIRCULATION: 16,500. MANUSCRIPT SELECTION: Editor. REPRINTS: Back issues from the publisher. BOOK REVIEWS. TARGET AUDIENCE: GP, SP. SAMPLE COPIES.

This quarterly's main purpose is to share among Christians news of how other Christians live and do mission work in various political circumstances in which they find themselves, especially in parts of the world with historical connections with the United Society for the Propagation of the Gospel. The articles are written mainly by British authors; Anglican missions are emphasized. Besides the newsy articles, there are letters to the editor and advertisements for mission workers needed in the field. The journal is very much like a very large newsletter. Some of the more interesting sections of the journal include quotations from various journals about the church in the world. The four, signed, 250 word reviews deal not only with popular approaches to missions but also with academic works as well. The journal's emphasis contrasts with that of some more conservative journals that deal with missions.

172. *New Blackfriars*. DATE FOUNDED: 1964; but numbering

of volumes runs from the founding of Blackfriars in 1920. MERGER: Life of the Spirit and Blackfriars, 1964. FREQUENCY: m. PRICE: 10.00 pounds/yr. or $23.00/yr.; through agents, 9.00 pounds/yr. or $20.00/yr. PUBLISHER: The English Dominicans, New Blackfriars, Blackfriars, Oxford OX1 3LY, England. EDITOR: The Rev. John Orme Mills, O. P. INDEX. ADVERTISEMENTS. CIRCULATION: 2,000. MANUSCRIPT SELECTION: Editor in consultation with an editorial board and a team of advisors. MICROFORMS: UMI. REPRINTS: UMI. BOOK REVIEWS. SPECIAL ISSUES: Occasionally. INDEXED/ABSTRACTED: BHI, CPLI, NTA, OTA. TARGET AUDIENCE: AC, GP, SP. SAMPLE COPIES.

This Roman Catholic monthly is the most open to the left among serious Catholic journals published in English. The articles first analyze the social or moral situation at hand first and then bring in the Christian response to that situation; in other words, the articles have a very strong bent toward social analysis; rarely is the Christian message first analyzed to determine if anything can be said. This journal is very much like Christianity and Crisis in emphasis. Each issue has an editorial; all four articles and eight, 1,000 word reviews are signed.

173. New REview. DATE FOUNDED: Autumn 1982. FREQUENCY: 3/yr. PRICE: 5.50 pounds/yr. or 7.50/yr which includes membership in the National Catechetical Association. PUBLISHER: The Rev. A. P. Purnell, S. J., National Catechetical Association, 23 Kensington Square, London W8 5HN, England. EDITOR: The Rev. Donald J. O'Leary. ILLUSTRATIONS. ADVERTISEMENTS. CIRCULATION: 2,000. MANUSCRIPT SELECTION: Authors are commissioned and submit articles to the editor and the editorial board. REPRINTS: Back issues available from the editor. BOOK REVIEWS. TARGET AUDIENCE: GP, HS, SP, UndSt. SAMPLE COPIES.

This journal, dedicated to religious education and renewal in Christian studies and the pastoral ministry, especially from the a Roman Catholic point of view, is very full and is of interest to all Christians. It is divided into ten sections which include news, teaching particular particular seasons in the Christian calendar, topical issues on Christian education, occasional articles, articles for parents, a forum for responses from the youth, and a section on art and education. The authors are mainly British and Irish. The ten, signed, 400 word book reviews not only cover books but audio visual materials as well. The articles are practical rather than philosophical.

174. Newsletter. DATE FOUNDED: 1983, new series. PUBLISHER: Christian Brethren Research Fellowship, c/o

Paternoster Press, 3 Mount Radford Crescent, Exeter EX2 4JW England. EDITOR: G. John Polkinghorne. TARGET AUDIENCE: GP.

This is the newsletter of the Christian Brethren Research Fellowship; it apparently appears every six months starting with September 1983. It is intended to be a forum for subscribers' ideas--what books they have recently read, what meetings they have gone to, or comments on what the Christian Brethren Research Fellowship should be doing. It is aimed at the laity of the Christian Brethren.

175. Orbit. DATE FOUNDED: 1982. TITLE CHANGES: King's Messengers, 1905, Adventurer and Trek, 1982; various title changes, 1905-1982 FREQUENCY: q. PRICE: 60p. PUBLISHER: United Society for the Propagation of the Gospel, 15 Tufton Street, London SW1P 3QQ, England jointly with the Church Missionary Society, 157 Waterloo Road, London SE1 8UU, England. EDITOR: Children's Work Secretary of USPG. ILLUSTRATIONS. CIRCULATION: 9,000. MANUSCRIPT SELECTION: Editors assign work and receive contributions. REPRINTS: Back issues available from the publisher. TARGET AUDIENCE: HS, UndSt. SAMPLE COPIES.

The purpose of this journal is aimed at exciting children about their world-wide church and family. Like Network it focuses on the social issues facing the church in various parts of the world. It emphasizes cooperation and sharing resources in response to God's goodness. It has puzzles. The articles are clearly written and will enlighten not only children but Christians in general about such issues as homelessness and apartheid and what the church is seeking to do about them. Each issue is devoted to one such topic, whether it be breaking down barriers or one's wildest dreams. The articles, unsigned, are written mainly by Britons.

176. The Pope Speaks: The Church Documents Quarterly. DATE FOUNDED: 1954. FREQUENCY: q. PRICE: Domestic, $13.00/yr., $25.00/2 yrs., $36.00/3 yrs.; foreign, $14.25/yr., $27.00/2 yrs., $39.00/3 yrs. PUBLISHER: Our Sunday Visitor, Inc., 200 Noll Plaza, Huntington, Indiana 46750. EDITOR: Albert J. Nevins, M. M. ILLUSTRATIONS. ADVERTISEMENTS. CIRCULATION: 5,000. MICROFORMS: UMI. REPRINTS: UMI; back issues from the publisher. INDEXED/ABSTRACTED: CPLI. TARGET AUDIENCE: GP.

This journal publishes recent papal letters and addresses and other church documents. They are translated into English if that was not their original language. The translations are based on texts in the English-language edition of L'Osservatore Romano and from revisions of versions derived from other sources. Each issue contains about eight such statements by the pope with a heading indicating the first two words of the address in its original language. The translations are very well done. Each issue ends with a "TPS Log" which lists the papal documents appearing in the last three months' issues of L'Osservatore Romano. This serial gives a very good indication of official Roman Catholic concerns.

177. Quaker History. DATE FOUNDED: 1906. TITLE CHANGES: Bulletin of the Friends Historical Association (1906-1961). FREQUENCY: sa. PRICE: $7.50/yr, individuals; libraries, $7.50/yr., $6.00/yr. if subscription is through an agent. PUBLISHER: Friends Historical Association, Quaker Collection, Haverford College Library, Haverford, Pennsylvania 19041. EDITOR: Arthur J. Mekeel. INDEX: Every four years. CIRCULATION: 830. MANUSCRIPT SELECTION: Editor and Editorial Committee of the Friends Historical Association. MICROFORMS: UMI, 1950 to date only. REPRINTS: Incomplete runs may be available from the publisher. BOOK REVIEWS. SPECIAL ISSUES. INDEXED/ABSTRACTED: America, HA DATABASE: America, HA. TARGET AUDIENCE: AC. SAMPLE COPIES: Not usually.

This journal is devoted to the study of Quaker history. The articles are well researched and documented, and the authors do not feel restrained from criticizing the founders of Quakerism. The authors are Americans who write mainly for scholars although well-educated laity could gain from these articles. Again, like so many other journals, it has a section on other publications concerned with the Friends, as well as a section on work in progress. There is also a section called "Briefer Notices" dealing with other publications and meetings that are to take place. In addition, each issue has, on the average, four to five signed book reviews, taking up 400 words each.

178. Quaker Religious Thought. DATE FOUNDED: 1959. FREQUENCY: irr. PRICE: $8.00/ four issues; $15.00 for eight issues. PUBLISHER: Quaker Religious Thought, Rt. 1, Box 549, Alburtis, Pennsylvania 18011; European distribution: Woodbrooke College, 1046 Bristol Rd., Birmingham B29 6LJ, England. EDITOR: Dean Freiday. CIRCULATION: 500. MANUSCRIPT SELECTION: Editor. BOOK REVIEWS. TARGET AUDIENCE: GP, SP.

This journal, sponsored by the Quaker Theological Discussion group, is a remarkable journal seeking to explore the meaning and implications of the Quaker faith. The approximately five articles are signed and are written primarily by American Quakers. While there are no special issues, an issue can be devoted to one topic such as the place of faith in Christ in Quakerism and what that means for a Jew who is a Quaker. The articles are clearly written, engaging and are relevant to all faiths. The journal does suffer from misprints and misspellings, however. A typical book review section contains one signed two page review.

179. Review and Expositor. DATE FOUNDED: 1904. TITLE CHANGES: Baptist Review and Expositor (1904-1906). FREQUENCY: q. PRICE: $9.00/yr., $23.00/3 yrs.; foreign, $10.00/yr. PUBLISHER: Review and Expositor, 2825 Lexington Road, Louisville, Kentucky 40280. EDITOR: Roy L. Honeycut. INDEX. ADVERTISEMENTS. CIRCULATION: 5,000. MANUSCRIPT SELECTION: Articles are commissioned by the editorial board. REPRINTS: Back issues available from the publisher; UMI. BOOK REVIEWS. INDEXED/ABSTRACTED: IZBG, NTA, OTA, RIO, RTA, SBPI. DATABASE: ATLA, RI. TARGET AUDIENCE: AC, SP. SAMPLE COPIES: For $3.50 per issue.

Published by the faculty of the Southern Baptist Theological Seminary in Louisville, Kentucky, each issue of this journal is devoted to a particular topic such as philosophy of religion, the book of Hebrews, or missions; it appears that at least one issue per year is dedicated to the study of a biblical book. Each issue begins with an editorial describing that issue's contributions. The seven or so articles follow, written by academics; many of the authors either have connections with the seminary or the Baptist tradition. The reviews are extensive and are arranged topically; they number forty one per issue, each one signed and occupying one page. In many ways it is similar to Interpretation or Theology Today; it has a broader horizon than the former.

180. St. Vladimir's Theological Quarterly. DATE FOUNDED: 1957, new series. TITLE CHANGES: St. Vladimir's Seminary Quarterly (1952-1957). FREQUENCY: q. PRICE: $15.00/yr.; foreign, $18.00/yr.; single issues, $4.00. PUBLISHER: Faculty, St. Vladimir's Orthodox Theological Seminary, 575 Scarsdale Road, Crestwood, Tuckahoe, New York 10707. EDITOR: John Breck. INDEX. ADVERTISEMENTS. CIRCULATION: 1,800. MANUSCRIPT SELECTION: Editor. MICROFORMS: UMI. REPRINTS: UMI. BOOK REVIEWS. INDEXED/ABSTRACTED: OTA, NTA, RIO, TRI. DATABASE: ATLA, RI. TARGET AUDIENCE: AC, SP.

Like other denominational theological journals such as Theology Today, this journal publishes two or three articles devoted its own theology or history, in this case that of the Orthodox Church. The authors are academics and are drawn from many different kinds of academic institutions. While no special issues exist, a regular issue may devote some or all of its articles to one topic, be it reform in the Orthodox Church or the role of the bishop. The articles are clearly written and will interest those outside the Orthodox Church. Each issue may contain anywhere from five to thirteen reviews that are signed and take up one to two pages apiece; the books reviewed are mostly, but not always, on the history and theology of the Orthodox Church.

181. Searching Together. DATE FOUNDED: 1972. TITLE CHANGES: Baptist Reformation Review (1972-1982). FREQUENCY: q. PRICE: $6.00/yr., United States; $7.00/yr., Canada; 4.00 pounds/yr., United Kingdom; A$5.00/yr., Australia; R6.00/yr., South Africa; $7.00/yr., all other foreign countries; $3.00/yr., libraries. PUBLISHER: Word of Life Church, 104 Dresser Street East, Dresser, Wisconsin 54009. EDITOR: Jon Zens. ILLUSTRATIONS. ADVERTISEMENTS. CIRCULATION: 3,000. MANUSCRIPT SELECTION: Editor, with advice from the church. MICROFORMS: Prairie Bible Institute, Three Hills, Alberta, Canada. REPRINTS. BOOK REVIEWS. SPECIAL ISSUES. INDEXED/ABSTRACTED: RIO, RTA. DATABASE: ATLA, RI. TARGET AUDIENCE: AC, GP, UndSt. SAMPLE COPIES.

This journal devotes each of its issues to a topic as perceived from a biblical point of view. The articles are written by scholars and elders of the church. The articles published in the journal are sometimes selected from other media, usually books. The signed, 500 word book reviews, which number four per issue, are more like notices rather than full, critical reviews. Although the journal claims to have no point view, the articles do espouse conservative ideas, such as the inerrancy of Scripture. Most of the articles are documented. The history of the journal seems to connect it with the Baptist tradition. Though the journal would like to have a scholarly audience, the periodical is aimed more at laypeople.

182. Sobornost. DATE FOUNDED: 1979. MERGER: with Eastern Churches Review, 1979. FREQUENCY: sa. PRICE: 5.00 pounds ($10.00.)/yr. PUBLISHER: Fellowship of St. Alban and St. Sergius, 52 Ladbroke Grove, London W11 2P8, England. EDITOR: The Very Reverend Sergei Hackell. ILLUSTRATIONS. ADVERTISEMENTS. CIRCULATION: 2,200. MANUSCRIPT SELECTION: Editorial board. REPRINTS: Back issues from the publisher. BOOK REVIEWS. SPECIAL ISSUES. INDEXED/ABSTRACTED: AHCI, BHI, CC, CPLI, RIO, RTA. DATABASE: AHSearch, ATLA, RI. TARGET AUDIENCE: AC, GP, UndSt.

Sobornost, begun in 1935 and incorporating Eastern Churches Review, is devoted to the history and theology of Orthodox Christianity or to movements that are related to it. The journal not only deals with academic subjects written primarily by Britons, but it also includes news of events that are coming up and notes about people in an obituary column. The illustrations are usually from illuminated medieval manuscripts. Each issue has fifteen book reviews, are signed, and occupy one half to one and a half pages apiece. This is an important journal for those interested in Eastern Orthodoxy, especially academics and educated laymen. The journal is comparable to the Greek Orthodox Theological Review; the latter, however, tends to draw its authors more from the ranks of academia.

183. Southwestern Journal of Theology. DATE FOUNDED: 1917-1924; 1958-present. FREQUENCY: sa. PRICE: $7.00/yr., domestic; $8.50/yr., foreign. PUBLISHER: Faculty, School of Theology, Southwestern Baptist Theological Seminary, Fort Worth, Texas 76122. EDITOR: Dr. Dan Gentry Kent. ILLUSTRATIONS. ADVERTISEMENTS. CIRCULATION: 2,500. MANUSCRIPT SELECTION: Editor, under the direction of the board of directors. MICROFORMS: UMI. REPRINTS: UMI. BOOK REVIEWS. INDEXED/ABSTRACTED: RIO, SBPI. DATABASE: ATLA, RI. TARGET AUDIENCE: AC, SP. SAMPLE COPIES: Occasionally.

This Baptist journal generally takes a conservative stance on the issues of the day, such as secularism, but it is a conservatism that rarely falls into fundamentalism. Each semiannual issue contains about four articles and is dedicated to one topic, either a social one in the spring issue or a biblical one in the fall. All of the articles are signed and documented; the authors are Baptist and most of them come from Southwestern Baptist Theological Seminary. The sixty five signed reviews consisting of one to two pages are organized according to whether the books are written by professors at the seminary; subsequent reviews are major or shorter, with the latter arranged by subject. For those who wish to know a Baptist view of things, this is a good journal. In some ways, it is similar to Interpretation, except that its views are more denominational and Interpretation draws its authors from a wider theological spectrum.

184. The Thomist. DATE FOUNDED: 1939. FREQUENCY: q. PRICE: $15.00/yr.; $17.00/yr., Canada and foreign subscribers. PUBLISHER: The Thomist Press, 487 Michigan Avenue, N. E., Washington, D. C. 20017. EDITOR: The Rev. Joseph A. DiNoia, O. P. INDEX. ADVERTISEMENTS. CIRCULATION: 1,175. MANUSCRIPT SELECTION: By a majority of the editorial staff; occasionally by a referee. REPRINTS: From the publisher. BOOK REVIEWS. SPECIAL ISSUES. INDEXED/ABSTRACTED: AHCI, CC, CPLI, Elenchus, IBPL, JPCI, NTA, PI, RBP, RTA, TvF. DATABASE: AHSearch,

PI. TARGET AUDIENCE: AC, SP. SAMPLE COPIES.

This journal, averaging about 170 pages per issue, is dedicated to the area of theology and philosophy, specializes in Thomistic thought, and aims at cultivating a dialogue between contemporary philosophy and the classical tradition of philosophy and Christian theology. The articles are signed and the authors are mainly English-speaking, drawn from an international pool. The ten to fifteen signed book reviews are printed in smaller print than the articles so that the three to five page reviews are very full. There is a books received section as well as a listing of off-prints that are available from the journal.

185. Trinity Seminary Review. DATE FOUNDED: 1979. TITLE CHANGES: The Seminary Bulletin (1977-1978). FREQUENCY: sa. PRICE: Free(?). PUBLISHER: Herald Printing, 625 South Kibler, New Washington, Ohio 44854; Trinity Lutheran Seminary, 2199 E. Main Street, Columbus, Ohio 43209. EDITOR: Walter F. Taylor, Jr. ILLUSTRATIONS: Rarely. CIRCULATION: 6,000. MANUSCRIPT SELECTION: Editor and editorial committee. REPRINTS: Limited back issues from the editor. BOOK REVIEWS. SPECIAL ISSUES. INDEXED/ABSTRACTED: RIO. DATABASE: ATLA, RI. TARGET AUDIENCE: AC, SP. SAMPLE COPIES.

This journal publishes signed articles that provide a forum for interaction between the theological disciplines and the practice of the ministry. It is also designed to aid in the continuing education of professional church leaders. In contrast to other journals like the International Bulletin of Missionary Research and the International Review of Mission that are more general, this one is aimed primarily at Lutherans. The issues may have a thematic emphasis, such as the meaning of baptism. The style of writing is direct and non-technical. Each issue contains eight to fifteen signed book reviews composed with 500 words.

186. U. S. Catholic Historian. DATE FOUNDED: 1980. FREQUENCY: q. PRICE: Full members and archivists, $20.00/yr.; associate members, $16.00/yr.; institutions, $25.00/yr. PUBLISHER: United States Catholic Historical Society, P. O. Box 97, Eltingville, Staten Island, New York 10312. EDITOR: Christopher J. Kauffman. ILLUSTRATIONS. ADVERTISEMENTS. MANUSCRIPT SELECTION: Editor. TARGET AUDIENCE: GP, SP.

This journal attempts to relate the meaning of Catholicism to Catholics through an historical analysis of Catholicism in America as it relates to a particular theme. Such themes include patriotism, Catholics and the international life, and the dialogue between bishops and historians. Each issue is broken into three sections: historical analysis, dialogue, and living witness. The last one uses documents to reveal something of the past with regard to that particular issue's theme. The signed articles are written by academics, laity, and clerics. The journal is very attractively produced and the print type is easy on the eyes. Not all laymen will find everything interesting; but both the specialist and the layman will find something. Some of the issues raised are not limited to Roman Catholics.

187. USPG Yearbook. DATE FOUNDED: 1966. FREQUENCY: a. PRICE: Free. PUBLISHER: United Society for the Propagation of the Gospel, 15 Tufton Street, London SW1P 3QQ, England. EDITOR: Anthony Richmond. ILLUSTRATIONS. CIRCULATION: 80,000. MANUSCRIPT SELECTION: Editors. REPRINTS: Back issues from the publisher. TARGET AUDIENCE: GP. SAMPLE COPIES.

This annual focuses on the people of the worldwide church supported by the United Society for the Propagation of the Gospel. Again, like its sister journals, Network and Orbit, it shows how the church is working throughout the world. After introducing various people, there is a suggestion for praying for their work. The unsigned articles are written mainly by British authors. All of illustrations are in color. The journal stresses sharing and cooperation and is not dogmatic.

188. Wesleyan Theological Journal. DATE FOUNDED: 1966. FREQUENCY: sa; annually, 1966-1978. PRICE: $6.00/yr. PUBLISHER: Wayne E. Caldwell, Wesleyan Theological Society, 215 East 43rd Street, Marion, Indiana 46953. EDITOR: Alex R. G. Deasley. INDEX: Every five years. CIRCULATION: 1,600. MANUSCRIPT SELECTION: Editorial committee; papers given at the annual meeting are given priority. MICROFORMS: UMI. REPRINTS: UMI; all issues are also for sale from the publisher. BOOK REVIEWS. INDEXED/ABSTRACTED: CPI, RIO. DATABASE: ATLA, RI. TARGET AUDIENCE: AC, SP, UndSt. SAMPLE COPIES: Supplied at discretion of the publisher.

This journal contains six or seven articles written by scholars on topics that are related to the Wesleyan-Arminian tradition. The spring issue contains papers and responses to those papers delivered at the annual conference of the Wesleyan Theological Society; many of the articles in the fall issue are also from the annual conference. Those who deliver papers at the annual conferences, must be members of the society which requires that each member believe in a creed that reflects conservative Christianity. Since fall 1981 the journal has included three or four book reviews comprising 250 to 350 words apiece. The book reviews are written from a Wesleyan point of view.

189. The Witness: An Ecumenical Journal of Social Concern. DATE FOUNDED: 1917; ran to 1972; resumed in 1974. FREQUENCY: m. PRICE: $12.00/yr.; $6.00/yr. for those on limited income. PUBLISHER: Episcopal Church Publishing Co., P. O. Box 359, Ambler, Pennsylvania 19002. EDITOR: Mary Lou Suhor. ILLUSTRATIONS. INDEX. CIRCULATION: 6,000. MANUSCRIPT SELECTION: An editorial committee. REPRINTS: Back issues from the publisher. SPECIAL ISSUES: Occasionally. INDEXED/ABSTRACTED: RIO. DATABASE: ATLA, RI. TARGET AUDIENCE: AC, GP, SP, UndSt. SAMPLE COPIES.

This monthly, averaging about five articles per issue written by American and Third World ministers, is devoted to interpreting the gospel as it relates to racism, sexism, peace, and classism. In terms of point of view, it is comparable to the Christian Century. There is little biblical exegesis; instead the emphasis is on the social situation with the appropriate Christian response being assumed. It should not be assumed that all of the articles espouse a liberal viewpoint or a viewpoint slanted toward the Third World. Some are critical of the Third World. This journal will be important for collections which aim to have journals emphasizing social issues from a Christian point of view.

Theology

190. Africa Theological Journal. DATE FOUNDED: 1968; discontinued 1973-1976; resumed 1977. FREQUENCY: Currently, 3/yr. PRICE: East Africa, TShs. 200/yr.; rest of Africa, $20.00/yr.; Europe, $25.00/yr.; United States and the Far East, $27.00/yr. PUBLISHER: Tanzania Litho, Box 200, Arusha, Tanzania. EDITOR: Dr. Howard S. Olson. INDEX. ADVERTISEMENTS: Not currently. CIRCULATION: 500. MANUSCRIPT SELECTION: Editorial committee. REPRINTS: Back issues from the Managing Editor, Box 7149, Arusha, Tanzania. BOOK REVIEWS. INDEXED/ABSTRACTED: RIO, TK. DATABASE: ATLA, RI. TARGET AUDIENCE: AC, SP, UndSt. SAMPLE COPIES: Upon request.

This journal, dedicated to an ecumenical approach and supported by the Lutheran Church, is a clearly written serial with articles signed and written mainly by academics. This journal forms a bridge between western theology and African Christian theologians who are trying to practice their faith among the African cultures; it does not come to to a discussion of this issue through a history of religions approach. Each issue contains five signed 1,500 word book reviews. The reviews of books by western theologians are highly enlightening for a western reader. Occasionally an issue will be dedicated to a particular issue such as Luther. Each issue is introduced by an editorial giving the main points of each article and the authority of each writer.

191. American Journal of Theology and Philosophy. DATE FOUNDED: 1980. FREQUENCY: 3/yr. PRICE: $9.00/yr,

individuals; $15.00/yr., libraries. PUBLISHER: American Society for Social Philosophy and Philosophical Theology, Dept. of Philosophy, Augusta College, Augusta, Georgia 30910. EDITOR: Dr. Creighton Peden. INDEX. CIRCULATION: 400. MANUSCRIPT SELECTION: Blind review process. REPRINTS: Back issues from the publisher. INDEXED/ABSTRACTED: PI, RIO. DATABASE: ATLA, PI, RI. TARGET AUDIENCE: AC. SAMPLE COPIES.

This journal is devoted to the discussion of three areas: (1) American theological efforts which are attentive of philosophical literature; (2) the history and development of liberalism in American religious thought; and (3) themes of relevance to the "Chicago School" of theology. Although this journal is in typescript, it is attractively produced with none of the "light spots" that occur in such types of printing. Computer formatted articles are invited. The articles are very clearly written, and no scholar or graduate student should find the articles difficult to read. Each issue is a dedicated to one topic and guest editors are invited.

192. Andrews University Monographs, Studies in Religion. DATE FOUNDED: 1966. FREQUENCY: irr. PRICE: Varies. PUBLISHER: Andrews University Press, Berrien Springs, Michigan 49104. EDITOR: Dr. Robert Firth. ILLUSTRATIONS: Rarely. INDEX: Occasionally. CIRCULATION: Variable. MANUSCRIPT SELECTION: Vote by the board after receiving opinions from the referees. REPRINTS: Back issues available from the publisher. TARGET AUDIENCE: AC, SP.

193. Andrews University Seminary Doctoral Dissertation Series. DATE FOUNDED: 1981. FREQUENCY: irr. PRICE: Price varies. PUBLISHER: Andrews University Press, Berrien Springs, Michigan 49104. EDITOR: Dr. Robert Firth. INDEX: Occasionally. CIRCULATION: Varies. MANUSCRIPT SELECTION: By recommendation by the seminary committee, followed by a vote by the board. REPRINTS: Back issues available from the publisher. TARGET AUDIENCE: AC, SP.

194. Andrews University Seminary Studies. DATE FOUNDED: 1963. FREQUENCY: 3/yr. PRICE: Individuals: $12.00/yr. (domestic), $13.50/yr. (foreign); institutions: $15.00/yr. (domestic), $16.50/yr. (foreign). PUBLISHER: Seventh-day Adventist Theological Seminary of Andrews University, Berrien Springs, Michigan 49104. EDITOR: Kenneth A. Strand. INDEX. CIRCULATION: 1,000. MANUSCRIPT SELECTION: Editor. BOOK REVIEWS. INDEXED/ABSTRACTED: BRM, ElencBibBib, IBHR, IZBG, MPI, NTA, OrientLit, OTA, RecPubArt, RIO, RTA, ZAW. DATABASE: ATLA, RI. TARGET AUDIENCE: AC, SP.

This journal publishes papers and brief notes on all subjects pertaining to the church and Christianity: from biblical studies to systematic and practical theology. Its nature and emphasis are very similar to those of Interpretation. The four or so articles and the reviews are written primarily by Americans. In addition to the ten signed two page book reviews, there are approximately twenty four book notices, or very short book reviews, of current books. The last issue of the journal has the index, a transliteration table for Hebrew, and a listing of the abbreviations for theological journals. Each issue usually has at least one exegetical article on a passage from the Bible.

195. Anglican Theological Review. DATE FOUNDED: 1919. FREQUENCY: q. PRICE: Individuals, $15.00/yr., $29.00/2 yrs., $43.00/3 yrs.; institutions, $18.00/yr., $35.00/2 yrs. PUBLISHER: Anglican Theological Review, 600 Haven St., Evanston, Illinois 60201. EDITOR: James Dunkley. INDEX. CIRCULATION: 12,300. MICROFORMS: UMI. REPRINTS: UMI. BOOK REVIEWS. INDEXED/ABSTRACTED: BullSig, IBZL, NTA, OTA, RIO, RTA. DATABASE: ATLA, Francis, RI. TARGET AUDIENCE: AC, SP.

While the journal's title seems to imply that only Anglicans write for it, authors from other traditions are invited to do so and are published. The journal's purpose is to relate one field of study to another so that readers can discover what those fields mean as they develop ideas about the Christian life and ministry; the four or five articles are written by academics who document their articles. In addition to the articles, there is a section for poetry which, it must be said, is not specifically Christian; the poetry reflects the human condition and could have appeared in any secular journal. The articles show no particular bias, and criticism of some Anglican positions are exhibited. The thirteen signed one page book reviews cover all types of books on biblical studies, history, and theology.

196. Augustinian Studies. DATE FOUNDED: 1970. FREQUENCY: a. PRICE: $15.00/yr. PUBLISHER: Augustinian Institute, Villanova, Pennsylvania 19085. EDITOR: Robert P. Russell. MANUSCRIPT SELECTION: Editor. BOOK REVIEWS. INDEXED/ABSTRACTED: CPLI, PI. DATABASE: PI. TARGET AUDIENCE: AC, SP.

This journal is devoted to scholarly studies on the life, teaching, and influence of St. Augustine. To this end, it publishes about fifteen articles written by experts from around the world; most of the articles are in English, however, with most of the authors being American. The articles are documented and are about ten to twenty pages long. There is no book review section as such; instead, there are review articles. In addition to the articles there is a section listing the St. Augustine Lectures. It appears that this journal is very slow in being published; the 1982 publication was copyrighted in 1985.

197. Augustiniana. DATE FOUNDED: 1951. FREQUENCY: q. PRICE: Belgium, Luxemburg, BF900.00/yr.; other countries, BF1,000.00/yr. PUBLISHER: Augustijns Historisch Instituut, Pakenstraat 109, B-3030 Hererlee-Lovain, Belgium. INDEX. CIRCULATION: 400. TARGET AUDIENCE: AC.

Dedicated to the study of Augustine, the Augustinian Order, and Jansenism, this journal is written by academics for academics. Although it is published in Belgium, a fair number of the articles are written in English. The five or so articles are signed. The journal is not for beginners in Augustinian theology; the articles can be very long, fifty or seventy pages, and the prose can be heavy. For scholars dedicated to the details of such theology, it is a must. While the journal is highly objective, and presents no particular point of view, it should be noted that it is published "cum approbatione ecclesiastica."

198. Bangalore Theological Forum. DATE FOUNDED: 1967. FREQUENCY: q. PRICE: Rs25.00/yr. (India, Pakistan, Bangladesh, Sri Lanka), Rs40.00/yr. (other Asian countries and South America), 5.00 pounds/yr. (England), $10.00/yr. (United States), DM24.00/yr. (Germany and Europe), A$8.00/yr. (Australia and New Zealand). PUBLISHER: Bangalore Theological Forum, United Theological College, 17, Millers Road, Bangalore-560 046, India. EDITOR: Eric J. Lott. CIRCULATION: 550. MANUSCRIPT SELECTION: Editor. INDEXED/ABSTRACTED: RIO. DATABASE: ATLA, RI. TARGET AUDIENCE: AC, SP.

This theological journal is written for Indians by Indians. Each issue, containing six to nine articles, is devoted to one particular theme, be it the future or the Sermon on the Mount. The articles are scholarly but not dry; an effort is made to apply the findings to solutions of problems in the world. For instance, the articles on the Sermon on the Mount try to apply the message to current society. Occasionally an issue will be published in collaboration with other theological schools in Europe or the United States.

199. Bibliotheca Sacra. DATE FOUNDED: 1843. FREQUENCY: q. PRICE: $8.00/yr.; $10.00/yr., foreign. PUBLISHER: Dallas Theological Seminary, 3909 Swiss Ave., Dallas, Texas 75204. EDITOR: Dr. Roy B. Zuck, Managing Editor. INDEX.

CIRCULATION: 9,000. MANUSCRIPT SELECTION: Editors. REPRINTS: Back issues from the publisher. BOOK REVIEWS. INDEXED/ABSTRACTED: Biblica, CPI, Elenchus, IZBG, NTA, OTA, OT/ANE, RIO. DATABASE: ATLA, RI. TARGET AUDIENCE: AC, SP.

Dedicated to an evangelical, conservative Christianity, this journal is the oldest continuously published theological journal in the western hemisphere. The authors of the five articles interpret subjects according to the theological stance of the journal which is conservative, evangelical, and premillenial. It is a kind of conservative blend of the Journal of Biblical Literature and Interpretation. The scholars writing for the journal are acquainted with the leading scholars who are cited in the footnotes. The review section usually contains thirty to thirty five book reviews, all signed and each taking up one half page. The emphasis may be jarring to some, but it contains a viewpoint needed to balance more standard, objective analyses of Scripture.

200. Chicago Studies. DATE FOUNDED: 1962. FREQUENCY: 3/yr. PRICE: $11.50/yr., $21.00/2 yrs., $30.00/3 yrs; 20% discount to agencies. PUBLISHER: Civitas Dei Foundation, Box 655, Mundelein, Illinois 60060. EDITOR: The Rev. George J. Dyer. INDEX. CIRCULATION: 10,000. MANUSCRIPT SELECTION: Editorial board. MICROFORMS: UMI. REPRINTS. SPECIAL ISSUES: Occasionally. INDEXED/ABSTRACTED: CPLI, NTA. TARGET AUDIENCE: GP, SP. SAMPLE COPIES: $2.00 per sample issue.

This journal, comprising about 100 pages per issue, is a Roman Catholic journal dedicated to the continued theological development of priests and religious educators; the material is designed to be used in theology classes. Two issues per year are dedicated to one subject apiece. The articles are signed and are written by clerics and theological educators. The articles are aimed toward well educated laymen, clerics, and educators in seminary. Although the journal is Roman Catholic and is aimed at Roman Catholics, the opinions are the responsibility of the authors. Moreover, the articles will be of interest to non-Catholics as well.

201. The Christian Century. DATE FOUNDED: 1884. TITLE CHANGES: Christian Oracle (1884-1899). MERGER: With New Christian in 1970. FREQUENCY: w; 40/yr. PRICE: $21.00/yr; $36.00/2 yrs.; $54.00/3 yrs.; foreign subscriptions, add $2.50 per year. PUBLISHER: Christian Century Foundation, 407 S. Dearborn St., Chicago, Illinois 60605. EDITOR: James M. Wall. ILLUSTRATIONS. INDEX: Twice each year. ADVERTISEMENTS. CIRCULATION: 35,000. MANUSCRIPT SELECTION: Editorial staff. MICROFORMS.

REPRINTS: Limited quantities from the the editorial offices; back issues also available from publisher. BOOK REVIEWS. INDEXED/ABSTRACTED: BRG, BRI, IAPV, MRD, RG, RIO DATABASE: ATLA, RG, RI. TARGET AUDIENCE: AC, SP. SAMPLE COPIES.

This weekly Christian journal is written by American clerics and academics, is liberal and is aimed at the clergy and concerned Christian layman. It contains an editorial page, news from and about denominations and people in the church and approximately two or three regular articles. It also has a section for letters to the editor, a book review section, short notices of books recently received, and an area for classified advertisements. The book review section contains two long, signed reviews and six short unsigned essays; the average length is 500 to 600 words. There is a book issue in the spring and fall as well as an issue in the fall dedicated to theological education. Generally speaking, the journal is concerned with ecumenical issues and societal topics as seen from a theological point of view. This journal's conservative counterpart is _Christianity Today_.

202. _Concordia Theological Quarterly_. DATE FOUNDED: 1959, new ser. TITLE CHANGES: _The Springfielder_ until 1976. FREQUENCY: q. PRICE: $5.00/yr., United States; $10.00/yr., foreign. PUBLISHER: Concordia Theological Seminary, 6600 North Clinton Street, Fort Wayne, Indiana 46825. EDITOR: Dr. David P. Scaer. INDEX: Every few years. ADVERTISEMENTS: Occasionally. CIRCULATION: 10,000. MANUSCRIPT SELECTION: Editor. MICROFORMS: UMI. REPRINTS: From the seminary library; some hard copy from the publisher. BOOK REVIEWS. INDEXED/ABSTRACTED: NTA, OTA, RIO. DATABASE: ATLA, RI. TARGET AUDIENCE: AC, SP, UndSt. SAMPLE COPIES: Occasionally, on request.

This quarterly is a journal of the Lutheran Church-Missouri Synod, and its main concern is to promote orthodox theology. The number of articles range from three to seven, and each issue may have as few as three reviews or as many as twenty; each review is usually signed and may occupy up to one page. There is also a books received section. While the goal of the journal does not necessarily skew the scholarship in the articles, it should be noted that many of the book reviews are written from a confessional stance; usually a recommendation is based on whether the book conforms to orthodox theology. The articles are informative, well written, and engaging.

203. _Criterion_. DATE FOUNDED: 1962. TITLE CHANGES: _Divinity Student_ (1924-1932); _Divinity School News_ (1934-1962). FREQUENCY: bm. PRICE: $5.00/yr., described

as a "contribution." PUBLISHER: University of Chicago Divinity School, 1025 E. 58th Street, Chicago, Illinois 60637. EDITOR: Janet I. Summers, Anne E. Carr, Martin E. Marty. ILLUSTRATIONS. CIRCULATION: 5,000. INDEXED/ABSTRACTED: RIO. DATABASE: ATLA, RI. TARGET AUDIENCE: SP.

This publication focuses upon the ideas of students and faculty at the University of Chicago Divinity School as they are displayed in sermons and addresses given at special functions of the divinity school or at religious services. It contains about four articles per issue which are preceded by a one page introduction to the contents of the journal. The journal concludes with a section on alumni news. As would befit an academic institution, the addresses and sermons are intellectual in tone. This journal is a good window for the church to look into to see how a major divinity school's scholars and students think.

204. Dialog: A Journal of Theology. DATE FOUNDED: 1962. FREQUENCY: q. PRICE: United States, Canada, $16.00/yr., $28.00/2 yrs.; foreign, $18.00/yr., $32.00/2 yrs.; students, $12.00/yr. PUBLISHER: Dialog, Inc., 2481 Como Ave., St. Paul, Minnesota, 55108. EDITOR: Carl E. Braaten. ADVERTISEMENTS. CIRCULATION: 3,000. MICROFORMS: UMI. REPRINTS: UMI. BOOK REVIEWS. INDEXED/ABSTRACTED: NTA, OTA, RIO, RTA. DATABASE: ATLA, RI. TARGET AUDIENCE: AC, SP.

This journal publishes about six articles devoted to one theme, be it evangelism or J. S. Bach. While the articles themselves may not be on Lutheran subjects, the authors are mostly from the Lutheran tradition as is the editorial board. Besides the articles, one will find here several editorials dealing with the Lutheran Church; "Merger Watch," containing statements on the merging of Lutheran churches; "Outside the Theme," presenting articles not germane to the theme of the issue; "Theology Update," reviewing current theological trends and debates; and "Views and Counterviews," which presents some criticisms of some of the articles that appeared in earlier issues of Dialog. A strong interest of the journal is the relationship between the church and the surrounding culture. The six signed one to two page book reviews are solid; this journal is for the Lutheran minister, scholar, and well-educated layman.

205. Durham University Journal. DATE FOUNDED: 1876. FREQUENCY: 2/yr. (academic year). PRICE: England, 13.00 pounds/yr.; overseas, 13.50 pounds/yr. PUBLISHER: The Senate of the University of Durham, Old Shire Hall, Durham DH1 3HP, England. EDITOR: Dr. J. W. Blench. ILLUSTRATIONS: Occasionally. INDEX. ADVERTISEMENTS.

CIRCULATION: 500. MANUSCRIPT SELECTION: Editor, with occasional aid from an advisory board or an outside reader. MICROFORMS: UMI, for the period of 1876-1967. REPRINTS: Some hard copy available from the publisher. BOOK REVIEWS. INDEXED/ABSTRACTED: America, HA. DATABASE: America, HA. TARGET AUDIENCE: AC, SP, UndSt. SAMPLE COPIES: Only to libraries.

This is an interdisciplinary journal devoted to discussing art, literature, classics, history, philosophy, and theology. There appears to be one article per issue on theology, especially British theology. The articles are written by academics, mostly British, with a short biographical sketch of each author at the back of the journal. The thirty three signed book reviews are arranged under subject headings; each reviewer composes his essay in 750 words. It has a section for letters from the readers, as well as a books received section. Each issue is at least 150 pages long with an average of eleven articles.

206. The East Asia Journal of Theology. DATE FOUNDED: 1983. TITLE CHANGES: South East Asia Journal of Theology (1959-1982) and North East Asia Journal of Theology (1968-1982). MERGER: Of the two journals in "Title Changes." FREQUENCY: sa. PRICE: Asia and the Third World: S$12.00 or $6.00/yr., S$22.00 or $11.00/2 yrs., S$32.00 or $16.00/3 yrs.; elsewhere: S$24.00 or $12.00/yr., S$44.00 or $22.00/2 yrs., S$64.00 or $32.00/3 yrs. PUBLISHER: The Association for Theological Education in South East Asia, No. 4 Mount Sophia, Singapore 0922, Republic of Singapore. EDITOR: Dr. Jeow Choo Lak. INDEX. CIRCULATION: 1,200. MANUSCRIPT SELECTION: Editor. MICROFORMS: UMI. REPRINTS: Single copies available from the publisher. BOOK REVIEWS. INDEXED/ABSTRACTED: IRPL, RIO, TK. DATABASE: ATLA, RI. TARGET AUDIENCE: AC, SP. SAMPLE COPIES.

The purpose of this journal is to encourage Asian biblical scholarship and theological thinking; to relate the gospel to the culture, history, and religions of East Asia; to study the problems of teaching theology; and to share information about the schools of the Association. The authors, mainly academics, are fully conversant with the theologies of both East and West. The three parts of the journal appear to be devoted first to papers given in seminars, secondly to papers given at the assembly of the North East Asia Association of Theological Schools, and thirdly to independent articles and dissertation abstracts. It is comparable to the Taiwan Journal of Theology. This publication has three signed reviews, each averaging one and one half pages. It reflects issues that are not only Asian but also are relevant to issues in the Christian church world-wide.

207. Eglise et theologie. DATE FOUNDED: 1970. FREQUENCY: 3/yr. PRICE: $30.00/yr.; $12.00 per issue. PUBLISHER: Eglise et theologie, Saint Paul University, 223 Main Street, Ottawa, Ontario, Canada K1S 1C4. EDITOR: Leo Laberge. INDEX. CIRCULATION: 500. MICROFORMS: UMI. REPRINTS: UMI. BOOK REVIEWS. SPECIAL ISSUES: Yes, but as part of the regular issue. INDEXED/ABSTRACTED: CLA, NTA, OTA, RIO, RTA. DATABASE: ATLA, RI. TARGET AUDIENCE: AC.

This Roman Catholic journal with a French title publishes most of its articles in English. The approximately four to five articles concentrate on exegesis and theology. While there is no explicit theme mentioned for each issue, the articles in it tend to center around one theme, such as moral theology. Its special issue does have a thematic interest, and some of the French articles are translated into English. Each issue has thirty signed one page reviews; the book reviews in the regular issues are arranged schematically, moving from Old Testament studies to theology; these reviews are either in French or English. The journal concludes with a section for books received. This journal is very similar to Princeton's Theology Today. The writing style tends to be heavy.

208. Encounter. DATE FOUNDED: 1940. TITLE CHANGES: Shane Quarterly until 1956. FREQUENCY: q. PRICE: $12.00/yr.; $20.00/2 yrs.; $28.00/3 yrs. PUBLISHER: Christian Theological Seminary, 1000 West 42nd Street, Indianapolis, Indiana 46208. EDITOR: Clark M. Williamson. ILLUSTRATIONS: Only if it is an integral part of the article. INDEX. ADVERTISEMENTS: Only if camera ready copy is provided; very few advertisements are used. CIRCULATION: 500. MANUSCRIPT SELECTION: Editor. MICROFORMS: UMI. REPRINTS: UMI; hard copy available from the publisher. BOOK REVIEWS. INDEXED/ABSTRACTED: IZBG, NTA, RIO, RTA. DATABASE: ATLA, RI. TARGET AUDIENCE: AC, SP. SAMPLE COPIES: Upon request.

This journal of approximately 100 pages per issue of camera ready articles, usually contains several essays on process theology, but the journal's interests are wide-ranging, having articles on ethics, pastoral care, and preaching, to name a few. The articles are unsolicited and are arranged in each issue dedicated to one topic, e. g. process theology or theological ethics. The authors are mainly Christian North Americans although people of other faiths and nationalities do contribute. The eleven signed 400 word book reviews are written by authorities in the field. The signed articles are well written and engaging. It makes a point of avoiding sexist language.

209. Ephemerides Theologicae Lovaniensis. DATE FOUNDED: 1924. FREQUENCY: a. (published in four fascicles.) PRICE: 2,000.00 Belgian francs/yr.; $34.00/yr. PUBLISHER: Editions Peeter s.p.r.l., Bodegenotenlaan, B-3000, Louvain, Belgium. INDEX. BOOK REVIEWS. INDEXED/ABSTRACTED: OTA, NTA, RTA, RIO. DATABASE: ATLA, RI. TARGET AUDIENCE: AC.

This publication, which seems to have many articles in English, is published annually in four fascicles covering about 1,000 pages. Fascicles one and four contain articles reflecting theological research, book reviews, books received, a "Chronica," listing theological events around the world, and a list of dissertations presented at the Catholic University of Louvain. There are almost seventy book reviews in each of the two fascicles, each one signed and taking up to one page. Fascicles two and three make up the Elenchus Bibliographicus, containing a bibliography of books and articles in the fields of Christianity and religion. About four articles and four "notes" can be found in fascicles one and four. The articles cover both biblical interpretation as well as the history of theology, usually Catholic theology. This is a very scholarly journal.

210. Eternity. DATE FOUNDED: 1950. MERGER: Superseded Revelation, founded in 1931; merged with Our Hope, 1958. FREQUENCY: 11/yr. PRICE: $17.50/yr.; $32.50/2 yrs.; foreign subscriptions, add $4.00. PUBLISHER: Evangelical Ministries, Inc., 1716 Spruce St., Philadelphia, Pennsylvania 19103. EDITOR: William J. Peterson. ILLUSTRATIONS. INDEX. ADVERTISEMENTS. CIRCULATION: 44,000. MANUSCRIPT SELECTION: Executive Editor and editorial department. MICROFORMS: UMI. REPRINTS. UMI; back issues from the publisher at $2.00 apiece. BOOK REVIEWS. SPECIAL ISSUES. INDEXED/ABSTRACTED: GSScRel, CPI. TARGET AUDIENCE: GP. SAMPLE COPIES: At $2.00 apiece.

This journal has been reformatted and has taken on a very attractive look. The articles are signed by authors who are mainly researchers and academics from the United States. The magazine espouses a conservative point of view which seeks interaction with the culture from a Christian point of view. There are monthly departments on science, fine arts, business, social commentary, and news analysis. Each issue has a special topic as well as a section for letters to the editor. There are three special supplements: "Directions" in the September issue; "Doors" in the November issue; and "Update" in the March publication. In addition to the five to ten signed, 300 word book reviews, there are many advertisements of books primarily from conservative Christian publishers. This journal aims at the same audience as Christianity Today, but it is much more attractively packaged.

211. The Evangelical Quarterly. DATE FOUNDED: 1929. FREQUENCY: q. PRICE: 7.80 pounds/yr.; $17.55/yr. PUBLISHER: The Paternoster Press, 3 Mount Radford Crescent, Exeter EX2 4JW, England. EDITOR: Professor I. H. Marshall. INDEX. ADVERTISEMENTS. CIRCULATION: 1,500. MANUSCRIPT SELECTION: Editor. MICROFORMS: Xerox. REPRINTS. BOOK REVIEWS. INDEXED/ABSTRACTED: CPI, NTA, OTA, RIO, RTA. DATABASE: ATLA, RI. TARGET AUDIENCE: AC, UndSt. SAMPLE COPIES.

The Evangelical Quarterly is devoted to biblical and theological studies for scholars and possibly for undergraduate students. The articles are signed, but neither the authority nor the addresses of the authors are noted. The articles generally deal with New Testament studies, but occasional articles on the history of theology in the church do appear. While the journal does represent an evangelical point of view, its conservatism is not rigid as can be seen from the ten book reviews, all of which are signed; each review is composed in a little less then one page. In some ways, this journal is comparable to Interpretation.

212. Explor. DATE FOUNDED: 1975. FREQUENCY: a. PRICE: Free; all copies over the one complimentary copy are $2.00 plus postage. PUBLISHER: Garrett-Evangelical Theological Seminary, 2121 Sheridan Rd., Evanston, Illinois 60201. EDITOR: T. Thomas Nustad, Managing Editor. ILLUSTRATIONS. CIRCULATION: 7,000. MANUSCRIPT SELECTION: Editorial committee. INDEXED/ABSTRACTED: RIO. DATABASE: ATLA, RI. TARGET AUDIENCE: AC, GP, SP, UndSt. SAMPLE COPIES.

Self-described as "A Journal of Theology," the eight or so articles in Explor are related to a particular theme that the issue is covering. The choice of themes seems to be guided by relating religion or Christianity to the current world. The authors are generally academics whose audience is primarily scholars and secondarily the religious public. Not only is there no section for book reviews; there is no books received section either. All the articles are signed and a brief biography of each author is provided at the end of the journal. The articles have very wide left hand margins where the important points of the article are noted.

213. Faith and Philosophy. DATE FOUNDED: 1984. FREQUENCY: q. PRICE: Individuals, $15.00/yr.; institutions, $25.00/yr.; others add $2.00; $5.00 per issue. PUBLISHER: Society of Christian Philosophers, Faith and Philosophy, Asbury College, Wilmore, Kentucky 40390. EDITOR: William P. Alston. INDEX. ADVERTISEMENTS.

CIRCULATION: 1,100. REPRINTS: Back issues from the managing editor. BOOK REVIEWS. INDEXED/ABSTRACTED: PI. DATABASE: PI. TARGET AUDIENCE: AC, SP.

Faith and Philosophy is devoted to publishing articles which address philosophical questions from a Christian perspective, discussions about the philosophical issues that arise from within Christianity, and articles that deal critically with the philosophical credentials of the Christian faith; articles by non-Christians are invited. The approximately four signed articles per issue fill these requirements very well. Each issue has four, signed, two to three page book reviews. This journal is definitely not for the novice in Christian philosophy; it is geared toward the academic world entirely. The prose does not read easily; but that is due to the close, logical reasoning of the authors.

214. Faith and Thought. DATE FOUNDED: 1983. FREQUENCY: sa. PRICE: $8.00/yr.; $4.00 per issue. PUBLISHER: First Baptist Church of Montclair, Church Street and Trinity Place, Montclair, New Jersey 07042. EDITOR: Robert M. Price. CIRCULATION: 600. BOOK REVIEWS. TARGET AUDIENCE: AC, GP, SP.

This journal was founded on the premise that evangelical Christians and liberal Christians are talking more to and appreciating one another more. The journal's emphasis is not on "how-to" but on theological issues. Its four articles are centered around one theme, such as Paul Tillich, the Princeton method of theology, or religious diversity. The articles are written primarily by academics. Other features of this journal are "Cover to Cover," an occasional book review section containing three, signed two page essays; "Cinema Classics," offering theology-of-culture analyses of important films; "Edifying Discourse," an analysis of issues facing Christianity; and a special interview with an important religious thinker.
Unique to this journal is the fact that it was founded and is published by a Christian congregation, rather than by a seminary, university, or academic press. Otherwise, it could be compared to Theology Today or other theological journals which are academic in tone, but whose intended audience also includes the educated laity.

215. Fides et Historia. DATE FOUNDED: 1968. FREQUENCY: sa; 3/yr in 1986. PRICE: $15.00/yr. PUBLISHER: Conference on Faith and History, Calvin College, Grand Rapids, Michigan 49506. EDITOR: Dr. James E. Johnson. INDEX: Not yet. ADVERTISEMENTS. CIRCULATION: 900. MANUSCRIPT SELECTION: Editor selects those to be sent to the readers who make recommendations. REPRINTS: Back

issues from Richard V. Pierard, Dept. of History, Indiana State University, Terre Haute, Indiana 47809. BOOK REVIEWS. INDEXED/ABSTRACTED: America, CERDIC, CPI, HA, OTA, RIC, RICSuppl, RIO, RTA. DATABASE: America, ATLA, HA, RI. TARGET AUDIENCE: AC, UndSt. SAMPLE COPIES.

This journal intends to concentrate on the relationship of Christian faith to insights into historical questions and developments. This purpose is best carried out in the book review section and the review essays where the criticism relates the historical concerns to current ones. The five or six articles tend to study the history of theology whose relationship to current concerns is implicit; the articles have no sectarian bias. Each issue has an average of ten signed 600-800 word book reviews; one notable feature of this journal is that the book reviews are documented.

216. Grace Theological Journal. DATE FOUNDED: 1980. FREQUENCY: sa. PRICE: $11.50/yr. PUBLISHER: Grace Theological Seminary, 200 Seminary Drive, Winona Lake, Indiana 46590. EDITOR: Dr. John C. Whitcomb. INDEX: Not yet. CIRCULATION: 2,500. MANUSCRIPT SELECTION: Editorial committee. REPRINTS: Back issues from the publisher. BOOK REVIEWS. SPECIAL ISSUES: Occasional festschriften. INDEXED/ABSTRACTED: CPI, NTA, OTA, RIO, RTA. DATABASE: ATLA, RI. TARGET AUDIENCE: AC, GP, SP. SAMPLE COPIES.

This conservative theological journal contains six to seven articles per issue which are signed and documented. The articles and the journal assume and espouse the inerrancy and inspiration of the Bible; some books and views are criticized on this basis. The articles deal with the Bible, theology, church history, archaeology, philosophy, and Christian literature. The authors are both ministers and academics; the articles definitely have an academic tone. They are directed toward other scholars and the religious public. In addition to the usual reviews, which are signed and number ten to fifteen covering one to two pages, there is also a section of shorter reviews. At the current time, the journal does not have an index.

217. Harvard Theological Review. DATE FOUNDED: 1908. FREQUENCY: q. PRICE: $12.00/yr. PUBLISHER: Scholars Press, P. O. Box 1608, Decatur, Georgia 30031. EDITOR: Helmut Koester. ADVERTISEMENTS: Only on the back cover. CIRCULATION: 1,800. MICROFORMS: On microfiche. INDEXED/ABSTRACTED: AHCI, CC, HI, NTA, OTA, RIO, RTA. DATABASE: AHSearch, ATLA, HI, RI. TARGET AUDIENCE: AC.

The four or five articles in each issue of this journal cover such fields as theology, ethics, the history and philosophy of religion, and other related subjects. The articles are arranged chronologically with the first article on an earlier period of Christianity and the last article on a later one. Following these signed articles is a section, "Notes and Observations," that contains short notes on subjects such as early Christian art or some detail of biblical exegesis. The journal's emphasis is historical rather than philosophical or theological. Its scope is comparable to journals devoted to the history of the church, but it is not denominationally centered.

218. The Hastings Center Report. DATE FOUNDED: 1971. FREQUENCY: bm. PRICE: $33.00/yr., individuals; $45.00/yr., libraries. PUBLISHER: The Hastings Center, 360 Broadway, Hastings-on-Hudson, New York 10706. EDITOR: Carol Levine. INDEX. CIRCULATION: 9,400. MANUSCRIPT SELECTION: Editorial board. MICROFORMS: UMI. REPRINTS: UMI; back issues from the publisher. BOOK REVIEWS. SPECIAL ISSUES. INDEXED/ABSTRACTED: CC, IM, ISI, PI, RIO, SSI. DATABASE: ATLA, PI, RI, SSI. TARGET AUDIENCE: AC, SP, UndSt. SAMPLE COPIES.

This journal is not really religious, but it deals with a topic close to religious sensitivities: ethical issues in medicine and in the social and behavioral sciences. The seven or eight articles are written primarily by American academics and are signed. Some of the articles are not written by medical professionals, but are composed by people completely outside the medical profession, e. g. Leslie A. Fiedler. In addition to the one or two signed three page book reviews there are also sections for letters to the editor, and a listing of current books and articles in the field of science and ethics. Some of the "Friends of the Center" are theologians and clerics. This journal will be of high interest to those who wish to be knowledgeable in the field of bioethics.

219. Henceforth. . .. DATE FOUNDED: 1972. FREQUENCY: 3/yr. PRICE: $4.00/yr. PUBLISHER: Berkshire Christian College, Lenox, Massachusetts 01240. EDITOR: Freeman Barton. ILLUSTRATIONS: Rarely. INDEX. CIRCULATION: 450. MANUSCRIPT SELECTION: Editor. REPRINTS: From the editor. BOOK REVIEWS. SPECIAL ISSUES: Irregularly. INDEXED/ABSTRACTED: MPI, RTA. TARGET AUDIENCE: GP, SP. SAMPLE COPIES.

This Adventist publication concentrates on the history, doctrine, and practice of Seventh-Day Adventists. It is supposedly aimed at the general public, but his would be a good journal for the Adventist minister to read; the articles, composed by Americans, are well written and do not get bogged down in jargon. While the point of view is evangelical and conservative, the tone of the journal is not strident. On the average, each issue has two, signed, one page book reviews. Occasionally it prints a reader's response to one of the articles.

220. The Heythrop Journal: A Quarterly Review of Philosophy and Theology. DATE FOUNDED: 1960. FREQUENCY: q. PRICE: 11.00 pounds/yr.; United States, $27.00/yr. PUBLISHER: Heythrop Journal, Business Manager, 114 Mount Street, London W1Y 6AH, England. EDITOR: Dr. J. Munitiz. ILLUSTRATIONS: Very rarely. INDEX. ADVERTISEMENTS. CIRCULATION: 1,000. MANUSCRIPT SELECTION: Based on approval from at least two members of the Heythrop College academic staff. REPRINTS: Back issues from the publisher. BOOK REVIEWS. SPECIAL ISSUES: Occasionally. INDEXED/ABSTRACTED: AHCI, CC, CLA, CPLI, IZBG, NTA, PI, RTA. DATABASE: AHSearch, PI. TARGET AUDIENCE: AC, SP, UndSt. SAMPLE COPIES: To libraries, by arrangement.

This academic journal is dedicated to exploring theology, philosophy, and related disciplines. All of the articles are signed; they tend to be devoted to Catholic doctrine, although not exclusively so. The very large book review section is followed by "short notices" on various books. Each one of the forty reviews is signed and takes up 500-800 words. An unusual feature of this journal is in the section on books received: they are arranged by publisher. This journal has no articles on biblical exegesis nor on comparative religion. It is attractively printed and should be of interest to those who attempt to relate reason to faith.

221. The Iliff Review. DATE FOUNDED: 1944. FREQUENCY: 3/yr. PRICE: $4.00/yr. PUBLISHER: Iliff School of Theology, 2201 S. University Blvd., Denver, Colorado 80210. EDITOR: Charles S. Milligan. INDEX: decennially. CIRCULATION: 600. MANUSCRIPT SELECTION: Editor, after advice based on blind readings. REPRINTS: Back issues from the business manager; from the author of the article. BOOK REVIEWS. SPECIAL ISSUES: Occasionally. INDEXED/ABSTRACTED: BI, OTA, RIO. DATABASE: ATLA, RI. TARGET AUDIENCE: AC, SP. SAMPLE COPIES.

As a publication supported by the Iliff School of Theology, this scholarly journal tends to draw both its authors and reviewers from the area around Colorado. In this regard it is very similar to the other journals published by seminaries and to Biblical Studies (Chicago). The journal emphasizes theology over biblical studies although there are some articles that relate to Scripture. All the articles are written by scholars for scholars and divinity students. Occasionally the same book will be reviewed twice in the journal's short section for book reviews; each issue contains approximately six, signed, one page book review essays.

222. The Indian Journal of Theology. DATE FOUNDED: 1952. FREQUENCY: q. PRICE: United Kingdom, 3.00 pounds/yr. if paid to the Rev. Dr. I. D. L. Clark at St. Catherine's College, 3.50 pounds/yr. if paid to the business manager of the journal; United States and Canada, $7.00/yr. if paid through an agent, $8.00/yr. if paid to directly to the business agent of the journal; India, Pakistan, and Bangladesh, Rs.15.00/yr. if paid by money order; Rs.20.00/yr. if paid by check; other countries, 3.00 pounds/yr. if paid through an agent, 3.50 pounds/yr. if paid directly to the business agent of the journal. PUBLISHER: Indian Journal of Theology, c/o Bishop's College, 224 Acharya Jagedish Bose Road, Calcutta-700 017, India. EDITOR: Dr. P. N. Hillyer. INDEX. CIRCULATION: 500. BOOK REVIEWS. INDEXED/ABSTRACTED: OTA, RTA, RIO. DATABASE: ATLA, RI. TARGET AUDIENCE: AC, GP.

This journal in most of its articles aims at discussing how Christianity is compatible with the culture of India. Other articles discuss topics, such as the baptism at Qumran. The authors are from around the world, but they are mostly drawn from those who are or have been in contact with the Indian culture; the authors also assume an ecumenical stance. An average book review section contains twenty eight signed, two page essays. The books reviewed deal not only with Indian Christianity, but also with important works by Americans and Europeans. It should be noted that several numbers may make up one issue; for instance, vol. 33, nos. 1-3 is one published issue covering January-September; it is no larger than any other issue, however.

223. International Journal for Philosophy of Religion. DATE FOUNDED: 1970. FREQUENCY: 3/yr. PRICE: Libraries, Dfl.150.00/$55.00/yr. plus Dfl.50.00/$20.00 for postage; individuals, Dfl.75.00/$28.00. PUBLISHER: Martinus Nijhoff Publishers, P. O. Box 163, 3300 AD Dordrecht, The Netherlands. EDITOR: Bowman L. Clarke. INDEX. ADVERTISEMENTS. BOOK REVIEWS. INDEXED/ABSTRACTED: AHCI, CC, HI, RIO, RTA. DATABASE: AHSearch, ATLA, HI, RI. TARGET AUDIENCE: AC.

The five to ten articles per issue written by scholars around the world contain discussions on the rational philosophical basis for religion and ethics. The journal can be technical, but if the reader is willing to take the time, the resulting understanding can be well worth the trouble. It should be noted that Western philosophies of religion are discussed here; there is little or no discussion of Eastern philosophies of religion. Not all issues have book reviews; in the issues that they do appear, there is an average of six, signed, two page essays; the books reviewed are also centered on the concerns of the journal. The journal is aimed at those discussing the rational grounds for any kind of theism.

224. Journal of Social Philosophy. DATE FOUNDED: 1970. FREQUENCY: 3/yr. PRICE: Individuals: domestic, $10.00/yr.; foreign $13.00/yr. Libraries: United States and Canada, $12.00; foreign, $13.00. PUBLISHER: North American Society for Social Philosophy, Villanova University, Dept. of Philosophy, Villanova, Pennsylvania, 19085. EDITOR: Joseph Betz. ADVERTISEMENTS: To be included. CIRCULATION: 325. MANUSCRIPT SELECTION: Recommendations from two blind readings to the editor who makes final decision. MICROFORMS: UMI. REPRINTS: Back issues also available from the editor. BOOK REVIEWS. SPECIAL ISSUES: Guest edited. INDEXED/ABSTRACTED: PI, PSA. DATABASE: PI. TARGET AUDIENCE: AC, GP, SP, UndSt. SAMPLE COPIES: Upon request.

This journal discusses current problems, both academic and non-academic, from the perspective of social philosophy. It attempts to use philosophy to illuminate some social issue. It does not discuss issues from a religious point of view, although occasionally there are articles that relate to religion. The society supports conferences that deal with such subjects as "American Philosophy and Religion." Guest editors are sometimes asked to put together a journal on a special topic. Many of the articles list the university where the author teaches or studies, but at times it is unclear what the authority of the writer is. Most of the authors are American and Canadian; no introduction of the authors is given, however. An average issue contains three, signed, 1,000 word book reviews.

225. Journal of the Evangelical Theological Society. DATE FOUNDED: 1958. TITLE CHANGES: Bulletin of the Evangelical Theological Society (1958-1969). FREQUENCY: q. PRICE: $15.00/yr. PUBLISHER: Bethany Fellowship, 6820 Auto Club Road, Minneapolis, Minnesota 55438. EDITOR: Ronald Youngblood. INDEX. CIRCULATION: 2,500. MANUSCRIPT SELECTION: Editor. MICROFORMS: UMI. REPRINTS: UMI; back issues also from the publisher. BOOK REVIEWS. INDEXED/ABSTRACTED: CPI, NEBPI, NTA, OTA, RBIC, RIO, RTA. DATABASE: ATLA, RI. TARGET AUDIENCE: AC, UndSt. SAMPLE COPIES: Upon request.

This journal, while published by a society that believes in the inerrancy of the autographs of Scripture, contains an average of six articles that contain good, solid scholarship that is not necessarily skewed by doctrinal considerations.

Most of the articles cover exegetical matters with one or two articles on theological issues. Each one of the twenty to twenty five signed book reviews takes up one to two pages. This publication is a good journal to have beside the Journal of Biblical Literature or Interpretation. The prose of this journal is somewhat livelier than that of the Journal of Biblical Literature.

226. Journal of Theology for Southern Africa. DATE FOUNDED: 1972. FREQUENCY: q. PRICE: Individuals: R6.50/yr, southern Africa; R10.00/yr., elsewhere; libraries: R12.00/yr., southern Africa; R18.00/yr. elsewhere. PUBLISHER: Mills Litho, P. O. Box 4503, Cape Town 8000, Union of South Africa. EDITOR: Prof. John de Gruchy. INDEX. ADVERTISEMENTS. CIRCULATION: 800. MANUSCRIPT SELECTION: Editor. REPRINTS: Back issues available from publisher. BOOK REVIEWS. INDEXED/ABSTRACTED: NTA, OTA, RIO. DATABASE: ATLA, RI. TARGET AUDIENCE: AC, SP. SAMPLE COPIES.

This journal is of interest to theologians, clergy, theological students, and informed laymen as it explores issues of ecumenism and social justice. Its editors claim that its focus on southern Africa is unique. All the articles and reviews are signed and are composed primarily by writers from the countries of southern Africa. The articles are documented with bibliographies listed at the end of each article. Each one of the eight signed book reviews is composed in 300 words.

227. Lexington Theological Quarterly. DATE FOUNDED: 1966. TITLE CHANGES: Superseded College of the Bible Quarterly (1910-1965); suspended between Jan. 1926 and Dec. 1937. FREQUENCY: q. PRICE: Free to alumni; sent to libraries on an exchange basis. PUBLISHER: Lexington Theological Seminary, 631 South Limestone, Lexington, Kentucky 40508. EDITOR: William O. Paulsell. CIRCULATION: 2,000. MANUSCRIPT SELECTION: Editorial committee. REPRINTS: Back issues available from the editor. BOOK REVIEWS: SPECIAL ISSUES: Occasionally. INDEXED/ABSTRACTED: NTA, OTA, RIO, RTA. DATABASE: ATLA, RI. TARGET AUDIENCE: AC, GP. SAMPLE COPIES: Only to individuals.

This journal, published by a seminary affiliated the Disciples of Christ, averages about 100 pages per issue, with the special issues being somewhat longer. The journal is aimed primarily at the clergy and interested laymen. Comparable to Interpretation and other journals like it, this journal has a more popular air about it. Contributors come from the secular academic world as well as the clerical. Footnotes are listed at the end of the article, giving the reader a short bibliography on the subject discussed. The articles are wide-ranging in their interests, including discussions of preaching, the social world of early Christianity, and a listing of papyri at Lexington Theological Seminary. Occasionally there is a signed book review.

228. The Modern Churchman. DATE FOUNDED: 1911; n.s. 1957. FREQUENCY: q. PRICE: 6.00 pounds/yr. PUBLISHER: The Modern Churchmen's Union, The School House, Leysters, Leominster, Hereford HR6 OHS, England. EDITOR: Professor A. O. Dyson. INDEX. ADVERTISEMENTS: Currently, no. CIRCULATION: 1,200. MANUSCRIPT SELECTION: Chief Editor and Section Editors who have expertise in various fields. MICROFORMS: UMI. REPRINTS: Hard copy also available from the publisher. BOOK REVIEWS. INDEXED/ABSTRACTED: NTA, RIO. DATABASE: ATLA, RI. TARGET AUDIENCE: GP, SP. SAMPLE COPIES.

This journal is comparable in coverage to Christianity Today, Christian Century, and the Quarterly Review in that all have articles on contemporary theology, pastoral theology, ethics, politics, and current affairs. The articles are clearly written and are directed toward pastors and educated laymen. All of the six articles are signed. An average issue contains fifteen signed 500 word book reviews; the books reviewed are not limited to those with a Christian perspective; a few are studies of politics or policies without any critique from the Christian point of view. The journal is relevant to both English and American circumstances.

229. Pacific Theological Review. DATE FOUNDED: 1967. TITLE CHANGES: Action/Reaction (1967-1975). FREQUENCY: 3/yr. PRICE: Free to selected individuals and institutions. PUBLISHER: San Francisco Theological Seminary, San Anselmo, California 94960. EDITOR: Robert B. Coote. ADVERTISEMENTS: Seminary advertisements. CIRCULATION: 8,000. MANUSCRIPT SELECTION: Editorial advisory board. REPRINTS: Very few back issues available from the publisher. BOOK REVIEWS: TARGET AUDIENCE: AC, GP, SP.

Each issue contains an average of twelve to fourteen signed one half page book reviews.

230. Perkins Journal. DATE FOUNDED: 1947. TITLE CHANGES: Perkins School of Theology Journal (1947-1972). FREQUENCY: q. PRICE: Free, upon request. PUBLISHER: Perkins School of Theology, Southern Methodist University, Dallas, Texas 75275. EDITOR: Leroy T. Howe. ILLUSTRATIONS. CIRCULATION: 4,500. MANUSCRIPT SELECTION: Editor, faculty of the Perkins School of Theology, and referees. REPRINTS:

Back issues available from Bridwell Library, Perkins School of Theology. BOOK REVIEWS. SPECIAL ISSUES: Occasionally. INDEXED/ABSTRACTED: RIO. DATABASE: ATLA, RI. TARGET AUDIENCE: AC, SP.

As a free journal, this has to be one of the best bargains in religious journals. The journal's three to five regular articles are signed and are directed toward the minister and seminary teacher. The articles are documented and each one has a bibliography. While the journal may not have a point view, Methodist theology and history are the main foci of this publication. Twelve to fifteen books are reviewed per issue; each one is signed. The book reviews are short (one half to one page) and cover areas from biblical studies to practical theology. Sometimes there is a books received section. Once in a while, there is an issue completely devoted to one subject and one approach, such as the issue on Genesis as told in the form of a folk tale.

231. The Princeton Seminary Bulletin. DATE FOUNDED: 1907; new ser., 1977. FREQUENCY: 3/yr. PRICE: Free to alumnae and alumni; or supplied upon exchange. PUBLISHER: Theological Seminary of the United Presbyterian Church at Princeton, Princeton, New Jersey 08542. EDITOR: Ronald C. White. ADVERTISEMENTS. MANUSCRIPT SELECTION: Editor; unsolicited material not acceptable. BOOK REVIEWS. INDEXED/ABSTRACTED: NTA, OTA, RIO. DATABASE: ATLA, RI. TARGET AUDIENCE: AC, SP.

This is surely one of the best journals published by a theological school; it is very comparable to Interpretation in both its tone and emphasis. The writing style is academic, but it is not nearly as dry as Criterion. Each issue has about seven or eight articles that are basically reflections on current theological issues; but the articles do cover biblical studies as well as the more "theological" and "social" concerns. Some of the articles are reprints of inaugural addresses, and there may be one article per issue on the history of Princeton Theological Seminary. Besides the sermons published, there is also in one of the issues a bibliography of publications by the faculty of Princeton. An average issue contains eight book reviews, each one signed and taking up one to two pages.

232. Process Studies. DATE FOUNDED: 1971. FREQUENCY: q. q. PRICE: Individuals, $12.00/yr., $22.00/2 yrs., $32.00/3 yrs.; institutions, $16.00/yr., $30.00/2 yrs., $44.00/3 yrs. PUBLISHER: Process Studies, Center for Process Studies, School of Theology at Claremont, 1325 N. College Ave., Claremont, California 91711. EDITOR: Lewis S. Ford. CIRCULATION: 1,000. MANUSCRIPT SELECTION: Editor. MICROFORMS: UMI. REPRINTS: UMI, ISI. BOOK REVIEWS.

INDEXED/ABSTRACTED: AHCI, CC, OTA, PI, RIO, RTA. DATABASE: AHSearch, ATLA, PI, RI. TARGET AUDIENCE: AC, SP.

This journal seeks to explore process thought as it appears in related philosophies and theologies and to apply Whiteheadian ideas to other fields such as aesthetics, mathematics, physics, biology, cosmology, history of religions, social science, and literary criticism. Each issue contains seventy two pages, with a variable number of articles; when there are more articles, there will be fewer book reviews and book notes. On the average there are ten signed reviews, each one taking up anywhere from two to seven pages. The articles are written by specialists in the field; while the reviews are also written by specialists, the language is more down to earth. Following the book reviews are dissertation abstracts, abstracts of current articles of interest to process philosophers, and announcements. Occasionally, an issue is devoted to one subject such as liberation theology.

233. Reformed Review. DATE FOUNDED: 1955. TITLE CHANGES: Western Seminary Bulletin (1946-1954). FREQUENCY: 3/yr. PRICE: $7.00/yr. PUBLISHER: Western Theological Seminary, Holland, Michigan 49423. EDITOR: Dr. M. Eugene Osterhaven. INDEX: Every ten years. ADVERTISEMENTS. CIRCULATION: 2,600. MANUSCRIPT SELECTION: Committee of professors at the seminary. MICROFORMS: UMI. REPRINTS: Some hard copy is available. BOOK REVIEWS. INDEXED/ABSTRACTED: IZBG, NTA, RIO, RTA. DATABASE: ATLA, RI. TARGET AUDIENCE: SP. SAMPLE COPIES.

This journal seeks to spur ministers' and others' thinking about theological and religious subjects. Such subjects are missions and ministering to ministers. The articles are short but very stimulating. The journal seeks to be catholic, evangelical, and Reformed; the journal is sponsored by a seminary supported by the Reformed Church of America. All the articles and reviews are signed; the latter number twenty five and are composed in 300 to 800 words. Compared to some other Protestant journals, such as Interpretation, this one is much more devoted to the practical ministry of the church; in terms of emphasis and target audience this journal is more comparable to the Quarterly Review.

234. Reformed World. DATE FOUNDED: 1971. TITLE CHANGES: The Catholic Presbyterian (1879-1883); The Quarterly Register (1886-1936); The Presbyterian Register (1927-1948); The Presbyterian World (1948-1955); The Reformed and Presbyterian World (1956-1970); Reformed World (1971-). FREQUENCY: q. PRICE: In U. S. dollars: $4.00/yr.; $7.50/2 yrs.; $11.00/3 yrs; in pounds sterling: 2.50

pounds/yr.; 4.75 pounds/2 yrs.; 7.00 pounds/3 yrs.; in Swiss francs: sfr8.00/yr.; sfr15.50/2 yrs.; sfr23.00/3 yrs. PUBLISHER: World Alliance of Reformed Churches, 150, Route de Ferney, 1211 Geneva 20, Switzerland. EDITOR: Dr. Edmond Perret. INDEX. ADVERTISEMENTS. CIRCULATION: 15,000. MANUSCRIPT SELECTION: Editorial board. MICROFORMS: UMI. BOOK REVIEWS. INDEXED/ABSTRACTED: RIO, RTA. DATABASE: ATLA, RI. TARGET AUDIENCE: SP. SAMPLE COPIES: Upon request.

This journal, which has gone through several title changes, is very ecumenical in its outlook. It has a very broad Reformed point of view and the articles seek to define what a "Reformed" point of view is. Some issues, instead of having the regular articles, are devoted to specific conferences such as the reports from the General Council held in Ottawa or the Cairo Consultation. In the issues that do not have special reports, there is news of various churches throughout the world; this is done on a larger scale in the Journal of Church and State. All the articles are signed and aimed at pastors and church members. Occasionally there are book reviews; such reviews are signed.

235. The Reformer. DATE FOUNDED: circa 1900. FREQUENCY: bm. PRICE: 2.00 pounds/yr. PUBLISHER: The Protestant Alliance, 112 Colin Gardens, London NW9 6ER, England. EDITOR: The Rev. A. G. Ashdown and Mr. A. N. R. Gutteridge. ILLUSTRATIONS. ADVERTISEMENTS. CIRCULATION: 4,000. MANUSCRIPT SELECTION: Editors. REPRINTS: Some. BOOK REVIEWS. SPECIAL ISSUES: Occasionally. TARGET AUDIENCE: GP. SAMPLE COPIES: Upon request.

The Reformer is dedicated to rebutting the views of the Roman Catholic Church, higher criticism, supports a conservative, fundamentalist theological position, and wants to encourage an interest in Protestant history. The journal definitely opposes anything that is Roman Catholic, and ecumenists and conservatives who wish to still be in dialogue with the Roman Catholic Church will be uncomfortable with this journal. The British authors praise the reformers. In every issue there is an editorial on the state of the reformed faith. Occasionally there will be signed 500 word book reviews. Some of the advertisements seem to be rather inflammatory.

236. The Review of Books and Religion. DATE FOUNDED: 1971. TITLE CHANGES: MERGER: FREQUENCY: m; except August and December. PRICE: $16.00/yr., United States; $20.00/yr., foreign. PUBLISHER: Review of Books, 1027 Gainesway Drive, Lexington, Kentucky 40502. EDITOR: Kendig Cully. ILLUSTRATIONS. ADVERTISEMENTS. CIRCULATION:

20,000. MICROFORMS: UMI. REPRINTS: UMI. BOOK REVIEWS. INDEXED/ABSTRACTED: RIO. DATABASE: ATLA, RI. TARGET AUDIENCE: GP, SP.

This journal, modeled after the New York Review of Books, is aimed at educating laypeople and the clergy with regard to the influence of religion in the modern world. It contains fifteen 600 word signed reviews of current books, critical essays on the larger issues which the books raise, and interviews with key figures in the religious, scholarly, and publishing communities. It tries to serve the same purpose as Religious Books Review, but the audience is more general; the reviews are written not only by clerics, but by scholars as well.

237. The Risk Book Series. DATE FOUNDED: 1977. TITLE CHANGES: Risk, a quarterly, 1965-1977. FREQUENCY: 3/yr. PRICE: $12.00/yr. PUBLISHER: World Council of Churches Publications, 150, Route de Ferney, 1211 Geneva 20, Switzerland. EDITOR: World Council of Churches Publications. ILLUSTRATIONS. CIRCULATION: 4,000. REPRINTS: Back issues from the publisher. TARGET AUDIENCE: GP. SAMPLE COPIES.

This series of books devoted to ecumenical interests publishes various titles per year. Each volume is dedicated to a subject such as Christian obedience, the media, technology, or the future. Books of poetry or fables may be included. While not strictly a journal, it is similar to those issues dedicated to one theme. The authors are from all over the world, although in the issues reviewed, the authors came from the Third World. The paperbound books are about sixty five pages per volume. The volumes address social issues in the world from a Christian perspective.

238. The Saint Luke's Journal of Theology. DATE FOUNDED: 1957. FREQUENCY: q. PRICE: Individuals: $10.00/yr.; $19.00/2 yrs.; $27.00/3 yrs.; libraries: $15.00/yr.; foreign subscriptions, add $2.50 for postage. PUBLISHER: School of Theology, The University of the South, Sewanee, Tennessee 37375. EDITOR: John M. Gessell. INDEX. ADVERTISEMENTS. CIRCULATION: 2,700. MANUSCRIPT SELECTION: Editor. MICROFORMS: UMI REPRINTS: UMI; back issues also available from the editor. BOOK REVIEWS. INDEXED/ABSTRACTED: OTA, RIO. DATABASE: ATLA, RI. TARGET AUDIENCE: SP. SAMPLE COPIES.

Averaging about three articles per issue, this journal is dedicated to relating theology to contemporary issues. While the journal does not advocate a particular point of view, the journal is Anglican in emphasis and is middle-of-the-road to liberal in the viewpoints expressed by the authors whose articles are signed by writers who are ministers and academics. Each issue seems to have one major book review article in addition to the fifteen reviews all of which are signed and take up 750 words. Judging by an editorial against another journal, this journal wishes to emphasize the rational aspects of the Anglican faith.

239. Saint Mark's Review. DATE FOUNDED: August 1955. FREQUENCY: q. PRICE: $10.00/yr., in Australia; $12.50/yr., overseas. PUBLISHER: St. Mark's Library, P. O. Box E 67, Canberra, A. C. T., 2600 Australia. EDITOR: The Rev. P. Mendham. INDEX: Apparently every 50 issues. ADVERTISEMENTS. CIRCULATION: 1,200. MANUSCRIPT SELECTION: Editorial committee. MICROFORMS: UMI. BOOK REVIEWS. TARGET AUDIENCE: AC, GP, HS, SP, UndSt. SAMPLE COPIES: To libraries only.

An average issue contains ten signed book reviews, each one composed in 1,200 words.

240. Scholars' Choice. DATE FOUNDED: 1960. FREQUENCY: sa. PRICE: $4.00/yr. PUBLISHER: Scholars' Choice, The Library, Union Theological Seminary, 3401 Brook Road, Richmond, Virginia 23227. EDITOR: Dr. John B. Trotti. CIRCULATION: 200. MANUSCRIPT SELECTION: Team of scholars. REPRINTS: Back issues from the editor. TARGET AUDIENCE: AC, SP. SAMPLE COPIES.

This is not a journal but an eight page semi-annual bibliography of books selected by a select group of scholars for American theological libraries. Besides the books selected, there is also a section on "books received." This could be helpful to book selectors in libraries, not to mention scholars and students attempting to build their own collections. Notable is the fact that it lists key publications not found in standard American book lists; it seeks to select current theological literature from abroad.

241. Scottish Journal of Theology. DATE FOUNDED: 1948. FREQUENCY: q. PRICE: Institutions: 27.50 pounds ($65.00)/yr., single copies, 7.50 pounds ($17.00); individuals: 12.00 pounds ($30.00)/yr., single copies, 3.00 ($7.50). PUBLISHER: Scottish Academic Press, Ltd., Edinburgh EH7 SJX, Scotland, United Kingdom. EDITOR: A. I. C. Heron, J. Houston. ILLUSTRATIONS: Sometimes. ADVERTISEMENTS. CIRCULATION: 1,200. MANUSCRIPT SELECTION: Editors. BOOK REVIEWS. INDEXED/ABSTRACTED: AHCI, CC, NTA, OTA, RIO, RTA. DATABASE: AHSearch, ATLA, RI. TARGET AUDIENCE: AC.

The Scottish Journal of Theology is a broadly based, ecumenical serial that seeks to establish modern theology on a sound scientific basis, commanding wide agreement. Its six articles cover areas of major theological and philosophical interest; it also has articles on biblical and applied theology for the preacher and teacher. Such a purpose means that there is a conversation between the practical and philosophical sides of Christianity. The articles are written by clerics as well as scholars, mostly from the United Kingdom. There is also a large section for books received which follows the book review section which contains an average of twenty five signed reviews, each one taking up one or two pages.

242. Sophia: A Journal for Discussion in Philosophical Theology. DATE FOUNDED: 1962. FREQUENCY: 3/yr. PRICE: A$6.00/yr.; United States, $7.50/yr.; United Kingdom, 3.00 pounds/yr. PUBLISHER: School of Humanities, Deakin University, Geelong, Victoria, Australia, 3217. EDITOR: M. J. Charlesworth. CIRCULATION: 500. MANUSCRIPT SELECTION: Editor. REPRINTS: Some back issues are available from the publisher. INDEXED/ABSTRACTED: PI. DATABASE: PI. TARGET AUDIENCE: AC, SP.

This journal is rightly subtitled A Journal for Discussion in Philosophical Theology; such questions as the philosophical basis for the belief in God's existence, religion and morality, Karma, and the self are discussed. The four or five articles are written by academics; the writers are drawn from around the world; many come from the United States. For a journal on the philosophical basis of religion, this serial is remarkably clearly written; people should not shun this journal because of a fear of technical jargon.

243. Taiwan Journal of Theology. DATE FOUNDED: 1979. FREQUENCY: a. PRICE: Taiwan$100.00/yr., domestic; $5.00/yr., overseas. PUBLISHER: Taiwan Theological College, 20, Lane 2, Sec. 2, Yang Teh Ta Road, Shihlin, Taipei, Taiwan, Republic of China. EDITOR: Graham S. Ogden. CIRCULATION: 500. MANUSCRIPT SELECTION: Editorial committee. REPRINTS: Back issues from the publisher. BOOK REVIEWS. INDEXED/ABSTRACTED: RIO. DATABASE: ATLA, RI. TARGET AUDIENCE: AC, SP, UndSt. SAMPLE COPIES.

This journal publishes about half of its articles in Chinese and half in English. The Chinese articles have English abstracts before the body of the discussion; English articles have Chinese abstracts. Whatever the primary language of the article may be, many of the footnotes cite English sources. All of the articles are signed and all authors are required to cite their own authority in the field. Occasionally there is a book review section that will contain two, signed, one page essays. Although the serial aims at promoting Asian theology, non-Asian readers will find many of the articles relevant. The publisher is Presbyterian. This journal compares very favorably with the East Asia Journal of Theology.

244. Themelios. DATE FOUNDED: Old ser., 1962; new ser., 1975. MERGER: Themelios (Old Series, vol. 1-vol. 11, no. 2) merged with TSF Bulletin (of the Theological Students Fellowship of the British Isles) in autumn 1975 issue which became vol. 1, no. 1 of the new series. FREQUENCY: 3/yr. PRICE: 1 yr.: 3.00 pounds; $6.00; Sfr10.00; 2 yrs.: 5.80 pounds; $11.00; Sfr18.00; 3 yrs.: 8.40 pounds; $16.00; Sfr25.00. PUBLISHER: Universities and Colleges Christian Fellowship, 38 De Montfort Street, Leicester LE1 7GP, England; and International Fellowship of Evangelical Students, 10 College Road, Harrow, Middlesex HA1 1BE, England. EDITOR: Dr. David Wenham. INDEX: Cumulative index planned for vol. 10, no. 3; separate index available from the Universities and Colleges Christian Fellowship. CIRCULATION: 5,500. MANUSCRIPT SELECTION: General Editor after consulting the Editorial Committee and Associate Editors. REPRINTS: Hard copy from publishers and from the Theological Students Fellowship, 233 Langdon, Madison, Wisconsin 53703; reprint series coming out in 1985 from the Universities and Colleges Christian Fellowship. BOOK REVIEWS. INDEXED/ABSTRACTED: NTA, OTA, RTA. TARGET AUDIENCE: AC, UndSt. SAMPLE COPIES: Free to libraries; at cost to individuals.

This journal contains about four articles on aspects of Christianity as seen from a conservative point of view. The authors' authority is noted and the articles are heavily documented. The articles take a jaundiced view of liberal theology, but the authors know all of the modern literature in the field and at times are positive toward it, e. g. the idea of a suffering God. Its appeals to conservative to a conservative viewpoint, however, are not shrill; the writers appeal to reason. The sixteen, signed, 600 word book reviews cover all aspects of biblical and religious literature. There is also a section that surveys other journal literature; the articles in the survey occasionally appear to have been selected according to the conservative stance of the journal.

245. Theologia Evangelica. DATE FOUNDED: 1968. FREQUENCY: 3/yr. PRICE: Republic of South Africa, R7.20/yr.; foreign countries, R10.20/yr. PUBLISHER: University of South Africa, P. O. Box 392, Pretoria, 0001, Republic of South Africa. EDITOR: Prof. I. J. du Plessis. ILLUSTRATIONS. CIRCULATION: 2,500. MANUSCRIPT SELECTION: Editorial board. REPRINTS: Limited number of hard copy from the publisher. BOOK REVIEWS. SPECIAL ISSUES:

Occasionally. INDEXED/ABSTRACTED: Miss., NTA, RIO. DATABASE: ATLA, RI. TARGET AUDIENCE: AC, SP, UndSt. SAMPLE COPIES: Only to libraries.

This journal, dedicated to producing research for graduate and postgraduate students, is written mainly by scholars from South Africa, although scholars from other countries also are published in this journal. While the journal is primarily written in English, there are some articles in Afrikaans. The articles are signed and documented, occasionally with a list of references after the notes; this is helpful for creating one's own bibliography even when the articles are not in English. The non-English articles have English summaries. The five signed book reviews are also written in either English or Afrikaans. The articles tend to discuss issues in an objective way without making an attempt to relate them specifically to debates going on in South Africa; but the implications for such debates are clear in the articles.

246. Theological Markings: A UTS Journal. DATE FOUNDED: 1971. FREQUENCY: irr.; currently annually. PRICE: Free, upon request. PUBLISHER: United Theological Seminary of the Twin Cities, 3000 Fifth St., N. W., New Brighton, Minnesota 55112. EDITOR: Dr. E. C. Jaberg. CIRCULATION: 2,900. MANUSCRIPT SELECTION: Editor and editorial board. REPRINTS: Back issues from the publisher. BOOK REVIEWS. INDEXED/ABSTRACTED: RIO. DATABASE: ATLA, RI. TARGET AUDIENCE: AC, SP. SAMPLE COPIES.

This currently annual journal of the United Theological Seminary contains four to six articles devoted to the issues confronting the theology of the United Church of Christ as they appear in teaching and practice. The articles are signed but the authority of the writers is not clear; it appears that most of the writers are from the United Theological Seminary. The articles are clearly printed and the ideas are clearly expressed. The energy evinced in the articles reflects very well the issues being reflected on in seminary. Occasionally some issues contain book reviews which, on the average, amount to four to eight signed 300 word essays. Other journals are published by theological seminaries, but this one reflects more and better the life within the seminary.

247. Theological Studies. DATE FOUNDED: 1940. FREQUENCY: q. PRICE: $14.00/yr., domestic; $17.00/yr., foreign. PUBLISHER: Theological Studies, Inc., Georgetown University, Washington, D. C. 20057. EDITOR: Walter J. Burghardt, S. J. INDEX. ADVERTISEMENTS. CIRCULATION: 6,500. MANUSCRIPT SELECTION: Editorial board. MICROFORMS: UMI. REPRINTS: Back issues also from the publisher. BOOK

REVIEWS. INDEXED/ABSTRACTED: AHCI, CPLI, IBBRev, IBPL, IRPL, IZBG. DATABASE: AHSearch. TARGET AUDIENCE: AC, SP. SAMPLE COPIES.

This journal, with an average of six or seven signed articles per issue, concentrates on various theological and historical issues; the historical articles are written with the purpose of illuminating a current problem. The issues investigated are soteriology, suffering, ecumenism, and the Orthodox Church. Every five years there is an article on the Orthodox Church. The reviews are numerous and cover all disciplines. Generally, there are twenty five long reviews accompanied by twenty five shorter ones; all are signed and are composed in 500 and 300 words, respectively. Although the journal does not espouse any point of view, most of the writers are American Roman Catholics and it is published by a Roman Catholic University.

248. _Theology_. DATE FOUNDED: 1920. FREQUENCY: bm. PRICE: 10.20 pounds/yr., United Kingdom; $20.00/yr., United States. PUBLISHER: SPCK, Holy Trinity Church, Marylebone Road, London NW1 4DU, England. EDITOR: The Right Reverend Peter Coleman. INDEX. ADVERTISEMENTS. CIRCULATION: 4,750. MANUSCRIPT SELECTION: Team of three editors. MICROFORMS. REPRINTS: Annual volumes from 1920-1940 from Kraus Reprints, FL-9491, Nendeln, Liechtenstein; back issues prior to 1983 available from publisher. BOOK REVIEWS. INDEXED/ABSTRACTED: UKCH. TARGET AUDIENCE: AC, SP, UndSt. SAMPLE COPIES: If available.

This British journal, containing about five articles per issue, an editorial, letters to the editor, book reviews, and a books received section, attempts to be comprehensive in its discussion of all sides of theological issues. The focus is Anglican and most of the authors are British. The editors try to use a unifying theme when publishing unsolicited papers. Each issue contains nineteen signed 700 word book reviews. This journal is comparable to many of its counterparts in the United States such as _Interpretation_, although _Theology_ is more "theological" and does not emphasize exposition of the Bible. It is more comparable to _Theology Today_. It gives the reader a wide perspective of what theologians in other countries are thinking.

249. _Theology Digest_. DATE FOUNDED: 1953. FREQUENCY: q. PRICE: Domestic: $9.00/yr., $17.00/2 yrs.; foreign: $10.50/yr; $20.00/2 yrs. PUBLISHER: St. Louis University, 3634 Lindell Boulevard, St. Louis, Missouri 63108-3395. EDITOR: Dr. Bernhard Asen. INDEX. ADVERTISEMENTS. CIRCULATION: 6,000-7,000. MANUSCRIPT SELECTION: Editors. MICROFORMS: UMI. REPRINTS. BOOK REVIEWS.

INDEXED/ABSTRACTED: CPLI, IZBG, OTA, RTA. TARGET AUDIENCE: AC, GP, SP. SAMPLE COPIES: Libraries, free; individuals may be asked to pay.

This journal abridges and translates into English about ten articles written in non-English journals; over 400 journals are surveyed. Each article is headed by the translator, the original title of the journal and where it was originally published. Each digested and translated article is approved by the author. Following the digested articles is a book survey containing 250 to 300 short descriptions of the contents of current books. The first three issues of a volume have digested articles; the fourth contains the annual Bellermine Lecture. The book review section is actually a book survey that contains six to seven book book notes covering forty one pages. This journal is directed not only toward scholars, but also toward educated laymen; in fact, laymen and Christian educators might find this journal helpful for discussion groups; scholars will find it helpful in its selection of articles on current debates; however, they will probably consult the article being translated rather than the digested ones here. Other journals translate non-English articles, but not as regularly as does Theology Digest.

250. Theology Today. DATE FOUNDED: 1944. FREQUENCY: q. PRICE: $14.00/yr., $25.00/2 yrs., United States; $19.00/yr., $35.00/2yrs., other countries. PUBLISHER: Theology Today, P. O. Box 29, Princeton, New Jersey 08542. EDITOR: Dr. Hugh Kerr. ILLUSTRATIONS. INDEX. ADVERTISEMENTS. CIRCULATION: 10,000. MANUSCRIPT SELECTION: Editor. MICROFORMS: UMI. REPRINTS: Upon permission; Microtext reprints from the American Theological Library Association. BOOK REVIEWS. INDEXED/ABSTRACTED: BRM, GSScRel, NTA, RGScRel, RIO, RTA, SISperLit. DATABASE: ATLA, RI. TARGET AUDIENCE: AC, SP. SAMPLE COPIES.

This journal contains about eight articles devoted to theological issues and written by scholars and ministers in an academic setting. Using non-technical language, the articles cover topics on history of theology as well as ones of current concern. Some of the articles have the character of personal statements, but not in the sense of testimonies of conversion experiences. The articles are not documented; they are signed and the authors' authority is noted. Articles of an exegetical nature are rare. An average issue contains twelve, signed, 500 to 750 word book reviews. There are no additional issues; special issues are created by devoting one issue to a special subject. Compared to Christianity Today and Christian Century, the journal is more scholarly. Theology Today appeals more to the professor of theology, the educated layman, and the minister. Occasionally, there is a poem.

251. Trinity Journal. DATE FOUNDED: 1980. TITLE CHANGES: Trinity Studies (1975-1980). FREQUENCY: sa. PRICE: $7.50/yr., domestic; $9.00/yr., overseas; $6.50/yr., students. PUBLISHER: Trinity Evangelical Divinity School, 2065 Half Day Road, Deerfield, Illinois 60015. EDITOR: D. A. Carson. CIRCULATION: 800. MANUSCRIPT SELECTION: Editor. REPRINTS: From the Managing Editor, Perry G. Downs; back issues from the publisher. BOOK REVIEWS. INDEXED/ABSTRACTED: BRI, CPI, GSScRel, IZBG, IZ, NTA, OTA, OT/ANE, RIO, RTA, Zdienst. DATABASE: ATLA, RI. TARGET AUDIENCE: AC.

This journal, concentrating on biblical, theological, philosophical, and ministerial issues, is written by scholars for scholars. Though the journal does not have a thematic approach, each issue does seem to have articles related to one another, such as the place of language in the study of Scripture. Each issue may have an article devoted to a subject as explained by a key theologian of the past. This journal reflects evangelical orthodoxy, but is not hard-nosed about it. The signed book reviews, while few--numbering about seven--are excellent and fair. It is a good journal, containing scholarly evangelical articles that are not narrow.

252. Tyndale Bulletin. DATE FOUNDED: 1956. TITLE CHANGES: Tyndale House Bulletin. FREQUENCY: a. PRICE: 5.95 pounds/yr. PUBLISHER: Inter-varsity Press, Norton Street, Nottingham NG7 3HR, England. EDITOR: M. J. Harris. INDEX. CIRCULATION: 800. MANUSCRIPT SELECTION: Editor. REPRINTS: Back issues from the publisher. INDEXED/ABSTRACTED: NTA, OTA, RIO, RTA. DATABASE: ATLA, RI. TARGET AUDIENCE: AC. SAMPLE COPIES: To libraries only.

This annual journal, dedicated to the study of the Bible and theology, is published directly from camera ready manuscripts. Recent issues average 170 pages, but the sample copy examined had 228 pages. The articles submitted for publication are expected to be compatible with the doctrinal views of the Tyndale Fellowship for Biblical and Theological Research; that viewpoint is conservative, but the conservatism is mild compared that exhibited to Bibliotheca Sacra. Some of the topics investigated are hope, and medical ethics; it also includes biblical studies which are related to contemporary life.

253. Union Seminary Quarterly Review. DATE FOUNDED: 1945. MERGER: The Union Review and Alumni Bulletin in 1945 to form the current title. FREQUENCY: q. PRICE: Institutions:

$12.00/yr., $22.00/2 yrs., $30.00/3 yrs., individuals: $10.00/yr., $18.00/2 yrs., $25.00/3 yrs. PUBLISHER: Union Theological Seminary, 3041 Broadway, New York, New York 10027. EDITOR: Margaret M. McGuinness. ILLUSTRATIONS: Occasionally. INDEX. ADVERTISEMENTS. CIRCULATION: 1,500. MANUSCRIPT SELECTION: Editorial staff. MICROFORMS: UMI. REPRINTS: Copies also available from the publisher. BOOK REVIEWS. SPECIAL ISSUES: One special supplement so far. INDEXED/ABSTRACTED: NTA, RIO, RTA. DATABASE: ATLA, RI. TARGET AUDIENCE: AC, GP, SP, UndSt. SAMPLE COPIES.

This journal, like Christianity and Crisis, Christianity Today, and Christian Century, concentrates primarily on the area of theology and culture; such an emphasis includes biblical studies, systematic theology, church history, and philosophy and religion. About one half of the issues are thematic, and occasionally two numbers are combined in one issue devoted to one subject. The articles are written by academics and researchers and documented, but laity as well as scholars can read the articles with profit. About five books are reviewed in each issue; each review is signed and is composed in three to five pages. While no viewpoint is explicitly stated, it tends to be liberal. In contrast to the journals mentioned above, this one tends to be more reflective and contains more historical background on the issues being discussed. The reviews are on books related to the theme of that particular issue.

254. Vox Evangelica. DATE FOUNDED: 1962. FREQUENCY: a. PRICE: 2.60 pounds/yr. PUBLISHER: Paternoster Press, 3 Mount Radford Crescent, Exeter EX2 4JW, England. EDITOR: Dr. Harold H. Rowdon. ADVERTISEMENTS. CIRCULATION: 1,000. MANUSCRIPT SELECTION: Editor. MICROFORMS: May be arranged. REPRINTS: Hard copy available from the publisher. BOOK REVIEWS. INDEXED/ABSTRACTED: ElencBibBib, NTA, OTA. TARGET AUDIENCE: AC, SP, UndSt. SAMPLE COPIES: Available at half price.

This evangelical journal, containing five articles per issue, is devoted to the study of particular issues from a biblical point of view. Those issues include biblical studies, history of Christianity, philosophy, study of religions, and missiology. All of the articles are signed and notes are printed at the end the end of each article. The articles are clearly and interestingly written and people of all Christian denominations will find something of value in them. Occasionally there are full articles that are book reviews.

255. The Way. DATE FOUNDED: 1961. FREQUENCY: q. PRICE: 11.95 pounds/yr.; $24.00/yr. PUBLISHER: Way Publications, Heythrop College, 11-13, Cavendish Square, London W1M 0AN,

England. EDITOR: The Rev. Philip Sheldrake, S. J.; the Rev. David Lonsdale, S. J. INDEX. ADVERTISEMENTS: Inserts only. CIRCULATION: 4,000. MANUSCRIPT SELECTION: Editor; articles solicited around chosen themes. REPRINTS: Back issues from Way Publications, 39, Fitzjohn's Ave., London NW3, England. BOOK REVIEWS. SPECIAL ISSUES. INDEXED/ABSTRACTED: CPLI, NTA, OTA. TARGET AUDIENCE: AC, GP, SP, UndSt. SAMPLE COPIES.

Each eighty page issue of this British Catholic journal contains about seven articles and is devoted to one topic from the point of view of general Christian spirituality or theology. The authors are drawn from the English-speaking world, and non-Catholic writers do contribute. All of the articles are signed, and there is a short biographical sketch of each author at the end of the journal. The book review section is really a bibliographical essay; after the the review article, the books are listed according to subject; approximately forty books are surveyed. The supplements, which come out three times a year, are also devoted to one subject.

256. The Westminster Theological Journal. DATE FOUNDED: 1938. FREQUENCY: sa. PRICE: $15.00/yr., individuals; $20.00/yr., libraries. PUBLISHER: Westminster Theological Seminary, Chestnut Hill, Philadelphia, Pennsylvania 19118. EDITOR: Moises Silva. ILLUSTRATIONS: Rarely. INDEX. ADVERTISEMENTS: Beginning in the near future. CIRCULATION: 1,400. MANUSCRIPT SELECTION: Editorial staff and other faculty members. REPRINTS: Limited back issues are available from the publisher. BOOK REVIEWS. INDEXED/ABSTRACTED: CPI, ElencBibBib, IZBG, NTA, OTA, RTA. TARGET AUDIENCE: AC, SP.

This journal's editors are committed to the exposition and promotion of Reformed theology and the patient, critical analysis of contemporary scholarship as it bears on theological study; the editors in their guidelines to contributors are very emphatic about the articles being scholarly. The articles are irenic and deal not only with the history of Reformed theology, but also with issues in biblical studies. All of the articles are signed and documented; the author's address is given at the end of the article. The sixteen, signed reviews are objective; the books reviewed, however, are different than those reviewed by the Journal of Biblical Literature or Interpretation.

257. Word and Spirit: A Monastic Review. DATE FOUNDED: 1979. FREQUENCY: a. PRICE: Price determined separately for each issue. PUBLISHER: St. Bede's Publications, P. O. Box 132, Still River, Massachusetts 01467. EDITOR: Sister May Joseph, OSB. CIRCULATION: 250.

MANUSCRIPT SELECTION: Editor. ILLUSTRATIONS. REPRINTS: Back issues from the publisher. INDEXED/ABSTRACTED: RTA. TARGET AUDIENCE: AC, SP, UndSt. SAMPLE COPIES.

This annual contains ten or twelve articles dedicated to scriptural, theological, and spiritual themes, or to the anniversary of a significant event in the history of Christianity. Two issues examined were dedicated to studies on Saint Basil the Great and on Saints Benedict and Scholastica respectively. The articles written by experts in the field are signed; some of them are reprinted from previous publications. The articles are clearly written and are documented. There are other journals devoted to the study of patristics, but the thematic approach used here concentrates the information on a subject in a way that informs the reader in a more concise way.

Practical Theology

258. America. DATE FOUNDED: 1909. TITLE CHANGES: Messenger (1866-1909). FREQUENCY: w; bw in the summer. PRICE: $23.00/yr.; $28.00/yr., Canada; $31.50/yr., foreign. PUBLISHER: America, 106 West 56th Street, New York, New York 10019. EDITOR: The Rev. George Hunt, S. J. INDEX. ADVERTISEMENTS. CIRCULATION: 33,000 per week. MANUSCRIPT SELECTION: Editor. MICROFORMS: UMI. REPRINTS: Some from the publisher. BOOK REVIEWS. SPECIAL ISSUES: Yes; but it does not appear that it is an additional issue, only a regular issue devoted to a special topic. INDEXED/ABSTRACTED: AbrRG, CPLI, RG. DATABASE: RG. TARGET AUDIENCE: GP, HS, SP, UndSt. SAMPLE COPIES.

This Jesuit journal of opinion, besides having about five articles per issue, has several special features. The journal opens with an introduction to the articles that are published; this is followed by an editorial page which contains several comments on the world situation and the place of theology in it; the "In Sight" section is a kind of short overview of some events that may have not been widely known, such as evidence of anti-Catholicism in publishing; the "Op Ed" page is an examination of an issue by someone other than one of the editors. An average issue has eight, signed 600 word book reviews. There are also film reviews, an occasional poem, and letters to the editor, not to mention a small classified section. The journal is addressed to Roman Catholics; its point of view is not necessarily traditional, however. This publication, in format and appeal is very similar to the Christian Century and Christianity Today.

259. The Bride of Christ: The Journal of Lutheran Liturgical Renewal. DATE FOUNDED: 1977. FREQUENCY: q. PRICE: $8.00/yr.; $5.00/yr. for students; add $2.00 for Canadian subscriptions; add $4.00 to other foreign subscriptions. PUBLISHER: Lutheran Liturgical Renewal, Inc., P. O. Box 2931, Lehigh Valley, Pennsylvania 18001-2931. EDITOR: Aubrey N. Bougher, chairman of the Publication Board. ILLUSTRATIONS: Line drawings. INDEX: Cumulated; last one covered vols. 1-9. ADVERTISEMENTS. CIRCULATION: 1,000. MANUSCRIPT SELECTION: Publication Board. BOOK REVIEWS. TARGET AUDIENCE: GP, SP.

This quarterly is committed to the free and open discussion of all matters related to the liturgical movement. To that end, about twelve articles and features are published in each issue. Each article is signed; most of the authors are Lutheran. The articles appear to be geared toward the particular time of the liturgical calendar in which that issue is published; for instance, in Advent, many articles were on that event with a special emphasis on Mary. There is also a section for letters from the readers. Each issue contains one signed book review covering two pages. Occasionally there is a news item and the publication of a Lutheran document pertaining to liturgy. All Lutheran points of view are presented, but the impression given is that the journal supports the ecumenical movement and high Lutheranism.

260. Call to Growth Ministry. DATE FOUNDED: 1975. FREQUENCY: q. PRICE: $12.00/yr., $20.00/2 yrs.,; foreign subscribers, add $3.00. PUBLISHER: National Conference of Religious Vocational Directors, 1307 S. Wabash Ave., No. 350, Chicago, Illinois 60605. EDITOR: Jeanne Schweickert, SSSF. ILLUSTRATIONS. ADVERTISEMENTS: In-house. CIRCULATION: 1,200. MANUSCRIPT SELECTION: Editor. REPRINTS: Permission required from the publisher. TARGET AUDIENCE: GP, SP.

This quarterly is devoted to exploring the meaning of Christian vocation in the Roman Catholic Church; many of the articles discuss the vocations of the priesthood or the sisterhood although other vocations within the church are mentioned. Here you will not find any articles on writing a sermon or teaching in the church; instead the articles discuss the social impact of the vocational ministry, the inner qualities that make good candidates for the priesthood, etc. This is not a journal for those already running a church and wanting help with everyday problems. Its emphasis is on being socially concerned.

261. Catechist. DATE FOUNDED: 1967. FREQUENCY: m. (8/yr., not published in May or June. PRICE: $15.95/yr.,

$29.90/2 yrs.; subscribers outside the U. S. should add $8.00. PUBLISHER: Catechist (Peter Li), 2451 East River Road, Dayton, Ohio 45439. EDITOR: Patricia Fischer. ILLUSTRATIONS. ADVERTISEMENTS. CIRCULATION: 40,000. MANUSCRIPT SELECTION: Editor. MICROFORMS: UMI. REPRINTS: UMI. INDEXED/ABSTRACTED: CPLI. TARGET AUDIENCE: GP, SP.

This periodical is aimed at religious educators in the Roman Catholic Church who teach pre-teens. Each issue is dedicated to a special subject although not all of the articles will be related to it. The articles deal with such items as stress, educational software, and suggestions on how to choose religious books. In addition to the articles, there are regular features that provide games and subjects to reflect on during the month; such reflections concentrate on events in the liturgical calendar. Of special value to religious educators is the availability of advertised educational materials for free. This journal is very attractively printed, using a lot of color.

262. Christian Education Journal. DATE FOUNDED: 1980. TITLE CHANGES: Journal of Christian Education until 1983. FREQUENCY: sa. PRICE: United States: $7.00/yr.; $13.00/2 yrs.; $18.00/3 yrs.; foreign: $8.00/1 yr.; $14.00/ 2 yrs.; $19.00/3 yrs. PUBLISHER: Scripture Press Ministries, P. O. Box 513, Glen Ellyn, Illinois 60138. EDITOR: James Kovalik. ILLUSTRATIONS. CIRCULATION: 2,000. MANUSCRIPT SELECTION: Staff. REPRINTS: Back issues from the publisher at $4.00 in the United States and $5.00 overseas. BOOK REVIEWS. INDEXED/ABSTRACTED: RTA. TARGET AUDIENCE: AC, SP, UndSt.

This journal aims to provide communication between segments of the Christian community in order to facilitate the thoughtful exchange of significant ideas and information regarding issues and problems of Christian education. The eight to ten articles are very practical; this is especially seen by the three questions of application at the end of each article; such questions are required of the authors. The journal gives awards for superior articles which are subsequently published in the Christian Education Journal. Of interest also is the section dedicated to review of the current research in Christian education. Four signed, one page book reviews grace this publication. This journal is focused much more on the practical application of ideas than Religious Education or the Journal of Christian Education which seeks to investigate how Christians can teach in a Christian way in secular institutions.

263. The Christian Ministry. DATE FOUNDED: 1969. TITLE CHANGES: The Pulpit (1929-1969). FREQUENCY: bm. PRICE: $8.50/yr.; Canada, $10.00/yr.; others, $10.00/yr.

PUBLISHER: Christian Century Foundation, 407 S. Dearborn St., Chicago, Illinois 60605. EDITOR: Alfred P. Klauser. ILLUSTRATIONS. MANUSCRIPT SELECTION: Editors. MICROFORMS: UMI. REPRINTS. BOOK REVIEWS. INDEXED/ABSTRACTED: RIO. DATABASE: ATLA, RI. TARGET AUDIENCE: SP. SAMPLE COPIES.

This bimonthly is aimed mainly at Protestant ministers although the laity would also find some of the articles interesting. The articles are written by American ministers and seminary teachers. The twelve or so short articles in two pages cover many aspects of the Christian minister's concerns, such as stewardship or the writing of sermons. One delightful facet of this journal is the various cartoons scattered throughout the journal that will hit a responsive chord among ministers. The book review section contains ten, signed, 150 to 500 word essays. Each review covers several books of related interests. There is also a section for letters to the editor. It is comparable of the Quarterly Review, though the latter is more scholarly.

264. Christianity and Crisis: A Christian Journal of Opinion. DATE FOUNDED: 1941. FREQUENCY: bw; 22/yr. PRICE: $21.00/yr., individuals; $24.00/yr., libraries; $10.00/yr., students; foreign subscribers, add $5.00. PUBLISHER: Christianity and Crisis, Inc., 537 W. 121 St., New York, New York 10027. EDITOR: Wayne Cowan. ILLUSTRATIONS. INDEX. ADVERTISEMENTS. CIRCULATION: 14,000. MANUSCRIPT SELECTION: Editors. MICROFORMS: NCR Corporation; Bell and Howell. REPRINTS: UMI. BOOK REVIEWS. INDEXED/ABSTRACTED: HI, PAIS, RIO. DATABASE: ATLA, HI, RI. TARGET AUDIENCE: AC, GP, SP. SAMPLE COPIES.

Christianity and Crisis is a semimonthly that addresses the issues of politics, economics, war and peace from a religious--especially a liberal Christian--point of view. Each issue opens up with letters from the readers, followed by editorials on various topics. Then come the main articles on timely subjects, averaging about five per issue; finally there are a couple of book reviews, signed, and covering one to two pages. The authors are clerics and academics. The counterpart of this journal is Christianity Today; its cousin is the Christian Century. The writing is lively and engaging and the reader is challenged.

265. Christianity Today. DATE FOUNDED: 1956. FREQUENCY: sm. (m. in January, May, June, July, August, December); 18/yr. PRICE: $2.00 per issue. PUBLISHER: Christianity Today, Inc., 465 Gunderson Drive, Carol Stream, Illinois 60188. EDITOR: Harold L. Myra. ILLUSTRATIONS. INDEX. ADVERTISEMENTS. CIRCULATION: 185,000. MANUSCRIPT SELECTION: No unsolicited manuscripts are accepted. MICROFORMS: Bell and Howell, UMI. REPRINTS: UMI. BOOK

REVIEWS. INDEXED/ABSTRACTED: BI, CPI, GSScRel, MI, NTA, PMR, RG, RIO, RTA. DATABASE: ATLA, RG, RI. TARGET AUDIENCE: GP.

Christianity Today, with its six articles, is the conservative counterbalance to the Christian Century. It too discusses contemporary issues, but from a conservative point of view. The journal begins with an editorial, about one column long by "Eutychus," followed by letters to the editor. Following these are the editorials and columns; then come the articles on such topics as abortion, religion and the schools, self-worship, to name a few. News about the church is reported in short paragraphs and there is a section for classified advertisements. Also included in an average issue is a book review section containing two, signed, one page essays. Although this journal is evangelical in its conviction, the tone does not exclude other Christians from reading nor from responding in the letters column; the journal reflects an evangelical faith seeking to maintain its roots while being open to the world and other Christian viewpoints.

266. Church. DATE FOUNDED: 1985. FREQUENCY: q. PRICE: Individuals, $24.00/yr.; institutions, $30.00/yr. PUBLISHER: National Pastoral Life Center, 299 Elizabeth Street, New York, New York 10012. EDITOR: Margaret O'Brien Steinfels. ILLUSTRATIONS. ADVERTISEMENTS: Back page only. MANUSCRIPT SELECTION: Editor. BOOK REVIEWS. TARGET AUDIENCE: GP, SP.

This quarterly is aimed at the general parish minister, seeks to educate lay people, and is directed toward those that help administer the church. Each issue contains about four articles dealing with various aspects of ministering to a church: preaching, the ministry of the laity, the use of computers in the church, etc. The articles are signed with the authority of the author noted in a vita at the bottom of the first page of the article. Well known figures such as Martin Marty and John Donahue write for this publication. In addition to the articles, there are sections called "Parish Bulletin" and "In Print"; the latter reviews the literature in a particular field. There are eleven, initialed book reviews, each covering one half page. The journal was started to fill a gap in religious periodical literature, but it is very similar to Quarterly Review. The articles are responsibly written and the authors do not patronize their readers.

267. The Clergy Review. DATE FOUNDED: 1931. FREQUENCY: m. PRICE: 14.50 pounds/yr.; 15.50 pounds/yr., overseas surface mail; 20.50 pounds/yr., airmail. PUBLISHER: The Tablet Publishing Company, 48 Great Peter Street, London

SW1P 2HB, England. EDITOR: The Rev. Michael Richards. ILLUSTRATIONS. INDEX. ADVERTISEMENTS. CIRCULATION: 2,500. MANUSCRIPT SELECTION: Editor. MICROFORMS. UMI. BOOK REVIEWS. SPECIAL ISSUES. INDEXED/ABSTRACTED: CPLI, NTA, OTA. TARGET AUDIENCE: SP. SAMPLE COPIES.

This Roman Catholic monthly is committed to communicating the gospel to the world and in its discussions of practical and academic matters is aimed primarily at the Roman Catholic clergy . The six articles are signed and are documented. Every issue contains about six, signed, 350 book reviews. Each book review usually covers several books that are related by subject. The reviews and books received are arranged by subject. The writing is clear and the layman should be attracted to this journal.

268. Contact. DATE FOUNDED: October, 1960. FREQUENCY: 3/yr. PRICE: 3.00 pounds/yr. PUBLISHER: Contact Pastoral Limited, c/o Department of Christian Ethics and Practical Theology, New College, The Mound, Edinburgh, Scotland. EDITOR: The Rev. David Lyall. INDEX: Only in issues 1-50. CIRCULATION: 2,000. MANUSCRIPT SELECTION: Editor in consultation with the Editorial Board. REPRINTS: Back issues available from C. M. Campbell, Brantwood, Manso Wynd, STOW, Galashiels TD1 2QS, Scotland. BOOK REVIEWS. TARGET AUDIENCE: AC, SP, UndSt. SAMPLE COPIES.

This Scottish quarterly is concerned with communication between people involved in interpersonal and social issues. Doctors, clergymen, social workers, nurses, teachers, *et al*. will find this journal interesting. The signed articles, however, do address the issues from a Christian perspective; the debate is lively. Each of the issues deals with one topic, whether it be health or the parish ministry; the articles are either documented or the references are clearly made in the articles themselves. Ten to twelve signed book reviews are included in each issue; each one occupies anywhere from one third to one page. The journal is sponsored by several professional organizations: the Clinical Theology Association, Institute of Religion and Medicine, Association of Pastoral Care and Counselling, Westminster Pastoral Foundation, and the Irish Pastoral Association.

269. Evangelical Missions Quarterly. DATE FOUNDED: 1964. FREQUENCY: q. PRICE: $10.95/yr.; airmail, $17.00/yr., $28.00/3 yrs.; airmail, $49.00/3 yrs. PUBLISHER: Evangelical Missions Information Service, Inc., 25W560 Geneva Road, Box 794, Wheaton, Illinois 60189. EDITOR: James Reapsome. INDEX. ADVERTISEMENTS. CIRCULATION: 7,000. MANUSCRIPT SELECTION: Editor. REPRINTS: Back issues are available. BOOK REVIEWS. SPECIAL ISSUES:

quarterly. INDEXED/ABSTRACTED: CPI, RIO. DATABASE: ATLA, RI. TARGET AUDIENCE: AC, SP. SAMPLE COPIES.

Like Missiology this journal, containing about eight articles, is devoted to Christian missions. Even though it is bit a more conservative, this journal is informative and packed with information. The articles, written by academics and missionaries, are not pollyanna pieces, but are serious analyses of missions by conservatives. Its six, signed book reviews are fairly short; opposite each review is a picture of the cover of the book being reviewed. A special section is called "AEFM News and Views" which in the issue examined was devoted to the rationale and technique of teaching courses on missions in seminaries. For different perspectives on missions, the International Review of Mission might be consulted.

270. Homiletic and Pastoral Review. DATE FOUNDED: 1900. FREQUENCY: 11/yr. PRICE: $18.00/yr.; $33.00/2yrs.; foreign, $22.00/yr., $37.00/yr. PUBLISHER: Catholic Polls, Inc., 86 Riverside Drive, New York, New York 10024. EDITOR: The Rev. Kenneth Baker, S. J. ILLUSTRATIONS. INDEX. ADVERTISEMENTS. CIRCULATION: 15,000. MANUSCRIPT SELECTION: Editor; sometimes consulting others. MICROFORMS: UMI. REPRINTS: UMI. BOOK REVIEWS. INDEXED/ABSTRACTED: CPLI. TARGET AUDIENCE: SP. SAMPLE COPIES.

This eighty page journal is dedicated to supporting Catholic orthodoxy and the teaching authority of the Catholic Church, especially the faith as prescribed by the pope and the councils of the church. The journal is a professional review for Catholic clergy and keeps them informed on the issues facing the Catholic Church. A special and attractive feature of the journal is a section of sermons for each Sunday and feast day of the year. Protestants might be put off by the lack of ecumenical spirit toward them. For instance, Luther is viewed as a revolutionary who simply wanted to reject Rome's authority. The writers are American professors and Catholics involved in pastoral work; occasionally a layman will write. There are five or six signed 700 word book reviews.

271. The Hymn. DATE FOUNDED: 1949. FREQUENCY: q. PRICE: $25.00/yr.; $28.00/yr., Canadian and foreign subscriptions. PUBLISHER: The Hymn Society of America, Inc., National Headquarters, Texas Christian University, Fort Worth, Texas 76129. EDITOR: Dr. Paul Westermeyer. ILLUSTRATIONS. INDEX. ADVERTISEMENTS. CIRCULATION: 3,500. MANUSCRIPT SELECTION: Editor. REPRINTS: Back issues from the publisher. BOOK REVIEWS. SPECIAL ISSUES. INDEXED/ABSTRACTED: CPI, MusInd, RIO. DATABASE: ATLA, RI.

TARGET AUDIENCE: AC, SP. SAMPLE COPIES.

This quarterly of research and opinion is aimed at church musicians, clergy, scholars, and poets, among others; it is the only hymn related publication in the United States. The writers are British and American. The articles are scholarly and practical. The journal opens with messages from the editor and the president of the society. The journal has one new hymn per issue, a listing of articles on hymnology in other journals, and a yearly listing of the dissertations written in the field of hymnology. All the articles are readable and are written in a lively and engaging style. The six, signed, 500 word book reviews not only review books, but new hymns as well. There is a section called "Hymnic News" that reports news around the world about Christian congregational singing.

272. International Bulletin of Missionary Research. DATE FOUNDED: 1977. TITLE CHANGES: Occasional Bulletin from the Missionary Research Library (1950-1977); Occasional Bulletin of Missionary Research (1977-1981); International Bulletin of Missionary Research (1981-). FREQUENCY: q. PRICE: $14.00/yr.; $26.00/2 yrs.; $37.00/3 yrs. PUBLISHER: Overseas Ministries Study Center, 6315 Ocean Avenue, Ventnor, New Jersey 08406. EDITOR: Gerald H. Anderson. ILLUSTRATIONS. INDEX. ADVERTISEMENTS. CIRCULATION: 9,000. MANUSCRIPT SELECTION: Editors. MICROFORMS: UMI. REPRINTS: Back issues available from publisher. BOOK REVIEWS. SPECIAL ISSUES. INDEXED/ABSTRACTED: BM, CPI, GSScRel, Miss., RIO, RTA. DATABASE: ATLA, RI. TARGET AUDIENCE: AC, SP. SAMPLE COPIES: Only to libraries.

This journal has the largest circulation of scholarly journals in its field of missiology. Each issue has about seven articles devoted to one particular area of missions; areas to be focused on are announced in each issue. All the articles are written by missiologists and are signed. In contrast to the journal published by the World Council of Churches, the International Review of Mission, all views are expressed and recognized in this journal; advertisers recognize this too. Twelve, signed, 350 word book reviews are written for each issue. The format is very much like Christianity Today or Christian Century. One special feature, also indexed, is a list of dissertations being written in the field of missiology.

273. International Review of Mission. DATE FOUNDED: 1912. TITLE CHANGES: International Review of Missions (1912-1969. FREQUENCY: q. PRICE: SFr32.50/yr.; $15.00/yr.; 8.95 pounds/yr.; there is a free exchange with some other publications. PUBLISHER: World Council of Churches, 150 rte. de Ferney, 1211 Geneva 20, Switzerland; L'Imprimerie

Corbaz S. A., 22 Ave. des Planches, 1820 Montreux, Switzerland (printer). EDITOR: The Rev. Eugene Stockwell. ILLUSTRATIONS: Occasionally. INDEX. ADVERTISEMENTS. CIRCULATION: 4,000. MANUSCRIPT SELECTION: Associate Editor. MICROFORMS: UMI. BOOK REVIEWS. INDEXED/ABSTRACTED: BHI, CPI, RIO, RTA. DATABASE: ATLA, RI. TARGET AUDIENCE: AC, SP. SAMPLE COPIES.

This quarterly has approximately ten articles per issue written by academics, theologians, and clerics on one subject per issue. "Cuttings," a special feature, cites statements about missions as printed in other publications. Following that is a section of signed book reviews, numbering sixteen, that are composed in 2,500 to 3,000 words. A selected bibliography on missions, arranged by subject, is located at the end of each issue. The journal currently seems to emphasize mission through social action.

274. Journal of Christian Education. DATE FOUNDED: 1957. FREQUENCY: 3/yr. PRICE: Individuals, $18.00/yr.; libraries, $24.00/yr. PUBLISHER: Australian Teachers' Christian Fellowship, 120 Chalmers Street, Surry Hills 2010, Australia. EDITOR: Prof. Brian V. Hill. ILLUSTRATIONS. INDEX. CIRCULATION: 1,000. MANUSCRIPT SELECTION: Articles solicited on themes by the editorial panel; or, more frequently, unsolicited material is assessed by a special review panel. REPRINTS: Back issues are available from publisher as well as specially selected articles. BOOK REVIEWS. SPECIAL ISSUES. INDEXED/ABSTRACTED: APAIS, AEI, CERDIC, CPI, EI, IZBG, RIO, RTA, ThDig. DATABASE: ATLA, RI. TARGET AUDIENCE: AC, GP. SAMPLE COPIES.

The purpose of this journal is to consider the implications of the Christian faith for the entire field of education and to examine its contribution to the solution of educational problems. It seeks to examine philosophically Christian views on education, to publish reports of experiments in curriculum and method based on Christian principles, and to discuss in the light of such principles some of the more important developments in modern education around the world. The journal has a basically Australian or British audience in view. The four or so articles will be of interest to everyone interested in education. For instance, an article on what it means for a Christian to teach English would have interest for the biblical exegete as well as those concerned with the accuracy of religious education. The publication attempts to be critical of the education in general while participating in it. Its focus is much wider than Religious Education. Two or three, signed, 500 to 600 word book reviews are found in each issue. Librarians may find this journal difficult to check in since no volume numbers or issue numbers are evident; each issue is distinguished by a "papers" number.

275. Journal of Pastoral Care. DATE FOUNDED: 1947. FREQUENCY: q. PRICE: $15.00/yr.; $28.00/2 yrs.; $50.00/4 yrs. PUBLISHER: Kutztown Publishing Co., P. O. Box 346, Rt. 222 and Sharadin Road, Kutztown, Pennsylvania 19530. EDITOR: Dr. Orlo Strunk. INDEX. ADVERTISEMENTS. CIRCULATION: 10,000. MANUSCRIPT SELECTION: Editor and editorial committee. MICROFORMS: UMI. REPRINTS: UMI; back issues from ACPE, 1549 Clairmont Road, Suite 103, Decatur, Georgia 30247. BOOK REVIEWS. INDEXED/ABSTRACTED: HLI, PA, RIO, RTA, TRI. DATABASE: ATLA, RI. TARGET AUDIENCE: AC, SP. SAMPLE COPIES: None to libraries; in a limited way only to individuals.

The eight or so signed articles of this journal are dedicated to the field of pastoral care. The authors are mostly American and are specialists in the field. Each issue is devoted to a theme on which about three articles are focused. The remaining articles, while not "theme" articles, are related to the topic of that particular issue. For instance, the issue focusing on biomedical ethics also had several articles on pastoral care in the hospital. Composed for each issue are four to six, signed, 750 word book reviews. The books reviewed are also on pastoral care. The language of the articles is very sexually inclusive.

276. Journal of Psychology and Theology. DATE FOUNDED: 1973. FREQUENCY: q. PRICE: United States: $20.00/yr.; $36.00/2 yrs.; $5.00 per back issue; $1.00 per each reprint of an article. All other countries: $24.00/yr.; $44.00/2 yrs.; $6.00 per back issue. PUBLISHER: Rosemead School of Psychology, Biola University, 13800 Biola Ave., La Mirada, California 90639. EDITOR: William F. Hunter. INDEX. CIRCULATION: 1,350. MANUSCRIPT SELECTION: A blind review procedure; recommendations made to the editor who makes final decision. MICROFORMS: UMI. REPRINTS: UMI; from the authors and publisher. BOOK REVIEWS. SPECIAL ISSUES. INDEXED/ABSTRACTED: AHCI, CPI, MPI, PA, PRG, RIO, RTA, SSCI. DATABASE: AHSearch, ATLA, RI, SocScisearch. TARGET AUDIENCE: AC, SP, UndSt.

The purpose of this journal is to communicate recent scholarly thinking on the interrelationships of psychological and theological concepts and to consider the application of these concepts to a variety of special settings. Although the journal is an "evangelical" forum, there are no strident tones emphasizing conservative Christianity. The articles are generally written by North American scholars and clinicians. Notable features of this journal are the listing of recent and important articles on

Christianity and psychology. The signed book reviews and the books received section are arranged by broad subject category. There are generally five "Featured Reviews," each one taking up one page and seven "Brief Reviews," composed in one half page each.

277. Joy and Light. DATE FOUNDED: 1843. FREQUENCY: 3/yr. PRICE: 1.00 pound/yr. for individuals; libraries, free. PUBLISHER: Mr. J. G. Roberts, 5, Victory Avenue, Morden, Surrey, England SM4 6DL. EDITOR: Mr. J. G. Roberts. ILLUSTRATIONS. CIRCULATION: 22,000. MANUSCRIPT SELECTION: Editor. REPRINTS: Back issues from the editor. BOOK REVIEWS. SPECIAL ISSUES. TARGET AUDIENCE: GP. SAMPLE COPIES.

As the organ of the Lord's Day Observation Society, Joy and Light advocates the importance and preservation of the Lord's Day primarily by opposing commercial activity on Sunday. The twenty five or so articles are unsigned and appear to be written in-house, covering news, meetings, and activities of the branches of the Society as well as the actions taken throughout the United Kingdom with regard to the correct observance of Sunday as the Lord's Day. The presence of reviews is haphazard; usually each issue has two, unsigned, thirty to fifty word reviews.

278. Leadership. DATE FOUNDED: 1980. FREQUENCY: q. PRICE: $18.00/yr.; $32.00/2 yrs.; $42.00/3 yrs; foreign subscriptions, add $4.00. PUBLISHER: Harold Myra, Christianity Today, Inc., 465 Gunderson Drive, Carol Stream, Illinois 60188. EDITOR: Terry C. Muck. ILLUSTRATIONS. INDEX: To be published. ADVERTISEMENTS. CIRCULATION: 85,000. MANUSCRIPT SELECTION: Editorial staff. REPRINTS: Back issues available from the Circulation Department at the publisher. BOOK REVIEWS. TARGET AUDIENCE: SP. SAMPLE COPIES: Only to libraries.

As a journal published by Christianity Today, it is not simply a conservative journal, but a journal that through twelve signed articles addresses common problems that ministers face in their calling. All ministers, no matter what theological stripes they may bear, will profit from this journal. Each issue has articles devoted to a theme, such as "Roles and Expectations," in addition to other articles on other subjects. There are special features which are shorter articles. Moreover, there is a bibliography on leadership in the church. Not only are the four, one half page reviews signed, but pictures of the author and the book being reviewed are supplied. This journal deals with some of the same concerns as the Quarterly Review, but it is aimed more at practical matters and is not as scholarly in tone. Humor is also supplied through cartoons that reflect the everyday life of a minister.

279. Missiology: An International Review. DATE FOUNDED: 1973. TITLE CHANGES: Practical Anthropology, 1953-1972. FREQUENCY: q. PRICE: Individual: $15.00/yr.; $29.00/2 yrs.; $40.00/3 yrs.; institutional: $20.00/yr.; $38.00/2 yrs.; $52.00/3 yrs.; students: $10.00/yr.; $19.00/2 yrs.; memberships for individuals, add $5.00. PUBLISHER: American Society of Missiology, 616 Walnut Ave., Scottdale, Pennsylvania. EDITOR: Ralph Covell. INDEX. ADVERTISEMENTS. CIRCULATION: 3,000. MANUSCRIPT SELECTION: Editor and two co-editors. MICROFORMS: UMI. REPRINTS: UMI. BOOK REVIEWS. INDEXED/ABSTRACTED: BM, CPI, GCP, Miss., RIO, RTA, SPD. DATABASE: ATLA, RI. TARGET AUDIENCE: AC, SP. SAMPLE COPIES.

This journal, written by professionals and academics in the field of missiology, is the academic journal in the field. Although it is academic, it should be attractive to all Christians interested in the place of Christianity in foreign lands. Each issue of the journal is dedicated to one topic. The ten to fifteen, 700 word book reviews are not only signed, but the credentials of each reviewer are outlined on an introductory page to the reviews. While the six or seven long articles are not documented, at the end of each one a list of sources used is supplied. This journal, while committed to missions, contains many articles that are historical.

280. Missionalia. DATE FOUNDED: 1973. FREQUENCY: 3/yr. PRICE: R7.00/yr., Republic of South Africa; R9.00/yr., elsewhere. PUBLISHER: South African Missiological Society, 31, Fourteenth Street, Menlo Park, 0081 Pretoria, Republic of South Africa. EDITOR: Prof. Dr. David J. Bosch. INDEX. CIRCULATION: 1,000. MANUSCRIPT SELECTION: Editorial Committee. REPRINTS: Back issues from the publisher. BOOK REVIEWS. INDEXED/ABSTRACTED: RIO. DATABASE: ATLA, RI. TARGET AUDIENCE: AC, SP, UndSt. SAMPLE COPIES.

This journal, written primarily for those in the mission field, has about four or five articles per issue plus a book review section. The authors are not afraid of tackling the issue of apartheid. Each issue has fifteen, signed, one and a half page book reviews. The most important contribution of each issue of this journal, however, is the section Missiological Abstracts which summarizes important articles devoted to missions published in books and journals. The list of publications so abstracted are indexed at the end of the year by author and subject. This information may be obtained in more general abstracting services, but to have it concentrated in one place is an advantage.

281. Pastoral Psychology. DATE FOUNDED: 1950. FREQUENCY: q. PRICE: Libraries, $76.00/yr.; individuals, $29.00/yr. PUBLISHER: Human Sciences Press, 72 Fifth Avenue, New York, New York 10011. EDITOR: Lewis R. Rambo. ADVERTISEMENTS. MANUSCRIPT SELECTION: Editor. MICROFORMS: UMI. REPRINTS: UMI, ISI. BOOK REVIEWS. INDEXED/ABSTRACTED: CC, GSScRel, RIC, RIO, RTA, SSCI. DATABASE: ATLA, RI, SocScisearch. TARGET AUDIENCE: AC, SP.

This journal provides a forum for the work of the ministry as it is illumined by other professions, by research into the behavioral sciences, and by theological awareness. The approximately five articles are written by professionals and academics in the field; most of the authors are American, but a few are from abroad. The articles do not discuss psychology in a vacuum or as an interest in and of itself; it is always related to the theology of Christianity. Each issue has two book reviews, each signed and lasting two to three pages. The journal is sponsored by Princeton Theological Seminary. It is aimed at practicing ministers who use psychology in their pastoral care.

282. PMC: The Practice of Ministry in Canada. DATE FOUNDED: 1984. FREQUENCY: q. PRICE: Cdn$15.00/yr.; in the United States, US$14.00/yr.; overseas, add Cdn$3.00. PUBLISHER: PMC Board of Directors, 60 St. Clair Ave., E., Suite 504, Toronto, Ontario M4T 1N5, Canada. EDITOR: James Taylor. ILLUSTRATIONS. ADVERTISEMENTS. CIRCULATION: 1,650 and rising. MANUSCRIPT SELECTION: Editor, in consultation with the editorial advisory committee. REPRINTS: Back issues available from the publisher. BOOK REVIEWS. TARGET AUDIENCE: GP, SP.

This quarterly is published by an interdenominational board representing the Anglican, Baptist, Lutheran, Presbyterian, Roman Catholic, and United Churches of Canada, under the umbrella of the Coordinating Committee on Theological Education in Canada and the Ecumenical Foundation; its five to six articles are dedicated to providing a resource for the Christian ministry. It is very ecumenical. It is not only for the clergy, but also for the laity. The articles are signed, but the authority of the authors is not always noted. It has a "News and Reports" section as well as a section listing opportunities for continuing education, a valuable service for clerics and laity alike. Each issue has three to eight, signed book reviews, composed in 200 to 400 words. This journal is very similar to the Christian Century and Christianity Today that deal with current problems in society and the church. Unlike the Quarterly Review, its tone is not as scholarly.

283. Printed Lectures. DATE FOUNDED: 1937. FREQUENCY: q. PRICE: 7.50 pounds/yr. for membership; 75p per printed lecture plus postage; 1.00 pound minimum order. PUBLISHER: Mr. P. Macaulife, 56 Milner Road, London SW19 3AA, England. EDITOR: Mr. Keith Ellis. CIRCULATION: 550. MANUSCRIPT SELECTION: Editorial Committee. REPRINTS: Back issues from the publisher. TARGET AUDIENCE: GP.

This serial comes out four times a year. Each staple bound booklet contains one of the Guild Lectures devoted to Jungian psychology and religion, the arts, myth, and other related topics. Some of the lectures are not current but are reprints of lectures given several years earlier. The Guild considers its series as on of the very few to deal with Jungian psychology and religion.

284. Quarterly Review: A Scholarly Journal for Reflection on Ministry. DATE FOUNDED: 1980. FREQUENCY: q.; but 5 issues in first year, 1980. PRICE: $15.00/yr. PUBLISHER: United Methodist Publishing House, 201 8th Avenue, South, Nashville, Tennessee 37202; and United Methodist Board of Higher Education and Ministry, Box 871, Nashville, Tennessee 37202. EDITOR: Charles E. Cole. INDEX. ADVERTISEMENTS. CIRCULATION: 5,800. MANUSCRIPT SELECTION: Evaluation by outside readers. MICROFORMS: UMI. REPRINTS: Back issues in print only available for past year. BOOK REVIEWS. SPECIAL ISSUES. INDEXED/ABSTRACTED: RIO. DATABASE: ATLA, RI. TARGET AUDIENCE: SP. SAMPLE COPIES.

This journal, while supported by the Methodist Church, will also be of interest to the clergy and laity of other Christian traditions. Dedicated to providing continuing educational resources for the professional ministry, it accepts articles in all fields of theological endeavor. Each issue includes homiletical resources based on the lectionary. In addition to the one or two signed reviews, there are review articles from time to time. Generally speaking the book reviews are 3,000 words long. Some articles have invited responses from other clergy; the writers are American. There is no section for books received. Other journals of this type have a thematic approach to each issue; the Quarterly Review has articles in each issue on various topics which are indexed in the last issue of each volume.

285. Radius. DATE FOUNDED: 1946. TITLE CHANGES: Christian Drama (1946-1965). FREQUENCY: q. PRICE: 10.00 pounds/yr., individuals; 3.00 pounds/yr., surface mail, 4.50 pounds/yr. air mail for libraries. PUBLISHER: Radius, St. Paul's Church, Covent Garden, Bedford Street, London WC2E 9ED, England. EDITOR: Margaret Hunt. CIRCULATION: 800-1,000. MANUSCRIPT SELECTION: Editor. REPRINTS: Back

issues from the the publisher. BOOK REVIEWS. TARGET AUDIENCE: GP, SP.

In this quarterly productions and new scripts or books are reviewed, controversial issues and new trends in religious drama discussed, and news is given of coming activities in religious drama. There are about six to eight short articles per issue about half of which are reviews of religious plays. It has a section called "Communication" which contains abstracts of publications in other journals. It includes news of drama workshops or of plays to be performed. Most to the authors are British. The number of book reviews varies; they are signed and consist of one page each. The journal has no table of contents. There apparently is no comparable publication to it, at least in the United Kingdom.

286. Religious Education. DATE FOUNDED: 1906. FREQUENCY: q. PRICE: United States and Canada, $25.00/yr.; others, $28.00/yr. PUBLISHER: Randolph Crump Miller, Executive Secretary, Religious Education Association of the United States and Canada, 409 Prospect Street, New Haven, Connecticut 06510. EDITOR: The Rev. Dr. John Westerhoff. INDEX. ADVERTISEMENTS. CIRCULATION: 4,000. MANUSCRIPT SELECTION: Editor's invitation; editor's choice; peer review. MICROFORMS: UMI. REPRINTS: Single copies available in print at $9.00 apiece. BOOK REVIEWS. SPECIAL ISSUES. INDEXED/ABSTRACTED: BRI, CC, EI, IJP, PA, RIO, RTA. DATABASE: ATLA, RI. TARGET AUDIENCE: AC, SP. SAMPLE COPIES: At $9.00 apiece.

Claiming to be the only interfaith journal for professionals in the field of religious education, this journal is devoted to one particular subject per issue. It is ecumenical as a glance at the members of the editorial board will show. Frequently there are written responses to published articles. The eight or ten articles are directed toward the education of Christian responsibility in the world as a list of the topics discussed and to be discussed shows. Scattered throughout the journal are short book reviews under the rubric, "Briefly Noted." The regular book reviews number ten, are signed and are composed in 750 words. The journal caters to the professionals in the field; it also offers an annual review of research in the field and abstracts of dissertations in religious education. The articles are well written and far from dry.

287. Search. DATE FOUNDED: 1924. TITLE CHANGES: YSL Magazine; Young Sower. FREQUENCY: m. PUBLISHER: Young Searchers League, 3 Eccleston Street, London SW1W 9LZ, England. ILLUSTRATIONS. CIRCULATION: 5,000. TARGET AUDIENCE: GP.

This little magazine is not for general circulation, but since it is aimed at teaching children about the meaning and history of Christianity, perhaps mention should be made of it for the benefit of those who teach children in church or similar institutions. The articles are written in-house, and they speak directly to the child rather than down to him. Apparently issues are only available from branches of the Youth Searchers League.

288. Signum: Documentation Service for Religious. DATE FOUNDED: 1974. FREQUENCY: bw; about 18 issues/yr. PRICE: 19.30 pounds/yr. PUBLISHER: Catholic Media Office, 39 Eccleston Square, London SW1V 1PD, England. EDITOR: Sr. Mary Helena Desmond, SHJC. INDEX. ADVERTISEMENTS. CIRCULATION: 1,500. MANUSCRIPT SELECTION: Editor. REPRINTS: Back issues available from Publications Officer, Ladyewell Press, Ashstead Lane, Godalming, Surrey GU7 1ST, England. BOOK REVIEWS. TARGET AUDIENCE: SP. SAMPLE COPIES.

This periodical, as a supplement to Briefing, publishes reports of various conferences held in England that are of interest to religious communities of men and women. The reports cover conferences on such social issues as poverty and ecology and such theological subjects as the relationship between Christianity and the other religions of the world. Most of the reports are written by religious women and are unsigned. There are also notices about future conferences and opportunities for continuing education. Occasionally there may be a book review that is not always signed. It is more like a newsletter.

289. Sisters Today. DATE FOUNDED: 1929. TITLE CHANGES: Sponsa Regis (1929-1964). FREQUENCY: 10/yr; June/July and August/September are separate issues. PRICE: \$10.00/yr.; \$11.50/yr., foreign. PUBLISHER: The Liturgical Press, St. John's Abbey, Collegeville, Minnesota 56321. ILLUSTRATIONS. INDEX. ADVERTISEMENTS. CIRCULATION: 10,000. MANUSCRIPT SELECTION: Some are requested; most are selected by editor. REPRINTS: Back issues from The Liturgical Press as well as occasional reprints of articles. BOOK REVIEWS. SPECIAL ISSUE. INDEXED/ABSTRACTED: CPG, CPLI. TARGET AUDIENCE: GP, SP. SAMPLE COPIES.

Each issue of this journal comprises about seventy pages and is full of opinions, articles, and information with regard to women and the church today. The articles cover the area of spirituality in all its forms, e. g. ministering to the sick, prayer, faith, etc. In addition to the articles it has poetry, illustrations, a book review section, an editorial, a section for letters to the editor and a section of announcements which includes want ads for employment. The journal is aimed at religious women, women seeking their own self-affirmation, and men seeking their own identity from the point of view of liberation. The writers are generally drawn from the United States and are both male and female. The journal is not strident in emphasizing its point of view; in fact, it is quite gentle. Each issue has five to six, signed book reviews, taking up one and a half to two columns per page. Compared to Pneuma, this journal is less esoteric and probably more understandable to the lay reader.

290. Studia Canonica: Revue canadienne de droit canonique/A Canadian Canon Law Review. DATE FOUNDED: 1967. FREQUENCY: sa. PRICE: $20.00/yr.; $10.00/single issue. PUBLISHER: Faculty of Canon Law, Saint Paul University, 223 Main Street, Ottawa, Ont., Canada K1S 1C4. EDITOR: Francis G. Morrissey, O. M. I. ILLUSTRATIONS: Tables, sometimes. INDEX. ADVERTISEMENTS: One, sometimes. CIRCULATION: 1,300. BOOK REVIEWS. INDEXED/ABSTRACTED: CLA, CPLI. TARGET AUDIENCE: SP.

This journal is devoted to exploring the implications of canon law for the Roman Catholic Church and its members. The articles, however, are not merely legal explanations; occasionally there is an article on the history of the canon law, e. g. a chapter from a thesis on the procedures for the resolution of conflicts in the early church. While there are no special issues, sometimes an issue is dedicated to one particular subject, such as the publication of a dissertation. The articles, about thirteen, are clearly written and readable for all who wish to know how the practitioners of Roman Catholic canon law formulate decisions. The articles are in French and English, the latter predominating. They are signed, and biographical notes on the authors appear at the end of each issue. An average issue contains seven, signed book reviews covering one to two pages.

291. Studia Liturgica. DATE FOUNDED: 1962. FREQUENCY: q. PRICE: Netherlands, Dfl. 40.00/yr.; United States, $17.50/yr.; United Kingdom, 8.50 pounds/yr.; Germany, DM 40.00/yr. PUBLISHER: Liturgical Ecumenical Center Trust, P. O. B. 25088, 3001 HB Rotterdam, The Netherlands. EDITOR: Wiebe Vos (Netherlands) and Geoffrey Wainwright are the chief editors. CIRCULATION: 2,000. MANUSCRIPT SELECTION: Editors. MICROFORMS: Back issues are available. BOOK REVIEWS. INDEXED/ABSTRACTED: RIO, RTA, NTA. DATABASE: ATLA, RI. TARGET AUDIENCE: SP.

This quarterly is a by-product of the Faith and Order Movement of the World Council of Churches although currently it is separate from it. It seeks to foster liturgical research and renewal in ecumenism. The articles, written by scholars from around the world, are directed toward their peers and are heavily documented. Besides the nine or ten articles that appear in each issue, there is a section called "Notes and Comments"; they average about two per issue. Occasionally there is a signed book review, written in one page.

292. The Tablet. DATE FOUNDED: 1840. FREQUENCY: w. PRICE: 26.90 pounds/yr., United Kingdom; 28.90 pounds/yr., overseas surface mail; United States and Canada, airmail, 32.90 pounds/yr.; airmail worldwide, 38.90 pounds/yr. PUBLISHER: Tablet Publishing Company, 48 Great Peter Street, Westminster, London SW1P 2HB, England. CIRCULATION: 9,300. MICROFORMS: UMI. REPRINTS: UMI. INDEXED/ABSTRACTED: CPLI. TARGET AUDIENCE: GP.

293. Theological Education. DATE FOUNDED: 1964. FREQUENCY: sa. PRICE: $5.00/yr. PUBLISHER: Association of Theological Schools, P. O. Box 130, Vandalia, Ohio 45377. EDITOR: David S. Schuller. CIRCULATION: 3,500. MANUSCRIPT SELECTION: Editorial staff. REPRINTS: Back issues available from the publisher. SPECIAL ISSUES. INDEXED/ABSTRACTED: CC, RIO. DATABASE: ATLA, RI. TARGET AUDIENCE: AC, SP.

This journal contains about four articles per issue devoted to one particular theme, e. g. the definition of issues in education. The articles are written by academics and are documented. The articles are objective, and while the authors are committed to the idea of a theological education, the approach is somewhat theoretical and based on the social sciences; what it gains in concerned objectivity it loses in concerned passion. This journal is requisite reading for all who wish to know the shape and emphases in theological education in the United States. There are occasional supplemental issues, such as the one on the future of theological libraries written by Stephen L. Peterson.

294. Worship. DATE FOUNDED: 1926. TITLE CHANGES: Orate Fratres until volume 26, 1951-1952. FREQUENCY: bm. PRICE: $15.00/yr., domestic; $16.50/yr., foreign. PUBLISHER: Monks of St. John's Abbey, Collegeville, Minnesota 56321. EDITOR: Aelred Tegels, O. S. B. INDEX. ADVERTISEMENTS. CIRCULATION: 6,700. MANUSCRIPT SELECTION: Editors with the two associate editors and editorial consultants. MICROFORMS: UMI. REPRINTS: UMI; back issues also available from Liturgical Press, Collegeville, Minnesota 56321. BOOK REVIEWS. SPECIAL ISSUES: July issue devoted to the proceedings of the North American Academy of Liturgy.

INDEXED/ABSTRACTED: CPLI, OTA, RIO, RTA. DATABASE: ATLA, RI. TARGET AUDIENCE: AC, GP, SP. SAMPLE COPIES.

Through the publication of about four articles per issue, this journal concentrates on the practice and rationale of the liturgy as it is performed in the Roman Catholic Church The articles, written by people from around the world, and the approximately ten, 750 word book reviews are signed. Other features of the journal include "Amen Corner," a kind of editorial page; "Chronicle," which comments on current liturgical practices in the Roman Catholic Church; "Forum," which contains shorter articles on liturgy; and finally there are announcements of workshops, new publications, positions open, etc. The journal, which considers itself the premier journal of the liturgical movement in the United States, sometimes discusses non-Roman liturgies, but only as they are relevant the Roman one. The articles are not documented, but neither are they filled with jargon.

295. Young Life Guard. PUBLISHER: Mr. J. G. Roberts, 5, Victory Avenue, Morden, Surrey, England SM4 6DL. EDITOR: Mr. J. G. Roberts. TARGET AUDIENCE: GP.

This children's four to six page leaflet as the companion to Joy and Light is devoted to leading children to understand the importance of Sunday and to preserve it as a day of rest and worship. The leaflet has a section on the animals of the Bible, facts about the Bible, a section on the importance of Sunday, little stories aimed at evangelizing children, puzzles and things to think about. This leaflet is a typical example of presenting the Christian message to children in a very simple way.

Christianity and Society

296. AFER: African Ecclesial Review. DATE FOUNDED: 1959. TITLE CHANGES: African Ecclesiastical Review (1959-1964). FREQUENCY: bm. PRICE: Kenya: KShs.110.00/yr.; Tanzania: TShs.150.00/yr.; Uganda: $10.00; other African countries: $12.00/yr.; outside Africa: $16.00/yr. PUBLISHER: AMECEA Pastoral Institute, Gaba Publications, P. O. Box 908, Eldoret, Kenya. EDITOR: Felician N. Rwihikiza. INDEX. CIRCULATION: 2,500. REPRINTS: Back issues available. REPRINTS. BOOK REVIEWS. INDEXED/ABSTRACTED: CLA, CPI, CPLI, NTA, RIO. DATABASE: ATLA, RI. TARGET AUDIENCE: GP, SP.

The journal's purpose is to make the Christian message relevant to present-day Africa; to that end it offers a platform for the exchange of views from those involved in the mission in Africa. The journal begins with a description of the contents of that particular issue, followed by a "News Commentary." The approximately seven articles are focused on Africa and written by clerics and lay people and are centered on social and theological issues that not only affect Africa, but the Third World at large. Such issues as abortion, liberation theology, and the confrontation and compromise of Christianity with native African religions are discussed. An average issue contains three to five signed book reviews, each one composed in one page. In addition, there is a section called "Platform" which offers readers' responses to articles previously published. The journal is Roman Catholic; its tone is irenic but not boring.

297. Ching Feng: Quarterly Notes on Christianity and Chinese Religion and Culture. DATE FOUNDED: 1957. FREQUENCY: q. PRICE: Hong Kong, Taiwan, Mainland China, HK$36.00/yr., HK$70.00/2 yrs., HK$100.00/3 yrs; overseas, $14.00/yr., $26.00/2 yrs., $38.00/3 yrs. PUBLISHER: Tao Fong Shan Ecumenical Centre, P. O. Box 33, Shatin N. T., Hong Kong. EDITOR: Peter K. H. Lee. ILLUSTRATIONS. CIRCULATION: 1,200. MICROFORMS: Newsbank. BOOK REVIEWS. INDEXED/ABSTRACTED: RIO. DATABASE: ATLA, RI. TARGET AUDIENCE: GP, SP.

This journal, as its subtitle suggests, is dedicated to relating Christianity and Chinese culture in a meaningful way; it seems to be closely tied with the Tao Fong Shan Ecumenical Center. The journal begins with an editorial outlining what the articles in that particular number are trying to say, usually under a broad thematic heading. This is followed by the "ecumenical centre chronicle" which relates some news of the center. Following this are the three or four signed articles. The ten reviews are signed or initialed and each one is composed in one or two pages. The book reviews are not only concerned about Christianity and Chinese culture, but books on Christian-Islam discussions, Gandhi, and Martin Luther King, Jr. are also assessed. For those who wish to see how Christians in other cultures maintain a common faith with their brothers and sisters in the rest of the world, this journal is a good place to start. One would wish for better editorial control; sometimes misspellings, incomplete sentences, and incorrect capitalization lead to confusion.

298. Christian Scholar's Review. DATE FOUNDED: 1970. TITLE CHANGES: Supersedes Gordon Review (1955-1970). FREQUENCY: q. PRICE: Individuals, $12.00/yr., $21.50/2 yrs, $30.00/3 yrs.; libraries, $15.00/yr., $27.50/2 yrs., $39.00/3 yrs. PUBLISHER: Christian Scholar's Review, RFD No. 2, Box 622, Union, Massachusetts 04862. EDITOR: Clifton J. Orlebeke. INDEX. ADVERTISEMENTS. CIRCULATION: 3,500. MICROFORMS: UMI; also available on microfiche. REPRINTS: Back issues also available. BOOK REVIEWS. INDEXED/ABSTRACTED: ALA, BELL, CPI, GSScRel, JES, NTA, PMLA, RIO, RTA. DATABASE: ATLA, RI. TARGET AUDIENCE: AC, SP.

This journal is dedicated to fostering both understanding between Christian scholars and between them and others. It seeks the integration of faith and learning on both the intra- and inter-disciplinary levels; it is also a forum for the discussion of issues in Christian higher education. The articles are written by academics and cover such topics as Ricoeur's ideas, biblical hermeneutics, and Augustine's ideas about civil government. The articles, about four in number, are written for scholars and very well educated laymen; they are documented. The journal does appeal to all Christian academics whether they be scholars in religious or secular fields. The book review section is rather extensive, containing thirty five essays which are signed and composed in one or two pages each. It is difficult to compare this journal to any other one publication; readers of the Journal of Biblical Literature, Interpretation, and the Journal of Church and State would find something of interest in this journal.

299. Churchman. DATE FOUNDED: 1879. TITLE CHANGES: The Churchman, changed in 1977. FREQUENCY: q. PRICE: 9.50 pounds/yr. or $15.00/yr. PUBLISHER: Church Society, Whitefield House, 186 Kennington Park Road, London SE11 4BT, England. EDITOR: The Rev. Dr. Gerald Bray. INDEX. ADVERTISEMENTS: Occasionally. MANUSCRIPT SELECTION: Editorial board. MICROFORMS: UMI. REPRINTS: From the Church Society. BOOK REVIEWS. INDEXED/ABSTRACTED: OTA, RIO. DATABASE: ATLA, RI. TARGET AUDIENCE: AC, GP, SP. SAMPLE COPIES.

This evangelical journal concentrates on historical and current interpretations of Protestant doctrines such as inerrancy and predestination. Its book review section is large and each book reviewed is listed at the end of the book review section. Only occasionally is the tone strident and overly polemical. Its appeal is to clerics and educated lay people; it would also be attractive to those who wish to learn more about the evangelical position. Forty signed book reviews are written for this journal, composed in 350 to 400 words each. It is very similar to Vox Evangelica except that the latter does not have a book review section. Churchman is also easier to read because of its use of boldface type to introduce sections of each article, which number anywhere from three to five.

300. The Japan Christian Quarterly. DATE FOUNDED: 1926. FREQUENCY: q. PRICE: 4,000 yen/yr.; $20.00/yr. outside Japan. PUBLISHER: The Japan Christian Quarterly, Kyo Bun Kwan, 4-5-1 Ginza, Chuo-ku, Tokyo 104, Japan. EDITOR: George L. Olson. INDEX. ADVERTISEMENTS. CIRCULATION: 5,000. BOOK REVIEWS. INDEXED/ABSTRACTED: RIO. DATABASE: ATLA, RI. TARGET AUDIENCE: GP.

This is a remarkable journal and is essential not only for understanding how Christianity may fit or be adapted to the Japanese culture, but it also covertly challenges assumptions made by Westerners about their own Christianity. Besides the approximately eight signed articles, the journal has sections on "Editor's Notes," letters to the editor, three two page book reviews, announcements of events and people, necrology, and features on Christian wholeness; poetry is also sometimes published. Besides the books reviewed, there is also a listing of Japanese books, some of which are translations of Western texts. The emphasis in this journal is on how Christianity can interact with the culture and not be totally acculturated, and on the wholeness of the religious spirit. World War II is the unspoken common guideline against which many Christian statements are made and compared; it is seen as a time when the church faltered. The articles are sound and are not patronizing.

301. Journal of Church and State. DATE FOUNDED: 1959. FREQUENCY: 3/yr. PRICE: $15.00/yr. PUBLISHER: J. M. Dawson Institute of Church-State Studies, Box 380, Baylor University, Waco, Texas 76798. EDITOR: James E. Wood, Jr. INDEX. ADVERTISEMENTS. CIRCULATION: 1,400. MANUSCRIPT SELECTION: Editor after Editorial Council members review the articles. MICROFORMS: Hein. REPRINTS: Hein. BOOK REVIEWS. INDEXED/ABSTRACTED: BRI, CLI, CPI, LRI, PAIS, RIO. DATABASE: ATLA, RI. TARGET AUDIENCE: AC, SP. SAMPLE COPIES.

This journal is the English language journal exploring the relationships between church and state. All of the six or seven articles are well written by scholars in the field; they are documented and signed. Each issue opens with an extensive editorial on a significant event in the relationship between religion and the state which is usually associated with the American scene. While the issues are not explicitly devoted to one topic, sometimes articles are dedicated to one aspect of church-state relations, such as Nazism and the Holocaust. The twenty five, signed, 500 word reviews are split into two sections: book reviews and book notes. The final sections of the journal list the dissertations on church-state relations and describe the state of those relations in various countries of the world. The indexes classify the articles by title, author, and subject; the book reviews by author, title, and reviewer; and the dissertations by author and title. This journal is a must for any collection that pretends to be relevant to the issues facing the church and the state.

302. Katallagete. DATE FOUNDED: 1965. FREQUENCY: irr. PRICE: $10.00/yr. (called a "contribution.") PUBLISHER: Katallagete, Inc., Box 2307, College Station, Berea, Kentucky 40404. EDITOR: James Holloway. ILLUSTRATIONS. REPRINTS. SPECIAL ISSUES: Occasionally. INDEXED/ABSTRACTED: RIO. DATABASE: ATLA, RI. TARGET AUDIENCE: GP.

This journal's articles are devoted to articulating what it

means to be a Christian in the United States today. The authors are mostly academics who write from a very committed point of view, which could be described as radical--radical in the sense that Christ's claims are permanent and the world's are contingent. Its articles on Jacques Ellul, William Stringfellow, Karl Barth and the Confessing Church and its meaning for today all point in this direction. All readers will be challenged--conservatives and liberals alike. The style of writing is very engaging, opinionated, editorializing, and exciting.

303. The Other Side. DATE FOUNDED: 1965. TITLE CHANGES: Freedom Now, changed January 1970. FREQUENCY: Every five weeks; every six weeks in January and July. PRICE: $21.75/yr. PUBLISHER: The Other Side, 300 W. Apsley Street, Philadelphia, Pennsylvania 19144. EDITOR: Mark W. Olson. ILLUSTRATIONS. ADVERTISEMENTS. CIRCULATION: 16,000. MANUSCRIPT SELECTION: Editorial staff. REPRINTS: Back issues available from the publisher. BOOK REVIEWS. SPECIAL ISSUES: In place of regular issues. INDEXED/ABSTRACTED: CPI, PII, RIO. DATABASE: ATLA, RI. TARGET AUDIENCE: AC, GP, SP, UndSt. SAMPLE COPIES: Upon request.

There are several book reviews, numbering about sixty; they are signed and take up about 300 words apiece.

304. RCDA: Religion in Communist Dominated Areas. DATE FOUNDED: 1962. FREQUENCY: q. PRICE: Unite States: Individuals, $15.00/yr.; institutions, $20.00/yr.; foreign countries: $20.00/yr.; air mail, $30.00/yr. PUBLISHER: Research Center for Religion and Human Rights in Closed Societies, Ltd., 475 Riverside Drive, New York, New York 10115. EDITOR: Blahoslav Hruby and Olga S. Hruby. MANUSCRIPT SELECTION: Editors. REPRINTS: Unbound volumes available at $20.00 apiece. TARGET AUDIENCE: GP.

The purpose of this publication is to make available and analyze information on the attitudes and practices of Communist parties with respect to the life and work of religious people in Communist countries. Particular attention is given to the violations of religious freedom and other human rights in closed societies. It is definitely anti-communist in tone; some of the articles are either adapted or translated from publications in communist lands showing how religious people are persecuted or manipulated in those countries. Other articles may be written by government or religious officials in the United States. There are about twenty-one articles. A good companion journal to this is Religion in Communist Lands.

305. Religion in Communist Lands. DATE FOUNDED: 1973.

FREQUENCY: 3/yr. PRICE: 16.00 pounds/yr., surface mail; air mail: North Africa and the Middle East, 18.00 pounds/yr.; the Americas and Africa, 19.00 pounds; Australia, 20.00 pounds/yr.; United States and Canada, $30.00/yr. from Keston College USA, Framingham, Massachusetts 01701. PUBLISHER: Keston College, Heathfield Road, Keston, Kent BR2 6BA, England. EDITOR: Jane Ellis. ILLUSTRATIONS. INDEX. ADVERTISEMENTS. CIRCULATION: 3,500. MANUSCRIPT SELECTION: Editorial board. MICROFORMS: UMI. REPRINTS: From the publisher. BOOK REVIEWS. INDEXED/ABSTRACTED: RIO. DATABASE: ATLA, RI. TARGET AUDIENCE: AC, SP. SAMPLE COPIES.

There are journals, such as the Journal of Church and State, which report news about church and state relations in the countries of the world, and other journals relate Christianity to the plight of the Third World, but this journal concentrates on religion in all Communist lands from Eastern Europe to Asia. In addition to the six articles, there are sections on sources which constitute an annotated bibliography of documents about the church in Communist countries. The eight, one page book reviews are signed. The journal also contains a news section about the activities of church and state. All articles are written and signed by academics and researchers.

306. SA: Sociological Analysis: A Journal in the Sociology of Religion. DATE FOUNDED: 1940. TITLE CHANGES: American Catholic Sociological Review (1940-1964); Sociological Analysis (1964-1973); SA (1973-). FREQUENCY: q. PRICE: $20.00/yr., individuals; $25.00/yr., libraries; add $2.00 for all subscribers outside the United States. PUBLISHER: Lorraine D'Antonio, Box U 68A, University of Connecticut, Storrs, Connecticut 06268. EDITOR: Roger O'Toole. INDEX. CIRCULATION: 1,400. MANUSCRIPT SELECTION: Editorial board. MICROFORMS: JAI, MIM, UMI. REPRINTS: UMI. BOOK REVIEWS. INDEXED/ABSTRACTED: CC, CPLI, LLBA, RIO, SA, SSCI. DATABASE: ATLA, RI, SA, SocScisearch. TARGET AUDIENCE: SP.

Each issue contains eight, signed, 800 word book reviews.

307. Sojourners. DATE FOUNDED: 1971. TITLE CHANGES: Post-American (1971-1975). FREQUENCY: m. PRICE: $15.00/yr., individuals; $12.00/yr., libraries. PUBLISHER: Sojourners, P. O. Box 29272, Washington, D. C. 20017. EDITOR: Jim Wallis. ILLUSTRATIONS. INDEX. ADVERTISEMENTS. CIRCULATION: 55,000. MANUSCRIPT SELECTION: Editorial staff. MICROFORMS: ATLA. REPRINTS: From the publisher. BOOK REVIEWS. INDEXED/ABSTRACTED: API, RIO. DATABASE: ATLA, RI. TARGET AUDIENCE: GP. SAMPLE COPIES.

Sojourners, printed in an attractive format, is devoted to exploring the meaning of Christian discipleship in dealing with the issues of justice, peace, and church renewal. There are eight to twelve articles, mostly written by Americans who are laymen, scholars, and activists. The journal, usually dedicated to one topic per issue, has an editorial page and a couple of news sections. Critical evaluations are made not only of books, but also of movies. Such reviews number three, are signed, and occupy about 700 words each. There is also a short annotated bibliography of books that might be of interest to Sojourners' readers. The viewpoint of the publication is liberal. It is very comparable to Christianity Century in both its interests and emphasis.

308. Thought: A Review of Culture and Idea. DATE FOUNDED: 1926. FREQUENCY: q. PRICE: $15.00/yr., individuals; $20.00/yr., libraries. PUBLISHER: Fordham University Press, Bronx, New York 10458. EDITOR: G. Richard Dimler. ADVERTISEMENTS. CIRCULATION: 1,400. MANUSCRIPT SELECTION: Decision based on recommendations made by readers. MICROFORMS: UMI. SPECIAL ISSUES. INDEXED/ABSTRACTED: CC, CPLI, HI, MLA Abstracts, PAIS, RTA. DATABASE: HI. TARGET AUDIENCE: AC, GP, SP, UndSt. SAMPLE COPIES.

309. United Evangelical Action. DATE FOUNDED: 1942. FREQUENCY: bm. PRICE: $10.00/yr., $17.00/2 yrs.; foreign, $15.00/yr., $25.00/2 yrs. PUBLISHER: Billy A. Melvin, Wheaton, Illinois 60189; National Association of Evangelicals, Box 28, Wheaton, Illinois 60189. EDITOR: Donald R. Brown. ILLUSTRATIONS. ADVERTISEMENTS. CIRCULATION: 7,800. MANUSCRIPT SELECTION: Editor. INDEXED/ABSTRACTED: CPI, GSScRel. TARGET AUDIENCE: GP.

For those who do think that conservative Christians are not socially active, this journal will correct that misconception. The three or so signed articles are focused on one theme, be it the sanctuary movement or liberation theology. All views are presented; comments contrary to an article's point of view are written in the margins. The articles are short and are written mainly by clerics and lay people. In addition to the regular articles, there are features such as "Focus on NAF," "News," "D. C. Dateline," and "Cutting Edge." It is the counterpart to the more liberal Christianity and Crisis; but some of its opinions are not much different than the ones found in that more liberal journal.

Christianity and Science

310. *Faith and Thought: The Journal of the Victoria Institute*. DATE FOUNDED: 1866. FREQUENCY: sa. PRICE: United Kingdom and the Commonwealth: 7.00 pounds/yr., 13.30 pounds/2 yrs., 19.40 pounds/3 yrs.; North America and Canada: $15.75/yr., $29.95/2 yrs., $43.65/3 yrs. PUBLISHER: Paternoster Press, Paternoster House, 3 Mount Radford Crescent, Exeter, England EX2 4JW. EDITOR: Dr. A. B. Robins. INDEX. CIRCULATION: 600. BOOK REVIEWS. TARGET AUDIENCE: AC, GP, SP.

This journal is dedicated to discussing the implications of new scientific thought; the Victoria Institute, in fact, was established during the controversy over evolution. Over the years, other subjects have also been examined in a Christian light: archaeology, history, philosophy, and sociology. The approximately six signed articles deal with such subjects to see what implications they have for the Christian faith; at times the papers are drawn from symposia held on such subjects as man's manipulation of nature. The articles are written by scholars and laymen; the prose is lively and engaging, and questions are raised that one may not have thought of before. The journal opens with an editorial and some news. The twenty-eight, signed, one page book reviews cover not only books on science and religion, but also those on theology, biblical studies, and philosophy. For those who feel that *Zygon* is over their heads, this a good place to begin on the subject of the relationships between the modern scientific culture and Christianity.

311. Journal of the American Scientific Affiliation. DATE FOUNDED: 1941. FREQUENCY: q. PRICE: $20.00/yr., individuals; $30.00/yr., libraries. PUBLISHER: Wilbur Bullock, P. O. Box J, Ipswich, Massachusetts 01938. EDITOR: Wilbur Bullock. ILLUSTRATIONS: Few. INDEX: Every third year. ADVERTISEMENTS. CIRCULATION: 4,200. MANUSCRIPT SELECTION: Editorial board. MICROFORMS: UMI. REPRINTS: From the publisher. BOOK REVIEWS. SPECIAL ISSUES. INDEXED/ABSTRACTED: CPI, RTA, TARGET AUDIENCE: AC, SP, UndSt. SAMPLE COPIES.

An average issue has ten, signed, two-page book reviews.

312. Zygon: Journal of Religion and Science. DATE FOUNDED: 1966. FREQUENCY: q. PRICE: $20.00/yr., individuals; $26.00/yr., libraries. PUBLISHER: Joint Publication Board, c/o Rollins College, Campus Box 2764, Winter Park, Florida 32789-4496. EDITOR: Karl E. Peters. ILLUSTRATIONS. INDEX. ADVERTISEMENTS. CIRCULATION: 2,000. MANUSCRIPT SELECTION: Editor in consultation with the Editorial Advisory Board and other referees. MICROFORMS: UMI. REPRINTS: Available from the authors; back issues also available in hard copy. BOOK REVIEWS. INDEXED/ABSTRACTED: AHCI, America, CC, GSScRel, HA, HI, PA, PI, RIO, RTA, SSCI. DATABASE: AHSearch, America, ATLA, HA, HI, PI, RI, SocScisearch. TARGET AUDIENCE: AC, SP, UndSt. SAMPLE COPIES.

Zygon seeks to provide a place where religious wisdom might be united with significant, recent scientific discoveries about the world and human nature, thereby providing basic values for enhancing human life. Each issue dedicates its five articles to one specific subject, e. g. genetics or sociobiology. All the articles and reviews are signed; it is difficult to compare this journal to any other since this one is almost unique in attempting to bring scholars in religion and science together. The six, signed, two to three page reviews are, broadly speaking, concerned with books that are written on science and religion. Occasionally there will be a commentary on a previous article as well as announcements of major meetings on science and religion. The articles are stimulating and are aimed at the specialist. No particular religion is discussed, only religion and philosophy in general.

Christianity and Literature

313. Christianity and Literature. DATE FOUNDED: 1950. TITLE CHANGES: Newsletter of the Conference on Christianity and Literature (1950-1973). FREQUENCY: q. PRICE: Individuals: $8.00/yr., United States; $10.00/yr., foreign; libraries: $12.00/yr., United States; $14.00/yr., foreign. PUBLISHER: Conference on Christianity and Literature, English Dept., Baylor University, Waco, Texas 76798. EDITOR: James Barcus. ADVERTISEMENTS. CIRCULATION: 1,200-1,400. MANUSCRIPT SELECTION: Editorial staff and qualified readers. REPRINTS: Some back issues from the publisher. BOOK REVIEWS. SPECIAL ISSUES: Occasionally. INDEXED/ABSTRACTED: AES, CPI, LCR, MLA, RIO. DATABASE: ATLA, RI. TARGET AUDIENCE: AC, GP, UndSt. SAMPLE COPIES: Available but not free.

This quarterly with its four articles per issue concentrates on the realm of English and American literature and their relationship to Christianity--a Christianity that is not understood in any sectarian manner. The articles are signed, usually written by American academics; the articles are documented with the footnotes at the end of the articles. An average issue contains fifteen to twenty book reviews, each one signed and composed in 1,000 words. One special feature, located at the end of each issue, is the annotated bibliographies of articles of interest that are published in other journals. A delightful section is "Poppycock" which wittily and accurately disects and discards bad English, even English written in grammar books. This journal will be of interest to Christians and non-Christians alike.

314. Religion and Literature. DATE FOUNDED: 1961. TITLE CHANGES: Notre Dame English Journal (1961-1984). FREQUENCY: 3/yr. PRICE: $12.00/yr., individuals; $15.00/yr., libraries; foreign subscriptions, add $3.00. PUBLISHER: University of Notre Dame, English Department, Notre Dame, Indiana 46556. EDITOR: Laura Marvel. INDEX. ADVERTISEMENTS. CIRCULATION: 450. MANUSCRIPT SELECTION: Board of readers advise editors; final decision made by editors, two faculty, and one graduate student. REPRINTS: Back issues available from the publisher for $5.00. BOOK REVIEWS. INDEXED/ABSTRACTED: AES, AHI, ChLit, CC, CPLI, EightCent, LCR, MHRA, MLAInt, RIC, RIO, RTA. DATABASE: ATLA, RI. TARGET AUDIENCE: AC, GP, SP, UndSt. SAMPLE COPIES.

This journal concentrates on the intersection between a writer's theology and his literary imagination. The four scholarly articles are essays in the interdisciplinary field of religion and literature. All of the articles and the rather long reviews are signed; the reviews occasionally become essays by the reviewer on the subject at hand; usually there are three such reviews, each occupying five to six pages. It is one of the very few journals to concentrate on the religious dimensions of literature; it is comparable to Christianity and Literature. While no additional issues are published each year, one issue, usually the spring one, is dedicated to a special topic. Scholars of biblical literature will find the approaches here interesting, since many of articles contain criticism from a structuralist point of view without the jargon. There is an occasional poem in this journal as well.

Ecumenism

315. Bulletin on Islam and Christian-Muslim Relations in Africa. DATE FOUNDED: 1983. FREQUENCY: q. PRICE: 7.50 pounds/yr. PUBLISHER: Centre for the Study of Islam and Christian-Muslim Relations, Selly Oak Colleges, Birmingham B29 6LE, United Kingdom. EDITOR: Sigvard von Sicard. INDEX. MANUSCRIPT SELECTION: Editor. BOOK REVIEWS. SPECIAL ISSUES: TARGET AUDIENCE: AC, SP.

There are one or two articles per issue in this typescript journal. Such articles are on the faith of Islam and what it means for Christians, on the ideas of religious freedom in Christianity and Islam, and on reports of meetings of Muslims and Christians. In addition to the well-documented articles, there are abstracts of several articles that pertain to the relations between Christians and Muslims in Africa. The section dedicated to book reviews has an average two or three signed essays that take up one page per review. Not only does this journal give one an insight into what others are thinking, it also provides a good list of journals devoted to the discussion of Islam.

316. Christian Jewish Relations. DATE FOUNDED: 1968. TITLE CHANGES: Christian Attitudes on Jews and Judaism, 1968-1980. FREQUENCY: q. PRICE: 9.50 pounds/yr. (airmail); $15.00/yr., United States and Canada (bulk airmail). PUBLISHER: Institute of Jewish Affairs, Ltd., 11 Hertford St., London W1Y 7DX, England. EDITOR: Norman Solomon. ADVERTISEMENTS: In-house. MANUSCRIPT SELECTION: Editor. INDEXED/ABSTRACTED: BullSig, Bowker, IAJS. DATABASE: Francis. TARGET AUDIENCE: AC, SP.

As the title suggests, this journal is devoted to the relationships between Jews and Christians, most notably, it seems, Roman Catholic Christians. On occasion, the journal is devoted to publishing reports from various meetings, such as a symposium on Nostra Aetate. Otherwise the journal contains four to five articles on how Jews are treated and related to by Christians in their teachings. The articles are signed and documented. Occasionally another journal's articles will be abstracted if they speak to social issues and how Jews and Christians have responded to them.

317. The Ecumenical Review. DATE FOUNDED: 1948. FREQUENCY: q. PRICE: $15.00/yr. PUBLISHER: World Council of Churches, 150 route de Ferney, P.O. Box 66, 1211 Geneva 20, Switzerland. EDITOR: Philip A. Potter. INDEX. ADVERTISEMENTS. CIRCULATION: 3,600. MANUSCRIPT SELECTION: Editor. MICROFORMS: UMI. REPRINTS: From the publisher. BOOK REVIEWS. INDEXED/ABSTRACTED: AHCI, CC, HI, NTA, OTA, RIO. DATABASE: AHSearch, ATLA, HI, RI. TARGET AUDIENCE: AC, SP, UndSt. SAMPLE COPIES.

This journal, which has approximately 100 pages and six articles per issue is and sponsored by the World Council of Churches, has several special features: ecumenical forum, a space for discussions of a particular ecumenical topic; ecumenical chronicle, a sort of news section; an ecumenical diary, another type of news section; significant ecumenical journals, a listing of the contents of major ecumenical journals, and a "Bibliographia Oecumenica." The articles describe and defend the activities of the World Council of Churches. The authors are drawn from all over the world. One will not find any article opposing ecumenism. The number of book reviews varies from one to six per issue; each is signed and averages 1,000 to 1,500 words.

318. The Ecumenist: A Journal for Promoting Christian Unity. DATE FOUNDED: 1962. FREQUENCY: bm. PRICE: Free. PUBLISHER: Paulist Press, 997 Macarthur Blvd., Mahwag, New Jersey 07430. EDITOR: Gregory Baum. CIRCULATION: 9,000. MICROFORMS: BLH, UMI. REPRINTS: UMI. BOOK REVIEWS. INDEXED/ABSTRACTED: CPLI, NTA, OTA. TARGET AUDIENCE: AC, SP.

Subtitled A Journal for Promoting Christian Unity, one would assume that this journal's articles would center on attempts to unite the various denominations of Christianity, but, in fact, very little of that kind of ecumenism is discussed. The "unity" that is attended to is that of the church with Marxism, women, worker coops, etc. In other words, union with those on the fringes of the church's structure is emphasized. Each issue contains about five signed articles written by scholars. Emphasis is placed on the Roman

Catholic Church's response to the ecumenical movement; it is quite objective, although its viewpoint seems to be somewhat left of center. While there may be one book review per issue, at times the articles are review articles covering books on Marxism, feminism, and church-state relations; such a review will average three pages. It is not really comparable to other journals devoted to ecumenism; it is more comparable to such journals as Christianity and Crisis and other journals focused on social concerns.

319. Journal of Ecumenical Studies. DATE FOUNDED: 1964. FREQUENCY: q.; 3/yr., 1964-1966. PRICE: $17.50/yr. PUBLISHER: Journal of Ecumenical Studies, Temple University (022-38), Philadelphia, Pennsylvania 19122. EDITOR: Dr. Leonard Swidler. INDEX. ADVERTISEMENTS. CIRCULATION: 2,200. MANUSCRIPT SELECTION: Editor and co-editor in consultation with readers. MICROFORMS: Hein. REPRINTS: From the publisher. BOOK REVIEWS. INDEXED/ABSTRACTED: America, BRM, CC, CPLI, ElencBibBib, GSScRel, HA, HI, Infodex, IZBG, NTA, RBIC, RIO, RTA, TLZ. DATABASE: America, ATLA, HA, HI, RI. TARGET AUDIENCE: AC, SP. SAMPLE COPIES: Occasionally to libraries; rarely to individuals.

This journal is one of the very scholarly journals devoted to the study of the ecumenical spirit, not only between Christian denominations, but also between religions of all kinds. The five major articles, signed and documented, tend to be rather long; they not only discuss current concerns but also historical movements that pertain to the ecumenical movement. In addition to the book review section, which contains forty signed essays averaging 600 to 1,200 words apiece, there are abstracts of articles published in other countries on ecumenism as well as announcements of ecumenical activities; finally there is a books received section. While no point of view is explicitly supported, some articles tend to assume that anything that stalls the ecumenical movement is bad.

320. Mid-Stream: An Ecumenical Journal. DATE FOUNDED: 1961. FREQUENCY: q. PRICE: United States, $15.00/yr.; foreign, $16.00/yr.; students, $8.00/yr. PUBLISHER: Council on Christian Unity of the Christian Church (Disciples of Christ), P. O. Box 1986, Indianapolis, Indiana 46206. EDITOR: Paul A. Crow. CIRCULATION: 1,000. MICROFORMS: UMI. BOOK REVIEWS. INDEXED/ABSTRACTED: RIO. DATABASE: ATLA, RI. TARGET AUDIENCE: AC, SP.

This serial in its four to six articles per issue is definitely dedicated to advancing the cause of ecumenism. In addition to the articles, there are two sections, one, "Ecumenical Documents," which reprints documents and statements from ecumenical bodies from around the world, and two, "Events in the oikoumene," which contains reports on ecumenical events. The articles are written by academics and lay people; some of the articles are heavily documented. The journal is enthusiastic in its claims for ecumenism. Each issue contains one to two signed book reviews, each averaging one to three pages; the books are reviewed in light of what contribution they make toward Christian unity; at times it is difficult to discern what expertise the reviewer has in the subject of the book being reviewed. Librarians should take note that the issue numbers on the spine of the journal may not match the issue number on the cover of the journal.

321. One in Christ: A Catholic Ecumenical Review. DATE FOUNDED: 1965. MERGER: Supersedes East Churches Quarterly (1936-1964) and absorbed Ecumenical Notes (1964-1969) FREQUENCY: q. PRICE: United Kingdom, 15.00 pounds/yr.; overseas surface mail, 15.35 pounds ($25.00)/yr.; overseas airmail, 19.35 pounds ($33.00)/yr.; Europe letter post, 17.35 pounds/yr. PUBLISHER: One in Christ, Turvey Abbey, Turvey, Bedfordshire MK43 3DE, England. EDITOR: Paschal Anne Hardiment. INDEX. CIRCULATION: 2,000. MANUSCRIPT SELECTION: Editor. MICROFORMS: UMI. REPRINTS: UMI; back issues also from the publisher. BOOK REVIEWS. INDEXED/ABSTRACTED: BHI, CPLI, OTA, RTA, RIO. DATABASE: ATLA, RI. TARGET AUDIENCE: AC, SP.

This quarterly is a Roman Catholic review that seeks to to further the movement toward Christian unity by giving information on ecumenical topics, by contributing to the dialogue between Christians, and by encouraging love between Christians. To this end, five articles are published in each issue which are written by various religious people who are mostly, but not all, Roman Catholics. While the articles are signed, the authority of each writer is not specified. Following the articles is a section, "Ecumenical Notes and Documentation," that includes descriptions of ecumenical reports and meetings. The articles are documented and clearly written. Controversial topics are not sidestepped. Not every issue has a book review section; the issues that do have an average of two signed four page reviews.

Islam

322. Bulletin of Christian Institutes of Islamic Studies. DATE FOUNDED: 1978. TITLE CHANGES: The Bulletin of Christian Institutes of Islamic Studies (1930-1971); Al-Basheer (1972-1976); The Bulletin of Christian Institutes of Islamic Studies (1978-). FREQUENCY: q. PRICE: $4.50/yr. PUBLISHER: Henry Martyn Institute, P.O. Box 153, Station Road, Hyderabad - 500 001, A. P., India. EDITOR: D. T. Lindell. INDEX. CIRCULATION: 400. MANUSCRIPT SELECTION: Editor and staff of the institute. REPRINTS: Back issues from the publisher. BOOK REVIEWS. INDEXED/ABSTRACTED: RIO. DATABASE: ATLA, RI. TARGET AUDIENCE: AC, GP, SP, UndSt. SAMPLE COPIES: Upon request.

This journal contains about two signed book reviews per issue, each containing about 700 to 1,000 words.

323. Hamdard Islamicus. DATE FOUNDED: 1978. FREQUENCY: q. PRICE: $15.00/yr., foreign countries; Rs75.00/yr., in Pakistan. PUBLISHER: Hamdard Foundation Press, Nazimabad No 3, Karachi-18, Pakistan. EDITOR: Hakim Mohammed Said. ILLUSTRATIONS. ADVERTISEMENTS. CIRCULATION: 2,000. SELECTION: Editorial committee. REPRINTS: Back issues available from the publisher. BOOK REVIEWS. INDEXED/ABSTRACTED: RIO. DATABASE: ATLA, RI. TARGET AUDIENCE: AC, SP. SAMPLE COPIES.

This journal is devoted to Islamic research and scholarship. Such a purpose includes not only the study of religion, but essays on all aspects of Islamic culture and history. It invites all schools of Islamic thought to participate. All of the five or so articles are signed, and while they are not documented, they do have a appended bibliographies.

Each issue has one to three signed reviews, each one taking up three pages. The articles are well and clearly written.

Modern Faiths

324. Dialogue: A Journal of Mormon Thought. DATE FOUNDED: 1966. FREQUENCY: q. PRICE: $25.00/yr.; students, $15.00/yr.; single issues, $7.00. PUBLISHER: Dialogue Foundation, Editorial Office, 202 West 300 North, Salt Lake City, Utah 84103. EDITOR: Linda King Newell; L. Jackson Newell. ILLUSTRATIONS. INDEX. CIRCULATION: 4,500. MICROFORMS: UMI. BOOK REVIEWS. TARGET AUDIENCE: AC, SP.

As the title suggests, this journal is dedicated to explicating the Mormon view on current topics, especially on the relevance of religion to secular life, and of the dialogue with the Judeo-Christian tradition. The journal opens with letters to the editor, expressing views on a potpourri of subjects, especially those that have been investigated in past issues. Approximately seven articles follow, dealing with all theological issues, whether it be ethics or the portrayal of religious values in literature; they are written by scholars and laymen and are well documented. Each book review section contains ten signed book reviews, each one taking up two pages. The books reviewed are usually on Mormon themes; occasionally a book is reviewed that is not. It is noteworthy that not only the theology of the Church of Jesus Christ of Latter-day Saints is explored, but also that of the Reorganized Church of Jesus Christ of Latter Day Saints. The journal is independent of the Mormon Church and all views are welcome. This journal is very much like mainline Protestant theological journals, such as Theology Today.

325. The Freethinker. DATE FOUNDED: 1881. FREQUENCY: m. PRICE: 3.60 pounds or $8.00/yr.; payment in foreign currency requires the additional payment, equaling $1.20 for

bank charges. PUBLISHER: G. W. Foote and Company, 702 Holloway Road, London N19 3NL, England. EDITOR: William McIlroy. CIRCULATION: 1,250. MANUSCRIPT SELECTION: Editor. REPRINTS: Back issues available from the publisher. BOOK REVIEWS. TARGET AUDIENCE: GP. SAMPLE COPIES.

This periodical is an advocate of secular humanism and atheism and will be of interest to all who are either religious sceptics or religious believers, especially Christians since the object of the journal's articles is Christianity both in its historical foundations and current practice. The three signed reviews of books or plays are well balanced and informative; each one comprisessof one page. It reports in bold type incongruous actions performed by religious people.

326. The Humanist. DATE FOUNDED: 1941. FREQUENCY: sa. PRICE: $18.00/yr., $30.00/2 yrs., $45.00/3 yrs.; foreign subscribers should add $3.00. PUBLISHER: The American Humanist Association, 7 Harwood Drive, P. O. Box 146, Amherst, New York 14226-0146. EDITOR: Lloyd L. Moran. ILLUSTRATIONS. INDEX. ADVERTISEMENTS. CIRCULATION: 17,000. MANUSCRIPT SELECTION: Editor. MICROFORMS: UMI. REPRINTS: UMI; back issues are available for $3.50. BOOK REVIEWS. INDEXED/ABSTRACTED: BRI, HI, MI, PAIS, PMR, RG, SSCI. DATABASE: HI, SocScisearch. TARGET AUDIENCE: GP.

This serial presents a non-theistic, secular, and naturalistic approach to philosophy, science, and broad areas of personal and social concerns; the Association believes that humans determine the moral principles by which they live. The nine or so articles are written by laymen and scholars on various subjects from a humanistic point of view. It would be fair to say that the tone of the articles, letters, and some of the classified advertising is not only non-theistic, but anti-theistic; many of the examples used against religion are straw men drawn from the actions of fundamentalistic Christians or the decisions of the hierarchy of the Roman Catholic Church. An average book review section contains three signed book reviews; each one is written in 300 to 675 words. In addition to the book review section, films are also reviewed. There are other sections featuring readers' opinions, humanism in literature, church and state, and noteworthy statements that debunk religion.

327. Religious Humanism. DATE FOUNDED: 1967. FREQUENCY: q. PRICE: $10.00/yr.; $18.00/2 yrs. PUBLISHER: Fellowship of Religious Humanists, P. O. Box 278, Yellow Springs, Ohio 45387. EDITOR: Paul Beattie, Lucinda

Beattie, co-editors. INDEX. ADVERTISEMENTS: Very seldom. CIRCULATION: 1,000. MANUSCRIPT SELECTION: Editors. MICROFORMS: UMI. REPRINTS: Publisher. BOOK REVIEWS. INDEXED/ABSTRACTED: AHCI, CC, GSScRel, PI, RIO, RTA. DATABASE: AHSearch, ATLA, PI, RI. TARGET AUDIENCE: AC, GP. SAMPLE COPIES.

This journal is dedicated to humanistic religion and ethics. The six articles per issue are signed and are concerned with the various aspects of humanism and ethics. On the average, there are five book reviews, each one composed in 500 words. The reviewed books are also centered on humanism; the reviews give a good description of the books being discussed. It should be noted that the tone of the journal tends to be against revelatory religion. The articles are written by scholars, but the appeal is broad. In addition to the essays there is also an editorial as well as some poetry.

328. World Order: A Baha'i Magazine. DATE FOUNDED: 1966. FREQUENCY: q. PRICE: United States: $10.00/yr., $18.00/2 yrs.; foreign: $18.00/yr., $34.00/2 yrs.; libraries receive 25% discount. PUBLISHER: National Spiritual Assembly of the Baha'is of the United States, 415 Linden Avenue, Wilmette, Illinois 60091. EDITOR: Dr. Firuz Kazemzadeh ILLUSTRATIONS. INDEX. CIRCULATION: 3,500. MANUSCRIPT SELECTION: Editorial board. MICROFORMS: UMI. BOOK REVIEWS. INDEXED/ABSTRACTED: IAPV, RIO. DATABASE: ATLA, RI. TARGET AUDIENCE: AC, GP, UndSt.

Each issue has one book review, signed, and written in two to four pages.

Geography Index

References are to item numbers, not page numbers

Australia
Australasian Catholic Record, 140
Australian Biblical Review, 81
Buried History, 99
Journal of Christian Education, 274
Journal of Religious History, 132
Lutheran Theological Journal, 165
Saint Mark's Review, 239
Sophia: A Journal for Discussion in Philos. Theology, 242
Belgium
Augustiniana, 197
Cistercian Studies, 152
Elenchus Bibliographicus, 7
Ephemerides Theologicae Lovaniensis, 209
Louvain Studies, 163
Social Compass, 50
Canada
Canadian Catholic Review, 146
Eglise et theologie, 207
Journal of the Canadian Church Historical Soc., 133
Newsletter for Targumic and Cognate Studies, 76
PMC: Practice of Ministry in Canada, 282
Studia Canonica, 290
Studies in Religion/Sciences Religieuses, 35
England
America: History and Life, 1
Baptist Quarterly, 142
Bull. of John Rylands Univ. Lib. of Manchester, 97
Bull. on Islam and Chris.-Musl. Relations in Africa, 315
Canon Law Abstracts, 6

Catena, 147
Christian Brethren Review, 151
Christian Jewish Relations, 316
Churchman, 299
Clergy Review, 267
Downside Review, 155
Durham University Journal, 205
English Historical Review, 129
^SFaith and Thought: The Journal of the Vict. Inst^S., 310
Freethinker, 325
Healing Review, 40
Heythrop Journal, 220
Historical Abstracts, 9
Horizons, 103
Iraq, 62
Journal for the Study of the New Testament, 107
Journal for the Study of the Old Testament, 108
Journal of Ecclesiastical History, 131
Journal of Jewish Studies, 72
Journal of Semitic Studies, 65
Journal of the United Ref. Church Hist. Soc., 162
Journal of Theological Studies, 110
Joy and Light, 277
Levant, 111
Middle Way, 57
Modern Churchman, 228
Network, 171
New Blackfriars, 172
New REview, 173
New Testament Studies, 112
Newsletter (Christian Brethren Research Fellowship), 174
One in Christ, 321
Orbit, 175
Palestine Exploration Quarterly, 67
Printed Lectures, 283
Radius, 285
Recusant History, 135
Reformer, 235
Religion, 29
Religion in Communist Lands, 305
Religious Studies, 31
Scripture Bulletin, 116
Search, 287
Signum, 288
Sikh Courier, 59
Sobornost, 182
Spectrum, 60
Studies in Comparative Religion, 34
Tablet, 292
Themelios, 244
Theology, 248

Trinitarian Bible Society Quarterly Record, 120
Tyndale Bulletin, 252
USPG Yearbook, 187
Vox Evangelica, 254
Way, 255
Word in Action: The Bible in the World, 122
Young Life Guard, 295

France
Bulletin signaletique, 5

Germany
Bibliographia Patristica, 4
Bulletin of the United Bible Societies, 98

Hong Kong
Ching Feng, 297

India
Bangalore Theological Forum, 198
Biblebhashyam, 90
Bulletin of Christian Inst. of Islamic Stud., 322
Divine Life, 52
Indian Journal of Theology, 222
Journal of Dharma, 24
Theosophist, 43

Ireland
Furrow, 156

Israel
Holy Land, 102
Israel Exploration Journal, 106

Italy
Biblica, 92
Christ to the World, 150
Elenchus Bibliographicus Biblicus, 8

Japan
Japan Christian Quarterly, 300
Japanese Journal of Religious Studies, 54
Japanese Religions, 55

Kenya
AFER: African Ecclesial Review, 296

Netherlands
International Bibliog. of the Hist. of Religions, 11
International Journal for Philosophy of Religion, 223
Journal for the Study of Judaism, 71
Journal of Religion in Africa, 36
Novum Testamentum, 113
Numen, 27
Studia Liturgica, 291
Vetus Testamentum, 121

Nigeria
Orita, 28

Norway
Studia Theologica, 119

Pakistan
Hamdard Islamicus, 323
Scotland
Bible Translator: Practical Papers, 88
Bible Translator: Technical Papers, 89
Contact, 268
Expository Times, 101
Innes Review, 130
Scottish Journal of Religious Studies, 33
Scottish Journal of Theology, 241
Singapore
East Asia Journal of Theology, 206
South Africa
Journal of Northwest Semitic Languages, 64
Journal of Theology for Southern Africa, 226
Missionalia, 280
Religion in Southern Africa, 30
Scriptura: Tydskrif vir Bybelkunde, 115
Theologia Evangelica, 245
Soviet Union
Journal of the Moscow Patriarchate, 161
Switzerland
Ecumenical Review, 317
International Review of Mission, 273
LWF Documentation, 166
LWF Report, 167
Reformed World, 234
Risk Book Series, 237
Taiwan
Taiwan Journal of Theology, 243
Tanzania
Africa Theological Journal, 190
United States
California
America: History and Life, 1
Creation, 39
Historical Abstracts, 9
Journal of Psychology and Theology, 276
Pacific Theological Review, 229
Process Studies, 232
Sources from the Ancient Near East, 68
Colorado
Bible Advocate, 82
Iliff Review, 221
Connecticut
Journal for the Scientific Study of Religion, 45
Journal of Religion and Psychical Research, 41
Religious Education, 286
Review of Religious Research, 49
SA: Sociological Analysis, 306
District of Columbia
American Historical Review, 123

Baptist World, 143
Bible Review, 86
Biblical Archaeology Review, 94
Catholic Biblical Quarterly, 100
Catholic Historical Review, 126
Old Testament Abstracts,
Sojourners, 307
Theological Studies, 247
Thomist, 184
Florida
Zygon, 312
Georgia
American Journal of Theology and Philosophy, 191
Eastern Buddhist, 53
Harvard Theological Review, 217
Journal of Biblical Literature, 109
Journal of Feminist Studies in Religion, 46
Journal of the American Academy of Religion, 26
Journal of the Interden. Theol. Ctr., 160
Religious Studies News, 32
Religious Studies Review, 17
Second Century, 136
Semeia, 117
Society of Biblical Literature Sem. Paper Ser., 118
Hawaii
Philosophy East and West, 58
Illinois
Anglican Theological Review, 195
Biblical Research, 95
Brethren Life and Thought, 144
Call to Growth Ministry, 260
Chicago Studies, 200
Christian Century, 201
Christian Education Journal, 262
Christian Ministry, 263
Christianity Today, 265
Criterion, 203
Evangelical Missions Quarterly, 269
Explor, 212
History of Religions, 23
Journal of Near Eastern Studies, 63
Journal of Religion, 25
Leadership, 278
Religion Index One: Periodicals, 30
Trinity Journal, 251
United Evangelical Action, 309
World Order: A Baha'i Magazine, 328
Indiana
Concordia Theological Quarterly, 202
Encounter, 208
Grace Theological Journal, 216

Journal of Religious Ethics, 48
Mennonite Quarterly Review, 169
Mid-Stream, 320
Pope Speaks, 176
Religion and Literature, 314
Wesleyan Theological Journal, 188

Kansas
Mennonite Life, 168

Kentucky
Catholic Theol. Soc. of Amer. Proceedings, 149
Faith and Philosophy, 213
Katallagete, 302
Lexington Theological Quarterly, 227
Review and Expositor, 179
Review of Books and Religion, 236

Maryland
Modern Judaism, 75

Massachusetts
American Journal of Archaeology, 124
Christian Scholar's Review, 298
Greek Orthodox Theological Review, 157
Henceforth. . ., 219
Journal of the American Scientific Affiliation, 311
New Testament Abstracts, 12
Word and Spirit: A Monastic Review, 257

Michigan
Andrews Univ. Monogr.: Studies in Religion, 192
Andrews Univ. Sem. Doctoral Diss. Ser., 193
Andrews University Seminary Studies, 194
Calvin Theological Journal, 145
Fides et Historia, 215
Institute of Archael. Publ. Assyr. Series, 61
Reformed Review, 233

Minnesota
Bible Friend, 85
Bible Today, 87
Catholic Digest, 148
Dialog, 204
Journal of the Evangelical Theological Soc., 225
Sisters Today, 289
Theological Markings: A UTS Journal, 246
Worship, 294

Missouri
Archives and History, 125
Concordia Historical Institute Quarterly, 153
Concordia Journal, 154
Lutheran Hist. Conf.: Essays and Reports, 164
Newsletter (Center for Reformation Research), 134
Sixteenth Century Journal, 137
Theology Digest, 249

New Jersey
BibleWorld, 91
Ecumenist, 318
Faith and Thought, 214
International Bulletin of Missionary Research, 272
Methodist History, 170
Princeton Seminary Bulletin, 231
Theology Today, 250
New York
America, 258
American Baptist Quarterly, 138
American Bible Society Record, 79
American Humanities Index, 2
Bible and Spade, 83
Biblical Theology Bulletin, 96
Bibliographia Patristica, 4
Christianity and Crisis, 264
Church, 266
Conservative Judaism, 69
Cross Currents, 44
Hastings Center Report, 218
Homiletic and Pastoral Review, 270
Humanist, 326
Humanities Index, 10
Journal of Ecclesiastical History, 131
Journal of Reform Judaism, 73
Journal of Religion and Health, 47
Journal of the Ancient Near Eastern Society, 66
Judaism, 74
New Testament Studies, 112
Pastoral Psychology, 281
RCDA: Religion in Comm. Dominated Areas, 304
Readers' Guide to Periodical Literature, 14
Reconstructionist, 77
Religious Studies, 31
St. Vladimir's Theological Quarterly, 180
Social Sciences Index, 19
Thought: A Review of Culture and Idea, 308
Tradition, 78
Union Seminary Quarterly Review, 253
U. S. Catholic Historian, 186
North Carolina
Early American Literature, 128
Greek, Roman, and Byzantine Studies, 22
North Dakota
American Benedictine Review, 139
Ohio
Catechist, 261
Religious Humanism, 327
Theological Education, 293
Trinity Seminary Review, 185

Pennsylvania
American Quarterly, 21
American Schools of Oriental Research Newsletter, 80
Anima: An Experiential Journal, 38
Arts and Humanities Citation Index, 3
Augustinian Studies, 196
Biblical Archaeologist, 93
Bride of Christ, 259
Church History, 127
Eternity, 210
Horizons in Biblical Theology, 104
Horizons: Jrnl. of the Col. Theol. Soc., 159
Jewish Quarterly Review, 70
Journal of Ecumenical Studies, 319
Journal of Pastoral Care, 275
Journal of Social Philosophy, 224
Latin American Indian Literatures Journal, 37
Missiology, 279
Other Side, 303
Quaker History, 177
Quaker Religious Thought, 178
Religious and Theological Abstracts, 16
Social Sciences Citation Index, 18
Studies in Formative Spirituality, 42
Westminster Theological Journal, 256
Witness, 189
Tennessee
Baptist History and Heritage, 141
Quarterly Review, 284
Saint Luke's Journal of Theology, 238
Soundings: An Interdisciplinary Journal, 51
Southern Baptist Periodical Index, 20
Texas
Bibliotheca Sacra, 199
Christianity and Literature, 313
Historical Magaz. of the Prot. Episc. Church, 158
Hymn, 271
Journal of Church and State, 301
Perkins Journal, 230
Restoration Quarterly, 114
Southwestern Journal of Theology, 183
Utah
Dialogue: A Journal of Mormon Thought, 324
Virginia
Interpretation: A Journal of Bible and Theology, 105
Scholars' Choice, 240
Wisconsin
Bible Collectors' World, 84
Journal of the Int. Assoc. of Buddhist Studies, 56
Searching Together, 181

Title Index

References are to item numbers, not page numbers

AFER: African Ecclesial Review, 296
Africa Theological Journal, 190
America, 258
America: History and Life, 1
American Baptist Quarterly, 138
American Benedictine Review, 139
American Bible Society Record, 79
American Historical Review, 123
American Humanities Index, 2
American Journal of Archaeology, 124
American Journal of Theology and Philosophy, 191
American Quarterly, 21
American Schools of Oriental Research Newsletter, 80
Andrews Univ. Monogr.: Studies in Religion, 192
Andrews Univ. Sem. Doctoral Diss. Ser., 193
Andrews University Seminary Studies, 194
Anglican Theological Review, 195
Anima: An Experiential Journal, 38
Archives and History, 125
Arts and Humanities Citation Index, 3
Augustinian Studies, 196
Augustiniana, 197
Australasian Catholic Record, 140
Australian Biblical Review, 81
Bangalore Theological Forum, 198
Baptist History and Heritage, 141
Baptist Quarterly, 142
Baptist World, 143
Bible Advocate, 82
Bible and Spade, 83

Bible Collectors' World, 84
Bible Friend, 85
Bible Review, 86
Bible Today, 87
Bible Translator: Practical Papers, 88
Bible Translator: Technical Papers, 89
Biblebhashyam, 90
BibleWorld, 91
Biblica, 92
Biblical Archaeologist, 93
Biblical Archaeology Review, 94
Biblical Research, 95
Biblical Theology Bulletin, 96
Bibliographia Patristica, 4
Bibliotheca Sacra, 199
Brethren Life and Thought, 144
Bride of Christ, 259
Bulletin of Christian Inst. of Islamic Stud., 322
Bulletin of John Rylands Univ. Lib. of Manchester, 97
Bulletin of the United Bible Societies, 98
Bulletin on Islam and Chris.-Musl. Relations in Africa, 315
Bulletin signaletique, 5
Buried History, 99
Call to Growth Ministry, 260
Calvin Theological Journal, 145
Canadian Catholic Review, 146
Canon Law Abstracts, 6
Catechist, 261
Catena, 147
Catholic Biblical Quarterly, 100
Catholic Digest, 148
Catholic Historical Review, 126
Catholic Theol. Soc. of Amer. Proceedings, 149
Chicago Studies, 200
Ching Feng, 297
Christ to the World, 150
Christian Brethren Review, 151
Christian Century, 201
Christian Education Journal, 262
Christian Jewish Relations, 316
Christian Ministry, 263
Christian Scholar's Review, 298
Christianity and Crisis, 264
Christianity and Literature, 313
Christianity Today, 265
Church, 266
Church History, 127
Churchman, 299
Cistercian Studies, 152
Clergy Review, 267
Concordia Historical Institute Quarterly, 153
Concordia Journal, 154

Concordia Theological Quarterly, 202
Conservative Judaism, 69
Contact, 268
Creation, 39
Criterion, 203
Cross Currents, 44
Dialog, 204
Dialogue: A Journal of Mormon Thought, 324
Divine Life, 52
Downside Review, 155
Durham University Journal, 205
Early American Literature, 128
East Asia Journal of Theology, 206
Eastern Buddhist, 53
Ecumenical Review, 317
Ecumenist, 318
Eglise et theologie, 207
Elenchus Bibliographicus, 7
Elenchus Bibliographicus Biblicus, 8
Encounter, 208
English Historical Review, 129
Ephemerides Theologicae Lovaniensis, 209
Eternity, 210
Evangelical Missions Quarterly, 269
Evangelical Quarterly, 211
Explor, 212
Expository Times, 101
Faith and Philosophy, 213
Faith and Thought, 214
Faith and Thought: The Journal of the Vict. Inst., 310
Fides et Historia, 215
Freethinker, 325
Furrow, 156
Grace Theological Journal, 216
Greek Orthodox Theological Review, 157
Greek, Roman, and Byzantine Studies, 22
Hamdard Islamicus, 323
Harvard Theological Review, 217
Hastings Center Report, 218
Healing Review, 40
Henceforth. . ., 219
Heythrop Journal, 220
Historical Abstracts, 9
Historical Magaz. of the Prot. Episc. Church, 158
History of Religions, 23
Holy Land, 102
Homiletic and Pastoral Review, 270
Horizons, 103
Horizons in Biblical Theology, 104
Horizons: Jrnl. of the Col. Theol. Soc., 159
Humanist, 326
Humanities Index, 10

Hymn, 271
Iliff Review, 221
Indian Journal of Theology, 222
Innes Review, 130
Institute of Archael. Publ., Assyr. Series, 61
International Bibliog. of the Hist. of Religions, 11
International Bulletin of Missionary Research, 272
International Journal for Philosophy of Religion, 223
International Review of Mission, 273
Interpretation: A Journal of Bible and Theology, 105
Iraq, 62
Israel Exploration Journal, 106
Japan Christian Quarterly, 300
Japanese Journal of Religious Studies, 54
Japanese Religions, 55
Jewish Quarterly Review, 70
Journal for the Scientific Study of Religion, 45
Journal for the Study of Judaism, 71
Journal for the Study of the New Testament, 107
Journal for the Study of the Old Testament, 108
Journal of Biblical Literature, 109
Journal of Christian Education, 274
Journal of Church and State, 301
Journal of Dharma, 24
Journal of Ecclesiastical History, 131
Journal of Ecumenical Studies, 319
Journal of Feminist Studies in Religion, 46
Journal of Jewish Studies, 72
Journal of Near Eastern Studies, 63
Journal of Northwest Semitic Languages, 64
Journal of Pastoral Care, 275
Journal of Psychology and Theology, 276
Journal of Reform Judaism, 73
Journal of Religion, 25
Journal of Religion and Health, 47
Journal of Religion and Psychical Research, 41
Journal of Religion in Africa, 36
Journal of Religious Ethics, 48
Journal of Religious History, 132
Journal of Semitic Studies, 65
Journal of Social Philosophy, 224
Journal of the American Academy of Religion, 26
Journal of the American Scientific Affiliation, 311
Journal of the Ancient Near Eastern Society, 66
Journal of the Canadian Church Historical Soc., 133
Journal of the Evangelical Theological Soc., 225
Journal of the Int. Assoc. of Buddhist Studies, 56
Journal of the Interden. Theol. Ctr., 160
Journal of the Moscow Patriarchate, 161
Journal of the United Ref. Church Hist. Soc., 162
Journal of Theological Studies, 110
Journal of Theology for Southern Africa, 226

Joy and Light, 277
Judaism, 74
Katallagete, 302
Latin American Indian Literatures Journal, 37
Leadership, 278
Levant, 111
Lexington Theological Quarterly, 227
Louvain Studies, 163
Lutheran Hist. Conf.: Essays and Reports, 164
Lutheran Theological Journal, 165
LWF Documentation, 166
LWF Report, 167
Mennonite Life, 168
Mennonite Quarterly Review, 169
Methodist History, 170
Mid-Stream, 320
Middle Way, 57
Missiology, 279
Missionalia, 280
Modern Churchman, 228
Modern Judaism, 75
Network, 171
New Blackfriars, 172
New REview, 173
New Testament Abstracts, 12
New Testament Studies, 112
Newsletter (Center for Reformation Research), 134
Newsletter (Christian Brethren Research Fellowship), 174
Newsletter for Targumic and Cognate Studies, 76
Novum Testamentum, 113
Numen, 27
Old Testament Abstracts, 13
One in Christ, 321
Orbit, 175
Orita, 28
Other Side, 303
Pacific Theological Review, 229
Palestine Exploration Quarterly, 67
Pastoral Psychology, 281
Perkins Journal, 230
Philosophy East and West, 58
PMC: Practice of Ministry in Canada, 282
Pope Speaks, 176
Princeton Seminary Bulletin, 231
Printed Lectures, 283
Process Studies, 232
Quaker History, 177
Quaker Religious Thought, 178
Quarterly Review, 284
Radius, 285
RCDA: Religion in Comm. Dominated Areas, 304
Readers' Guide to Periodical Literature, 14

Reconstructionist, 77
Recusant History, 135
Reformed Review, 233
Reformed World, 234
Reformer, 235
Religion, 29
Religion and Literature, 314
Religion in Communist Lands, 305
Religion in Southern Africa, 30
Religion Index One: Periodicals, 15
Religious and Theological Abstracts, 16
Religious Education, 286
Religious Humanism, 327
Religious Studies, 31
Religious Studies News, 32
Religious Studies Review, 17
Restoration Quarterly, 114
Review and Expositor, 179
Review of Books and Religion, 236
Review of Religious Research, 49
Risk Book Series, 237
SA: Sociological Analysis, 306
Saint Luke's Journal of Theology, 238
Saint Mark's Review, 239
St. Vladimir's Theological Quarterly, 180
Scholars' Choice, 240
Scottish Journal of Religious Studies, 33
Scottish Journal of Theology, 241
Scriptura: Tydskrif vir Bybelkunde, 115
Scripture Bulletin, 116
Search, 287
Searching Together, 181
Second Century, 136
Semeia, 117
Signum, 288
Sikh Courier, 59
Sisters Today, 289
Sixteenth Century Journal, 137
Sobornost, 182
Social Compass, 50
Social Sciences Citation Index, 18
Social Sciences Index, 19
Society of Biblical Literature Sem. Paper Ser., 118
Sojourners, 307
Sophia: A Journal for Discussion in Philos. Theology, 242
Soundings: An Interdisciplinary Journal, 51
Sources from the Ancient Near East, 68
Southern Baptist Periodical Index, 20
Southwestern Journal of Theology, 183
Spectrum, 60
Studia Canonica, 290
Studia Liturgica, 291

Studia Theologica, 119
Studies in Comparative Religion, 34
Studies in Formative Spirituality, 42
Studies in Religion/Sciences religieuses, 35
Tablet, 292
Taiwan Journal of Theology, 243
Themelios, 244
Theologia Evangelica, 245
Theological Education, 293
Theological Markings: A UTS Journal, 246
Theological Studies, 247
Theology, 248
Theology Digest, 249
Theology Today, 250
Theosophist, 43
Thomist, 184
Thought: A Review of Culture and Idea, 308
Tradition, 78
Trinitarian Bible Society Quarterly Record, 120
Trinity Journal, 251
Trinity Seminary Review, 185
Tyndale Bulletin, 252
Union Seminary Quarterly Review, 253
United Evangelical Action, 309
U. S. Catholic Historian, 186
USPG Yearbook, 187
Vetus Testamentum, 121
Vox Evangelica, 254
Way, 255
Wesleyan Theoloogical Journal, 188
Westminster Theological Journal, 256
Witness, 189
Word and Spirit: A Monastic Review, 257
Word in Action: The Bible in the World, 122
World Order: A Baha'i Magazine, 328
Worship, 294
Young Life Guard, 295
Zygon, 312

Publisher Index

References are to item entry numbers, not page numbers

ABC-Clio
America: History and Life, 1
Historical Abstracts, 9
Academic Press
Religion, 29
Academy of Religion and Psychical Research
Journal of Religion and Psychical Research, 41
AMECEA Pastoral Institute
AFER: African Ecclesial Review, 296
America
America, 258
American Baptist Historical Society
American Baptist Quarterly, 138
American Benedictine Review
American Benedictine Review, 139
American Bible Society
American Bible Society Record, 79
American Historical Association
American Historical Review, 123
American Humanist Association
Humanist, 326
American Jewish Congress
Judaism, 74
American Schools of Oriental Research
American Schools of Oriental Research Newsletter, 80
Biblical Archaeologist, 93
American Soc. for Social Philosophy & Philosophical Theology
American Journal of Theology and Philosophy, 191
American Society of Church History
Church History, 127

American Society of Missiology
Missiology, 279
American Theological Library Association
Religion Index One: Periodicals, 30
Ancient Near Eastern Society
Journal of the Ancient Near Eastern Society, 66
Andrews University Press
Andrews Univ. Monogr.: Studies in Religion, 192
Andrews Univ. Sem. Doctoral Diss. Ser., 193
Institute of Archael. Publ., Assyr. Series, 61
Anglican Theological Review
Anglican Theological Review, 195
Archaeological Institute of America
American Journal of Archaeology, 124
Association for the Study of Religion
Religion in Southern Africa, 30
Association for Theological Education in South East Asia
East Asia Journal of Theology, 206
Association of Theological Schools
Theological Education, 293
Augustijns Historisch Instituut
Augustiniana, 197
Augustinian Institute
Augustinian Studies, 196
Australian Institute of Archaeology
Buried History, 99
Australian Teachers' Christian Fellowship
Journal of Christian Education, 274
Bangalore Theological Forum
Bangalore Theological Forum, 198
Baptist Historical Society
Baptist Quarterly, 142
Baptist World Alliance
Baptist World, 143
Baylor University
Conference on Christianity and Literature
Christianity and Literature, 313
Berkshire Christian College
Henceforth. . ., 219
Bethany Fellowship
Journal of the Evangelical Theological Soc., 225
Bethel College
David A. Haury
Mennonite Life, 168
Bible Advocate Press
Bible Advocate, 82
Bible Collectors' World
Bible Collectors' World, 84
Bible Society
Word in Action: The Bible in the World, 122
Biblical Archaeology Society
Bible Review, 86

Biblical Institute Press
Biblica, 92
Biola University
Rosemead School of Psychology
Journal of Psychology and Theology, 276
Board of Publications (Christian Reformed Church)
Calvin Theological Journal, 145
Brethren Press
Brethren Life and Thought, 144
British School of Archaeology in Iraq
Iraq, 62
British School of Archaeology in Jerusalem
Levant, 111
British Wheel of Yoga
Spectrum, 60
Buddhist Society
Middle Way, 57
Cambridge University Press
Journal of Ecclesiastical History, 131
New Testament Studies, 112
Religious Studies, 31
Canadian Catholic Review Corporation
Canadian Catholic Review, 146
Canadian Church Historical Society
Journal of the Canadian Church Historical Soc., 133
Canon Law Society
Canon Law Abstracts, 6
Catechist (Peter Li)
Catechist, 261
Catenian Association
Catena, 147
Catholic Biblical Association
Catholic Biblical Quarterly, 100
Old Testament Abstracts, 13
Catholic Biblical Association of Great Britain
Scripture Bulletin, 116
Catholic Media Office
Signum, 288
Catholic Polls
Homiletic and Pastoral Review, 270
Catholic Record Society
Recusant History, 135
Catholic Theological Society of America
Catholic Theol. Soc. of Amer. Proceedings, 149
Catholic University of America Press
Catholic Historical Review, 126
Center for Process Studies
Process Studies, 232
Center for Reformation Research
Newsletter, 134
Central Conference of American Rabbis
Journal of Reform Judaism, 73

Centre de documentation sciences humaines
Bulletin signaletique, 5
Centre de recherches socio-religieuses
Social Compass, 50
Centre for the Study of Islam and Christian-Muslim Relations
Bulletin on Islam and Chris.-Musl. Relations in Africa, 315
Christ to the World
Christ to the World, 150
Christian Brethren Research Fellowship
Newsletter, 174
Christian Century Foundation
Christian Century, 201
Christian Ministry, 263
Christian Scholar's Review
Christian Scholar's Review, 298
Christian Theological Seminary
Encounter, 208
Christianity and Crisis
Christianity and Crisis, 264
Christianity Today
Christianity Today, 265
Leadership, 278
Church Society
Churchman, 299
Cisterciensia
Cistercian Studies, 152
Civitas Dei Foundation
Chicago Studies, 200
College of St. Thomas
Catholic Digest, 148
Concordia Historical Institute
Archives and History, 125
Concordia Historical Institute Quarterly, 153
Concordia Theological Seminary
Concordia Theological Quarterly, 202
Conference on Faith and History
Fides et Historia, 215
Conococheague Associates
Anima: An Experiential Journal, 38
Contact Pastoral Limited
Contact, 268
Convergence
Cross Currents, 44
Council of Societies for the Study of Religion
Religious Studies Review, 17
Council on Christian Unity of the Christian Church
Mid-Stream, 320
Dallas Theological Seminary
Bibliotheca Sacra, 199
Deakin University
School of Humanities
Sophia, 242

Dharma Research Association
  Journal of Dharma, 24
Dialog
  Dialog, 204
Dialogue Foundation
  Dialogue: A Journal of Mormon Thought, 324
Divine Life Society
  Divine Life, 52
Downside Review
  Downside Review, 155
Duke University
  Greek, Roman, and Byzantine Studies, 22
E. J. Brill
  International Bibliog. of the Hist. of Religions, 11
  Journal for the Study of Judaism, 71
  Journal of Religion in Africa, 36
  Novum Testamentum, 113
  Numen, 27
  Vetus Testamentum, 121
Editions Peeter
  Ephemerides Theologicae Lovaniensis, 209
English Dominicans
  New Blackfriars, 172
Episcopal Church Publishing Co.
  Witness, 189
Evangelical Ministries
  Eternity, 210
Evangelical Missions Information Service
  Evangelical Missions Quarterly, 269
Federation of Reconstructionist Congregations and Havurot
  Reconstructionist, 77
Fellowship for Biblical Studies
  Australian Biblical Review, 81
Fellowship of Religious Humanists
  Religious Humanism, 327
Fellowship of St. Alban and St. Sergius
  Sobornost, 182
First Baptist Church of Montclair
  Faith and Thought, 214
Fordham University Press
  Thought: A Review of Culture and Idea, 308
Franciscan Printing Press
  Holy Land, 102
Friends Historical Association
  Quaker History, 177
Friends of Creation Spirituality
  Creation, 39
Furrow Trust
  Furrow, 156
G. W. Foote and Company
  Freethinker, 325

Garrett-Evangelical Theological Seminary
Explor, 212
General Commission on Archives and History of the United Methodist Church
Methodist History, 170
Geneva College
Latin American Indian Literatures Journal, 37
Grace Theological Seminary
Grace Theological Journal, 216
H. W. Wilson Co.
Humanities Index, 10
Readers' Guide to Periodical Literature, 14
Social Sciences Index, 19
Hamdard Foundation Press
Hamdard Islamicus, 323
Hastings Center
Hastings Center Report, 218
Henry Martyn Institute
Bulletin of Christian Inst. of Islamic Stud., 322
Hershel Shanks
Biblical Archaeology Review, 94
Heythrop Journal
Heythrop Journal, 220
Historical Commission of the Southern Baptist Convention
Baptist History and Heritage, 141
Southern Baptist Periodical Index, 20
Historical Society of the Episcopal Church
Historical Magaz. of the Prot. Episc. Church, 158
Holy Cross Orthodox Press
Greek Orthodox Theological Review, 157
Human Sciences Press
Pastoral Psychology, 281
Hymn Society of America
Hymn, 271
Iliff School of Theology
Iliff Review, 221
Indian Journal of Theology
Indian Journal of Theology, 222
Institute for Scientific Information
Arts and Humanities Citation Index, 3
Social Sciences Citation Index, 18
Institute of Formative Spirituality
Studies in Formative Spirituality, 42
Institute of Jewish Affairs
Christian Jewish Relations, 316
Institutes of Religion and Health
Journal of Religion and Health, 47
Inter-varsity Press
Tyndale Bulletin, 252
Interdenominational Theological Center
Journal of the Interden. Theol. Ctr., 160
International Association of Buddhist Studies
Journal of the Int. Assoc. of Buddhist Studies, 56

International Bible Society
BibleWorld, 91
Israel Exploration Society
Israel Exploration Journal, 106
J. G. Roberts
Joy and Light, 277
Young Life Guard, 295
J. M. Dawson Institute of Church-State Studies
Journal of Church and State, 301
Japan Christian Quarterly
Japan Christian Quarterly, 300
Jewish Quarterly Review
Jewish Quarterly Review, 70
John Rylands University Library
Bulletin of John Rylands Univ. Lib. of Manchester, 97
Johns Hopkins University Press
Modern Judaism, 75
Joint Publication Board
Zygon, 312
Journal of Ecumenical Studies
Journal of Ecumenical Studies, 319
JSOT Press
Journal for the Study of the New Testament, 107
Journal for the Study of the Old Testament, 108
Katallagete
Katallagete, 302
Keston College
Religion in Communist Lands, 305
Kutztown Publishing Co.
Journal of Pastoral Care, 275
Leslie Hoppe
Biblical Research, 95
Lexington Theological Seminary
Lexington Theological Quarterly, 227
Liturgical Ecumenical Center Trust
Studia Liturgica, 291
Liturgical Press
Bible Today, 87
Sisters Today, 289
Longman Group
English Historical Review, 129
Lutheran Historical Conference
Lutheran Hist. Conf.: Essays and Reports, 164
Lutheran Liturgical Renewal
Bride of Christ, 259
Lutheran Publishing House
Lutheran Theological Journal, 165
Lutheran World Federation
LWF Documentation, 166
LWF Report, 167
Martinus Nijhoff Publishers
International Journal for Philosophy of Religion, 223

Mennonite Historical Society
  Mennonite Quarterly Review, 169
Mercer University
  Second Century, 136
Mills Litho
  Journal of Theology for Southern Africa, 226
Modern Churchmen's Union
  Modern Churchman, 228
Monks of St. John's Abbey
  Worship, 294
Moskovskaya Patriarkhiya Novodevichii pr
  Journal of the Moscow Patriarchate, 161
Nanzan Institute for Religion and Culture
  Japanese Journal of Religious Studies, 54
National Association of Evangelicals
  United Evangelical Action, 309
National Catechetical Association
  New REview, 173
National Conference of Religious Vocational Directors
  Call to Growth Ministry, 260
National Federation of Spiritual Healers
  Healing Review, 40
National Pastoral Life Center
  Church, 266
National Spiritual Assembly of the Baha'is of the U. S
  World Order: A Baha'i Magazine, 328
NCC Center for the Study of Japanese Religions
  Japanese Religions, 55
North American Society for Social Philosophy
  Journal of Social Philosophy, 224
One in Christ
  One in Christ, 321
Osterhus Publishing House
  Bible Friend, 85
Other Side
  Other Side, 303
Our Sunday Visitor
  Pope Speaks, 176
Overseas Ministries Study Center
  International Bulletin of Missionary Research, 272
Ovid Bell Press
  Concordia Journal, 154
Oxford Centre for Postgraduate Hebrew Studies
  Journal of Jewish Studies, 72
Oxford University Press
  Journal of Semitic Studies, 65
  Journal of Theological Studies, 110
P. Macaulife
  Printed Lectures, 283
Palestine Exploration Fund
  Palestine Exploration Quarterly, 67
Paternoster Press

Christian Brethren Review, 151
Evangelical Quarterly, 211

Faith and Thought: The Journal of Vict. Inst., 310
Vox Evangelica, 254
Paulist Press
Ecumenist, 318
Perennial Books
Studies in Comparative Religion, 34
Perkins School of Theology
Perkins Journal, 230
Pittsburgh Theological Seminary
Horizions in Biblical Theology, 104
PMC Board of Directors
PMC: Practice of Ministry in Canada, 282
Pontifical Institute
Elenchus Bibliographicus Biblicus, 8
Protestant Alliance
Reformer, 235
Quaker Religious Thought
Quaker Religious Thought, 178
Rabbinical Assembly/Jewish Theological Seminary of America
Conservative Judaism, 69
Rabbinical Council of America
Tradition, 78
Radius
Radius, 285
Religious and Theological Abstracts
Religious and Theological Abstracts, 16
Religious Education Association of the U. S. and Canada
Religious Education, 286
Religious Research Association
Review of Religious Research, 49
Research Ctr. for Relig. & Human Rights in Closed Societies
RCDA: Religion in Comm. Dominated Areas, 304
Restoration Quarterly Journal
Restoration Quarterly, 114
Review and Expositor
Review and Expositor, 179
Review of Books
Review of Books and Religion, 236
Saint Bede's Publications
Word and Spirit: A Monastic Review, 257
Saint John's University
Theology Dept.
Biblical Theology Bulletin, 96
Saint Louis University
Theology Digest, 249
Saint Mark's Library
Saint Mark's Review, 239
Saint Patrick's College
Australasian Catholic Record, 140

Saint Paul University
Eglise et theologie, 207
Faculty of Canon Law
Studia Canonica, 290
Saint Thomas Apostolic Seminary
Biblebhashyam, 90
Saint Vladimir's Orthodox Theological Seminary
St. Vladimir's Theological Quarterly, 180
San Francisco Theological Seminary
Pacific Theological Review, 229
Scholars Press
Eastern Buddhist, 53
Harvard Theological Review, 217
Journal of Biblical Literature, 109
Journal of Feminist Studies in Religion, 46
Journal of the American Academy of Religion, 26
Religious Studies News, 32
Semeia, 117
Society of Biblical Literature Sem. Paper Ser., 118
Scottish Academic Press
Scottish Journal of Theology, 241
Scottish Catholic Historical Association
Innes Review, 130
Scripture Gift Mission
Horizons, 103
Scripture Press Ministries
Christian Education Journal, 262
Senate of the University of Durham
Durham University Journal, 205
Seventh-day Adventist Theol. Sem. of Andrews University
Andrews University Seminary Studies, 194
Sikh Cultural Society of Great Britain
Sikh Courier, 59
Sixteenth Century Journal Publishers
Sixteenth Century Journal, 137
Society for the Scientific Study of Religion
Journal for the Scientific Study of Religion, 45
Society of Christian Philosophers
Faith and Philosophy, 213
Sojourners
Sojourners, 307
South African Missiological Society
Missionalia, 280
Southwestern Baptist Theological Seminary
School of Theology
Southwestern Journal of Theology, 183
SPCK
Theology, 248
Sydney University Press
Journal of Religious History, 132

T. and T. Clark
Expository Times, 101
Tablet Publishing Company
Clergy Review, 267
Tablet, 292
Taiwan Theological College
Taiwan Journal of Theology, 243
Tanzania Litho
Africa Theological Journal, 190
Tao Fong Shan Ecumenical Centre
Ching Feng, 297
Theological Sem. of the United Presb. Church at Princeton
Princeton Seminary Bulletin, 231
Theological Studies
Theological Studies, 247
Theology Today
Theology Today, 250
Theosophical Publishing House
Theosophist, 43
Thomist Press
Thomist, 184
Trinitarian Bible Society
Trinitarian Bible Society Quarterly Record, 120
Trinity Evangelical Divinity School
Trinity Journal, 251
Trinity Lutheran Seminary
Trinity Seminary Review, 185
Undena Publications
Sources from the Ancient Near East, 68
Union Theological Seminary
Union Seminary Quarterly Review, 253
Union Theological Seminary in Virginia
Interpretation: A Journal of Bible and Theology, 105
Library
Scholars' Choice, 240
United Bible Societies
Bible Translator: Practical Papers, 88
Bible Translator: Technical Papers, 89
Bulletin of the United Bible Societies, 98
United Methodist Publishing House
Quarterly Review, 284
United Reformed Church History Society
Journal of the United Ref. Church Hist. Soc., 162
United Society for the Propogation of the Gospel
Network, 171
Orbit, 175
USPG Yearbook, 187
United States Catholic Historical Society
U. S. Catholic Historian, 186
United Theological Seminary of the Twin Cities
Theological Markings: A UTS Journal, 246

Universite Catholique de Louvain
  Elenchus Bibliographicus, 7
Universitetsforlaget
  Studia Theologica, 119
Universities and Colleges Christian Fellowship
  Themelios, 244
University of Chicago Divinity School
  Criterion, 203
University of Chicago Press
  History of Religions, 23
  Journal of Near Eastern Studies, 63
  Journal of Religion, 25
University of Connecticut
  SA: Sociological Analysis, 306
University of Hawaii Press
  Philosophy East and West, 58
University of Ibadan
  Dept. of Religious Studies
    Orita, 28
University of Louvain
  Faculty of Theology
    Louvain Studies, 163
University of North Carolina Press
  Early American Literature, 128
University of Notre Dame
  English Department
    Religion and Literature, 314
University of Notre Dame Press
  Journal of Religious Ethics, 48
University of Pennsylvania (trustees)
  American Quarterly, 21
University of South Africa
  Theologia Evangelica, 245
University of Stellenbosch
  Department of Semitic Languages
    Journal of Northwest Semitic Languages, 64
  Dept. of Biblical Studies
    Scriptura: Tydskrif vir Bybelkunde, 115
University of Stirling
  Scottish Journal of Religious Studies, 33
University of Tennessee
  Soundings: An Interdisciplinary Journal, 51
University of the South
  School of Theology
    Saint Luke's Journal of Theology, 238
University of Toronto
  Department of Near Eastern Studies
    Newsletter for Targumic and Cognate Studies, 76
Villanova University
  Horizons: Jrnl. of the Col. Theol. Soc., 159
Walter de Gruyter
  Bibliographia Patristica, 4

Way Publications
Way, 255
Wesleyan Theological Society
Wesleyan Theological Journal, 188
Western Theological Seminary
Reformed Review, 233
Westminster Theological Seminary
Westminster Theological Journal, 256
Weston School of Theology
New Testament Abstracts, 12
Whitston Publishing Co.
American Humanities Index, 2
Wilbur Bullock
Journal of the American Scientific Affiliation, 311
Wilfrid Laurier University Press
Studies in Religion/Sciences religieuses, 35
Word of Life Church
Searching Together, 181
Word of Truth Productions
Bible and Spade, 83
World Alliance of Reformed Churches
Reformed World, 234
World Council of Churches
Ecumenical Review, 317
International Review of Mission, 273
World Council of Churches Publications
Risk Book Series, 237
Young Searchers League
Search, 287

Subject Index

References are to item entry numbers, not page numbers.

Africa
  Religion
    AFER: African Ecclesial Review, 296
    Africa Theological Journal, 190
Archaeology
  American Journal of Archaeology, 124
Atheism
  Freethinker, 325
Australia
  Religion
    Journal of Religious History, 132
Baha'is
  World Order: A Baha'i Magazine, 328
Baptists
  Baptist World, 143
  Review and Expositor, 179
  Searching Together, 94
  Doctrines
    Review and Expositor, 179
    Southwestern Journal of Theology, 183
  History
    American Baptist Quarterly, 138
    Baptist History and Heritage, 141
    Baptist Quarterly, 142
Bible
  Archaeology
    American Schools of Oriental Research Newsletter, 80
    Bible and Spade, 83
    Biblical Archaeologist, 93
    Biblical Archaeology Review, 94

Buried History, 99
Holy Land, 102
Israel Exploration Journal, 106
Levant, 111
Criticism and interpretation
Australian Biblical Review, 81
Bible Advocate, 82
Bible Friend, 85
Bible Review, 86
Bible Today, 87
Biblebhashyam, 90
Biblica, 92
Biblical Research, 95
Biblical Theology Bulletin, 96
Bulletin of John Rylands Univ. Lib. of Manchester, 97
Catholic Biblical Quarterly, 100
Evangelical Quarterly, 211
Expository Times, 101
Holy Land, 102
Horizons in Biblical Theology, 104
Interpretation: A Journal of Bible and Theology, 105
Journal of Biblical Literature, 109
Journal of Theological Studies, 110
Restoration Quarterly, 114
Scriptura: Tydskrif vir Bybelkunde, 115
Scripture Bulletin, 116
Semeia, 117
Society of Biblical Literature Sem. Paper Ser., 118
Studia Theologica, 119
New Testament
Criticism and interpretation
Journal for the Study of the New Testament, 107
New Testament Studies, 112
Novum Testamentum, 113
Old Testament
Criticism and interpretation
Journal for the Study of the Old Testament, 108
Vetus Testamentum, 121
Study and teaching
Word in Action: The Bible in the World, 122
Theology
Biblical Theology Bulletin, 96
Interpretation: A Journal of Bible and Theology, 105
Journal of Theological Studies, 110
Translation
American Bible Society Record, 79
Bible Collectors' World, 84
Bible Translator: Practical Papers, 88
Bible Translator: Technical Papers, 89
BibleWorld, 91
Bulletin of the United Bible Societies, 98

Horizons, 103
Trinitarian Bible Society Quarterly Record, 120
Word in Action: The Bible in the World, 122
Bio-ethics
Hastings Center Report, 218
Brethren
Christian Brethren Review, 151
Newsletter (Christian Brethren Research Fellowship), 174
History
Brethren Life and Thought, 144
Buddhism
Eastern Buddhist, 53
Journal of the Int. Assoc. of Buddhist Studies, 56
Middle Way, 57
Canada
Religion
Journal of the Canadian Church Historical Soc., 133
Catholic Church
Canadian Catholic Review, 146
Christ to the World, 150
Clergy Review, 267
Downside Review, 155
Horizons: Jrnl. of the Col. Theol. Soc., 159
New Blackfriars, 172
New REview, 173
U. S. Catholic Historian, 186
Worship, 294
Congresses
Catholic Theol. Soc. of Amer. Proceedings, 149
Controversial literature
Reformer, 235
Doctrines
Australasian Catholic Record, 140
Catholic Theol. Soc. of Amer. Proceedings, 149
Eglise et theologie, 207
Ephemerides Theologicae Lovaniensis, 209
Furrow, 156
Homiletic and Pastoral Review, 270
Louvain Studies, 163
Pope Speaks, 176
Studia Canonica, 290
Thomist, 184
England
Recusant History, 135
History
American Benedictine Review, 139
Catholic Historical Review, 126
Cistercian Studies, 152
U. S. Catholic Historian, 186
Popular works
Catholic Digest, 148

Religious education
Chicago Studies, 200
Scotland
Innes Review, 130
Study and teaching
Catechist, 261
China
Religion
Ching Feng, 297
Christian ethics
Journal of Religious Ethics, 48
Christian theology
American Journal of Theology and Philosophy, 191
Andrews Univ. Monogr.: Studies in Religion, 192
Andrews Univ. Sem. Doctoral Diss. Ser., 193
Andrews University Seminary Studies, 194
Anglican Theological Review, 195
Augustinian Studies, 196
Augustiniana, 197
Bangalore Theological Forum, 198
Bibliotheca Sacra, 199
Christian Century, 201
Criterion, 203
Dialog, 204
Durham University Journal, 205
East Asia Journal of Theology, 206
Eglise et theologie, 207
Encounter, 208
Ephemerides Theologicae Lovaniensis, 209
Eternity, 210
Evangelical Quarterly, 211
Explor, 212
Faith and Philosophy, 213
Faith and Thought, 214
Fides et Historia, 215
Grace Theological Journal, 216
Harvard Theological Review, 217
Henceforth. . ., 219
Iliff Review, 221
Indian Journal of Theology, 222
Journal of the Evangelical Theological Soc., 225
Journal of Theology for Southern Africa, 226
Lexington Theological Quarterly, 227
Modern Churchman, 228
Pacific Theological Review, 229
Perkins Journal, 230
Princeton Seminary Bulletin, 231
Process Studies, 232
Reformed Review, 233
Reformed World, 234
Reformer, 235

Review of Books and Religion, 236
Risk Book Series, 237
Saint Luke's Journal of Theology, 238
Saint Mark's Review, 239
Scottish Journal of Theology, 241
Sophia, 242
Taiwan Journal of Theology, 243
Themelios, 244
Theologia Evangelica, 245
Theological Markings: A UTS Journal, 246
Theological Studies, 247
Theology, 248
Theology Digest, 249
Theology Today, 250
Trinity Journal, 251
Tyndale Bulletin, 252
Union Seminary Quarterly Review, 253
Vox Evangelica, 254
Way, 255
Westminster Theological Journal, 256
History
Word and Spirit: A Monastic Review, 257
Christianity
Catena, 147
Searching Together, 181
Afro-Americans
Journal of the Interden. Theol. Ctr., 160
Australia
Journal of Religious History, 132
Bibliography
Scholars' Choice, 240
Canada
Journal of the Canadian Church Historical Soc., 133
England
Journal of Religious History, 132
History
American Historical Review, 123
Archives and History, 125
Church History, 127
Journal of Ecclesiastical History, 131
Early church
Second Century, 136
Reformation
Newsletter (Center for Reformation Res.), 134
Sixteenth Century Journal, 137
Japan
Japanese Religions, 55
Juvenile literature
Orbit, 175
Young Life Guard, 295

- Missions
  - Evangelical Missions Quarterly, 269
  - International Bulletin of Missionary Research, 272
  - International Review of Mission, 273
  - Missiology, 279
  - Missionalia, 280
  - USPG Yearbook, 187
- Music
  - Hymn, 271
- Southeast Asia
  - East Asia Journal of Theology, 206
- Study and teaching
  - Christian Education Journal, 262
  - Religious Education, 286
  - Theological Education, 293
  - Juvenile literature
    - Search, 287

Christianity and culture
- Africa Theological Journal, 190
- Ching Feng, 297
- Japan Christian Quarterly, 300

Christianity and education
- Journal of Christian Education, 274

Christianity and literature
- Christianity and Literature, 313
- Early American Literature, 128
- Religion and Literature, 314

Christianity and other religions
- Cross Currents, 44
- Islam
  - Bull. on Islam & Chris.-Musl. Relat. in Africa, 315
- Judaism
  - Christian Jewish Relations, 316

Christianity and philosophy
- American Journal of Theology and Philosophy, 191
- Faith and Philosophy, 213
- Heythrop Journal, 220
- Sophia, 242

Christianity and science
- Faith and Thought: The Jrnl. of the Vict. Inst, 310
- Journal of the American Scientific Affiliation, 311
- Zygon, 312

Christianity and society
- AFER: African Ecclesial Review, 296
- America, 258
- Christian Scholar's Review, 298
- Christianity and Crisis, 264
- Christianity Today, 265
- Eternity, 210
- Explor, 212
- Journal of Church and State, 301

Joy and Light, 277
Katallagete, 302
Modern Churchman, 228
New Blackfriars, 172
Other Side, 303
RCDA: Religion in Comm. Dominated Areas, 304
Religion in Communist Lands, 305
SA: Sociological Analysis, 306
Saint Luke's Journal of Theology, 238
Signum, 288
Sojourners, 307
Thought: A Review of Culture and Idea, 308
Union Seminary Quarterly Review, 253
United Evangelical Action, 309
Witness, 189
Church of England
Missions
Network, 171
Disciples of Christ
Lexington Theological Quarterly, 227
Early Christian literature
Second Century, 136
Eastern religions
Philosophy East and West, 58
Ecumenism
Ecumenical Review, 317
Ecumenist, 318
Journal of Ecumenical Studies, 319
Mid-Stream, 320
One in Christ, 321
England
Religion
Baptist Quarterly, 142
Downside Review, 155
English Historical Review, 129
Journal of Religious History, 132
Recusant History, 135
Episcopal Church
History
Historical Magaz. of the Prot. Episc. Church, 158
Ethics
Hastings Center Report, 218
Religious aspects
Journal of Religious Ethics, 48
Faith healing
Healing Review, 40
Health
Religious aspects
Journal of Religion and Health, 47
Hinduism
Divine Life, 52

History of religions
American Journal of Archaeology, 124
American Quarterly, 21
Greek, Roman, and Byzantine Studies, 22
History of Religions, 23
Journal of Dharma, 24
Journal of Religion, 25
Journal of the American Academy of Religion, 26
Numen, 27
Orita, 28
Religion, 29
Religion in Southern Africa, 30
Religious Studies, 31
Religious Studies News, 32
Scottish Journal of Religious Studies, 33
Studies in Comparative Religion, 34
Studies in Religion/Sciences religieuses, 35
Humanism
Freethinker, 325
Humanist, 326
Religious Humanism, 327
Indexes and abstracts
America: History and Life, 1
American Humanities Index, 2
Arts and Humanities Citation Index, 3
Bibliographia Patristica, 4
Bulletin signaletique, 5
Canon Law Abstracts, 6
Elenchus Bibliographicus, 7
Elenchus Bibliographicus Biblicus, 8
Historical Abstracts, 9
Humanities Index, 10
International Bibliog. of the Hist. of Religions, 11
New Testament Abstracts, 12
Old Testament Abstracts, 13
Readers' Guide to Periodical Literature, 14
Religion Index One: Periodicals, 15
Religious and Theological Abstracts, 16
Religious Studies Review, 17
Social Sciences Citation Index, 18
Social Sciences Index, 19
Southern Baptist Periodical Index, 20
India
Religion
Divine Life, 52
Indian Journal of Theology, 222
Irag
Religion
History
Iraq, 62
Islam
Bulletin of Christian Inst. of Islamic Stud., 322

Hamdard Islamicus, 323
Islam and other religions
Christianity
Bull. on Islam & Chris.-Musl. Relations in Arica, 315
Japan
Religion
Japanese Journal of Religious Studies, 54
Japanese Religions, 55
Judaism
Conservative Judaism, 69
Jewish Quarterly Review, 70
Journal of Jewish Studies, 72
Journal of Reform Judaism, 73
Judaism, 74
Modern Judaism, 75
Reconstructionist, 77
History
Journal for the Study of Judaism, 71
Newsletter for Targumic and Cognate Studies, 76
Orthodox
Tradition, 78
Judaism and other religions
Christianity
Christian Jewish Relations, 316
Judaism and society
Judaism, 74
Liturgy and worship
Bride of Christ, 259
Hymn, 271
Studia Liturgica, 291
Worship, 294
Lutheran Church
Concordia Journal, 154
Dialog, 204
Lutheran Hist. Conf.: Essays and Reports, 164
LWF Documentation, 166
LWF Report, 167
Trinity Seminary Review, 185
Doctrines
Africa Theological Journal, 190
Concordia Theological Quarterly, 202
Lutheran Theological Journal, 165
History
Concordia Historical Institute Quarterly, 153
Mennonites
Mennonite Life, 168
Mennonite Quarterly Review, 169
Methodist Church
Doctrines
Wesleyan Theological Journal, 188

History
Methodist History, 170
Monasticism
American Benedictine Review, 139
Cistercian Studies, 152
Mormons
Dialogue: A Journal of Mormon Thought, 324
Near Eastern religions
Institute of Archael. Publ. Assyr. Series, 61
Journal of Near Eastern Studies, 63
Journal of Northwest Semitic Languages, 64
Journal of the Ancient Near Eastern Society, 66
Palestine Exploration Quarterly, 67
Sources
Sources from the Ancient Near East, 68
Orthodox Church
Doctrines
Greek Orthodox Theological Review, 157
Sobornost, 182
St. Vladimir's Theological Quarterly, 93
History
Greek Orthodox Theological Review, 157
St. Vladimir's Theological Quarterly, 180
Sobornost, 182
Practical theology
Call to Growth Ministry, 260
Christian Ministry, 263
Church, 266
Clergy Review, 267
Contact, 268
Journal of Pastoral Care, 275
Journal of Psychology and Theology, 276
Leadership, 278
Pastoral Psychology, 281
PMC: Practice of Ministry in Canada, 282
Quarterly Review, 284
Signum, 288
Sisters Today, 289
Tablet, 292
Primal religions
Journal of Religion in Africa, 36
Latin American Indian Literatures Journal, 37
Process theology
Process Studies, 232
Protestant churches
Doctrines
Churchman, 299
Quakers
Doctrines
Quaker Religious Thought, 178

History
Quaker History, 177
Reconstructionism
Reconstructionist, 77
Reformed Church
Calvin Theological Journal, 145
History
Journal of the United Ref. Church Hist. Soc., 162
Religion
Psychological aspects
Journal of Religion and Psychical Research, 41
Religion and drama
Radius, 285
Religion and health
Journal of Religion and Health, 47
Religion and philosophy
Cross Currents, 44
International Journal for Philosophy of Religion, 223
Journal of Social Philosophy, 224
Religion and psychology
Printed Lectures, 283
Religion and society
Cross Currents, 44
Journal for the Scientific Study of Religion, 45
Journal of Feminist Studies in Religion, 46
Journal of Religion and Health, 47
Journal of Religious Ethics, 48
Review of Religious Research, 49
Social Compass, 50
Soundings: An Interdisciplinary Journal, 51
Religion and women
Journal of Feminist Studies in Religion, 46
Religious education
New REview, 173
Scotland
Religion
Innes Review, 130
Semitic languages
Journal of Northwest Semitic Languages, 64
Journal of Semitic Studies, 65
Semitic literature
Journal of Semitic Studies, 65
Seventh Day Adventists
Henceforth. . ., 219
Sikhism
Sikh Courier, 59
South Africa
Religion
Religion in Southern Africa, 30

Soviet Union
   Religion
      Journal of the Moscow Patriarchate, 161
Spiritualism
   Anima: An Experiential Journal, 38
   Creation, 39
   Healing Review, 40
   Journal of Religion and Psychical Research, 41
   Studies in Formative Spirituality, 42
   Theosophist, 43
Targums
   Newsletter for Targumic and Cognate Studies, 76
Theosophy
   Theosophist, 43
United States
   Religion
      American Baptist Quarterly, 138
      American Benedictine Review, 139
      Brethren Life and Thought, 144
      Concordia Historical Institute Quarterly, 153
      Concordia Journal, 154
      Early American Literature, 128
      Journal of the Interden. Theol. Ctr., 160
Yoga
   Spectrum, 60

Audience Index

References are to item entry numbers, not page numbers.

AC
American Benedictine Review, 139
American Journal of Archaeology, 124
American Journal of Theology and Philosophy, 191
Augustiniana, 197
Bibliographia Patristica, 4
Eglise et theologie, 207
Elenchus Bibliographicus Biblicus, 7
Ephemerides Theologicae Lovaniensis, 209
Harvard Theological Review, 217
International Journal for Philosophy of Religion, 223
Journal for the Scientific Study of Religion, 45
Journal for the Study of the New Testament, 107
Journal of Biblical Literature, 109
Journal of Feminist Studies in Religion, 46
Journal of Northwest Semitic Languages, 64
Journal of Religion, 25
Journal of the American Academy of Religion, 26
Journal of the Canadian Church Historical Soc., 133
Journal of Theological Studies, 110
Novum Testamentum, 113
Numen, 27
Orita, 28
Quaker History, 177
Religious and Theological Abstracts, 16
Religious Studies, 31
Religious Studies Review, 17
Scottish Journal of Theology, 241
Semeia, 117
Social Compass, 50

Society of Biblical Literature Sem. Paper Ser., 118
Soundings: An Interdisciplinary Journal, 51
Trinity Journal, 251
Tyndale Bulletin, 252
Vetus Testamentum, 121
AC GP
Indian Journal of Theology, 222
Journal of Christian Education, 274
Lexington Theological Quarterly, 227
Religious Humanism, 327
Restoration Quarterly, 114
AC GP HS SP UndSt
Mennonite Life, 168
Saint Mark's Review, 239
AC GP HS UndSt
Furrow, 156
AC GP SP
Anima: An Experiential Journal, 38
Arts and Humanities Citation Index, 3
Bible Review, 86
Biblical Archaeologist, 93
Brethren Life and Thought, 144
Christian Brethren Review, 151
Christianity and Crisis, 264
Church History, 127
Churchman, 299
Faith and Thought, 214
Faith and Thought: The Journal of the Vict. Inst., 310
Grace Theological Journal, 216
Humanities Index, 10
Japanese Religions, 55
New Blackfriars, 172
Old Testament Abstracts, 13
Pacific Theological Review, 229
Religion Index One: Periodicals, 15
Social Sciences Citation Index, 18
Social Sciences Index, 19
Theology Digest, 249
Thought: A Review of Culture and Idea, 308
Worship, 294
AC GP SP UndSt
Baptist Quarterly, 142
Biblical Theology Bulletin, 96
Bulletin of Christian Inst. of Islamic Stud., 322
Concordia Historical Institute Quarterly, 153
English Historical Review, 129
Explor, 212
Greek Orthodox Theological Review, 157
Journal of Social Philosophy, 224
Latin American Indian Literatures Journal, 37

Mennonite Quarterly Review, 169
Other Side, 303
Religion and Literature, 314
Sikh Courier, 59
Union Seminary Quarterly Review, 253
Way, 255
Witness, 189
AC GP UndSt
Christianity and Literature, 313
Holy Land, 102
Searching Together, 181
Sobornost, 182
World Order: A Baha'i Magazine, 328
AC SP
America: History and Life, 1
American Baptist Quarterly, 138
American Historical Review, 123
American Humanities Index, 2
American Quarterly, 21
American Schools of Oriental Research Newsletter, 80
Andrews Univ. Monogr.: Studies in Religion, 192
Andrews Univ. Sem. Doctoral Diss. Ser., 193
Andrews University Seminary Studies, 194
Anglican Theological Review, 195
Augustinian Studies, 196
Bangalore Theological Forum, 198
Baptist History and Heritage, 141
Bible Collectors' World, 84
Bible Translator: Practical Papers, 88
Bible Translator: Technical Papers, 89
Biblica, 92
Biblical Research, 95
Bibliotheca Sacra, 199
Bulletin of John Rylands Univ. Lib. of Manchester, 97
Bulletin on Islam and Chris.-Musl. Relations in Africa, 315
Bulletin signaletique, 5
Calvin Theological Journal, 145
Canon Law Abstracts, 6
Catholic Biblical Quarterly, 100
Catholic Historical Review, 126
Catholic Theol. Soc. of Amer. Proceedings, 149
Christian Century, 201
Christian Jewish Relations, 316
Christian Scholar's Review, 298
Cistercian Studies, 152
Conservative Judaism, 69
Dialog, 204
Dialogue: A Journal of Mormon Thought, 324
Downside Review, 155
East Asia Journal of Theology, 206
Eastern Buddhist, 53

Ecumenist, 318
Elenchus Bibliographicus, 7
Encounter, 208
Evangelical Missions Quarterly, 269
Expository Times, 101
Faith and Philosophy, 213
Greek, Roman, and Byzantine Studies, 22
Hamdard Islamicus, 323
Historical Abstracts, 9
Historical Magaz. of the Prot. Episc. Church, 158
Horizons in Biblical Theology, 104
Horizons: Jrnl. of the Col. Theol. Soc., 159
Hymn, 271
Iliff Review, 221
Innes Review, 130
Institute of Archael. Publ., Assyr. Series, 61
International Bibliog. of the Hist. of Religions, 11
International Bulletin of Missionary Research, 272
International Review of Mission, 273
Interpretation: A Journal of Bible and Theology, 105
Iraq, 62
Israel Exploration Journal, 106
Japanese Journal of Religious Studies, 54
Jewish Quarterly Review, 70
Journal for the Study of Judaism, 71
Journal of Church and State, 301
Journal of Dharma, 24
Journal of Ecclesiastical History, 131
Journal of Ecumenical Studies, 319
Journal of Jewish Studies, 72
Journal of Near Eastern Studies, 63
Journal of Pastoral Care, 275
Journal of Religion in Africa, 36
Journal of the Int. Assoc. of Buddhist Studies, 56
Journal of Theology for Southern Africa, 226
Louvain Studies, 163
Methodist History, 170
Mid-Stream, 320
Middle Way, 57
Missiology, 279
Modern Judaism, 75
New Testament Studies, 112
Newsletter (Center for Reformation Research), 134
Newsletter for Targumic and Cognate Studies, 76
One in Christ, 321
Palestine Exploration Quarterly, 67
Pastoral Psychology, 281
Perkins Journal, 230
Philosophy East and West, 58
Princeton Seminary Bulletin, 231
Process Studies, 232

Recusant History, 135
Religion, 29
Religion in Communist Lands, 305
Religion in Southern Africa, 30
Religious Education, 286
Religious Studies News, 32
Review and Expositor, 179
Review of Religious Research, 49
St. Vladimir's Theological Quarterly, 180
Scholars' Choice, 240
Scripture Bulletin, 116
Sophia, 242
Sources from the Ancient Near East, 68
Southwestern Journal of Theology, 183
Studia Theologica, 119
Studies in Comparative Religion, 34
Studies in Formative Spirituality, 42
Studies in Religion/Sciences religieuses, 35
Theological Education, 293
Theological Markings: A UTS Journal, 246
Theological Studies, 247
Theology Today, 250
Theosophist, 43
Thomist, 184
Tradition, 78
Trinity Seminary Review, 185
Westminster Theological Journal, 256
AC SP UndSt
Africa Theological Journal, 190
Archives and History, 125
Australian Biblical Review, 81
Bulletin of the United Bible Societies, 98
Christian Education Journal, 262
Concordia Journal, 154
Concordia Theological Quarterly, 202
Contact, 268
Cross Currents, 44
Durham University Journal, 205
Early American Literature, 128
Ecumenical Review, 317
Hastings Center Report, 218
Heythrop Journal, 220
History of Religions, 23
Journal for the Study of the Old Testament, 108
Journal of Psychology and Theology, 276
Journal of Religion and Psychical Research, 41
Journal of Religious Ethics, 48
Journal of Religious History, 132
Journal of Semitic Studies, 65
Journal of the American Scientific Affiliation, 311
Journal of the Ancient Near Eastern Society, 66

Journal of the Interden. Theol. Ctr., 160
Journal of the United Ref. Church Hist. Soc., 162
Levant, 111
Lutheran Hist. Conf.: Essays and Reports, 164
Missionalia, 280
New Testament Abstracts, 12
Scottish Journal of Religious Studies, 33
Scriptura: Tydskrif vir Bybelkunde, 115
Second Century, 136
Sixteenth Century Journal, 137
Taiwan Journal of Theology, 243
Theologia Evangelica, 245
Theology, 248
Vox Evangelica, 254
Wesleyan Theological Journal, 188
Word and Spirit: A Monastic Review, 257
Zygon, 312

AC UndSt

Evangelical Quarterly, 211
Fides et Historia, 215
Journal of the Evangelical Theological Soc., 225
Themelios, 244

GP

American Bible Society Record, 79
Baptist World, 143
Bible Advocate, 82
BibleWorld, 91
Biblical Archaeology Review, 94
Catholic Digest, 148
Christ to the World, 150
Christianity Today, 265
Creation, 39
Divine Life, 52
Eternity, 210
Freethinker, 325
Humanist, 326
Japan Christian Quarterly, 300
Joy and Light, 277
Katallagete, 302
Newsletter (Christian Brethren Research Fellowship), 174
Pope Speaks, 176
Printed Lectures, 283
RCDA: Religion in Comm. Dominated Areas, 304
Readers' Guide to Periodical Literature, 14
Reformer, 235
Risk Book Series, 237
Search, 287
Sojourners, 307
Tablet, 292
United Evangelical Action, 309
USPG Yearbook, 187

Word in Action: The Bible in the World, 122
Young Life Guard, 295
GP HS SP
Healing Review, 40
GP HS SP UndSt
America, 258
New REview, 173
GP HS UndSt
Bible Today, 87
GP SP
AFER: African Ecclesial Review, 296
Australasian Catholic Record, 140
Bride of Christ, 259
Buried History, 99
Call to Growth Ministry, 260
Canadian Catholic Review, 146
Catechist, 261
Catena, 147
Chicago Studies, 200
Ching Feng, 297
Church, 266
Henceforth. . ., 219
Horizons, 103
Journal of Reform Judaism, 73
Journal of the Moscow Patriarchate, 161
Judaism, 74
Modern Churchman, 228
Network, 171
PMC: Practice of Ministry in Canada, 282
Quaker Religious Thought, 178
Radius, 285
Reconstructionist, 77
Review of Books and Religion, 236
Sisters Today, 289
Spectrum, 60
Trinitarian Bible Society Quarterly Record, 120
U. S. Catholic Historian, 186
GP UndSt
Bible and Spade, 83
HS UndSt
Orbit, 175
SP
Bible Friend, 85
Christian Ministry, 263
Clergy Review, 267
Criterion, 203
Homiletic and Pastoral Review, 270
Journal of Religion and Health, 47
Leadership, 278
Lutheran Theological Journal, 165
LWF Documentation, 166

LWF Report, 167
Quarterly Review, 284
Reformed Review, 233
Reformed World, 234
SA: Sociological Analysis, 306
Saint Luke's Journal of Theology, 238
Signum, 288
Southern Baptist Periodical Index, 20
Studia Canonica, 290
Studia Liturgica, 291
UndSt
Biblebhashyam, 90

About the Compiler

EUGENE C. FIEG, JR., holds advanced degrees in both library science and religious studies. He is currently a Cataloger at the American Theological Library Association Preservation Board.